KU-700-494

Studies in Education (new series) 16

Changing English
Essays for Harold Rosen

edited by Margaret Meek and Jane Miller

with contributions by:

Manuel Alvarado
Dorothy Barnes
Douglas Barnes
Myra Barrs
James Berry
Garth Boomer
James Britton
Tony Burgess
Phillip Drummond
Bob Ferguson
Judith Graham
Gerald Gregory
Michael Hamerston
Heather Kay

Keith Kimberley
Josie Levine
Alex McLeod
Nancy Martin
Peter Medway
Margaret Meek
Nick Otty
Martyn Richards
John Richmond
Betty Rosen
Connie Rosen
Michael Rosen
Margaret Sandra

HEINEMANN EDUCATIONAL BOOKS
for the Institute of Education, University of London

Heinemann Educational Books Ltd
22 Bedford Square, London WC1B 3HH

LONDON   EDINBURGH   MELBOURNE   AUCKLAND
HONG KONG   SINGAPORE   KUALA LUMPUR   NEW DELHI
IBADAN   NAIROBI   JOHANNESBURG
EXETER (NH)   KINGSTON   PORT OF SPAIN

ISBN 0 85473 174 1
ISBN 0 435 80882 6

© Institute of Education, University of London, 1984
First published 1984

British Library Cataloguing in Publication Data

Changing English. – (Studies in Education. New series, 16). –
   (Studies in education. New series (University of London
   Institute of Education)   ISSN 0458-2101, 16)
   1. English language – Study and teaching
   I. Meek, Margaret, *1925–*   II. Miller, Jane
   3. Rosen, Harold   IV. University of London, *Institute of Education.*
   5. Series
   420'.7'1   LB 1576

ISBN 0-435-80882-6
ISBN 0-85473-174-1 Institute of Education

KING ALFRED'S COLLEGE
WINCHESTER

420
MEE   22468

Printed in Great Britain by
Biddles Ltd, Guildford, Surrey

Changing English

A

Tr

Acc

KA 0024765 0

Studies in Education

ISSN 0458-2101

A series of monographs published by Heinemann Educational Books for the Institute of Education, University of London. Other titles in the series:

For Harold,
to whom change is always challenge,
from all his friends.

Contents

Foreword

Denis Lawton

Retirement was once defined by a colleague at the Institute, Ian Michael (now himself retired), as 'an opportunity to read books by daylight'. There is probably enough truth in that view to make Harold Rosen not completely reluctant to give up his full-time role within the department of English and Media Studies. He has always given the impression of enjoying his work immensely, but the possibility of day-time reading (and writing) must also have its attractions. What is quite clear from the contributions which make up this volume is that we shall miss him. His colleagues, past colleagues and ex-students, have put together a collection of papers which not only makes a significant contribution to the study of English teaching, but also illustrates the kind of work that Harold has been so centrally involved in during his career at the Institute of Education and before.

A number of school subjects have changed dramatically during the last twenty years but perhaps none so excitingly as English and, as Margaret Meek points out in her Introduction, English is now much more than just another curriculum subject. A good deal of that change has been associated with English teaching at the Institute of Education, as well as with the London Association for the Teaching of English (LATE) and the National Association for the Teaching of English (NATE). Harold Rosen has been active in all of these change agencies, and has played a dynamic part in many of the most important developments.

Once upon a time I was a teacher of English, and I can imagine how stimulated I would have been if a book like this had been available at the beginning of my career. I am sure that many young teachers will be inspired by it, now and for many years to come. One of the most depressing aspects of the current educational scene is the emphasis on tests, objectives, monitoring and a very narrow view of accountability; the richness of the contributions to this

book is a splendid counterblast to the Gradgrinds of the 1980s. An important aim of education is to encourage the tolerance of ambiguity; even the
title of the book goes some way towards achieving that!

I am sure that all my colleagues at the Institute of Education who have not
had an opportunity of putting their tribute into writing would wish to join
me in thanking Harold for his contributions to our life and work in the past,
and wishing him well for the future.

Director,
University of London Institute of Education.
13 April, 1984.

Notes on Contributors

Manuel Alvarado was formerly Lecturer in Television and Film at the Institute of Education, and has edited and contributed to *Screen Education*. He is joint author of a forthcoming British Film Institute book on the work of Euston Films.

Douglas Barnes is now Senior Lecturer in Education in the University of Leeds. He was Chairman of the National Association for the Teaching of English (NATE) between 1967 and 1969 and taught English for many years. He is author (or co-author) of *Language, the Leaver and the School,* *From Communication to Curriculum, Communication and Learning in Small Groups,* and *Practical Curriculum Study* (the last two published by Routledge and Kegan Paul).

Dorothy Barnes is also an English teacher and has worked as Research Officer in the Schools Council English 16–19 Project and in the Social Science Research Council 'Versions of English' Project at the University of Leeds.

Myra Barrs is Adviser for English in the London Borough of Brent, a regular contributor to *The Times Educational Supplement*, and the editor of several anthologies, including the Penguin, *Shakespeare SuperScribe*.

James Berry is a well-known poet and a friend of Harold Rosen.

Garth Boomer is Director of Wattle Park Teachers' Centre in South Australia. He studied under Harold Rosen in 1972–3 and became interested in the relationship of language, class and politics at that time. Two of his books, *The Spitting Image* (Rigby, with Dale Spender) and *Negotiating the Curriculum* (Ashton Scholastic) explore these topics. He is President of the Australian Association for the Teaching of English.

James Britton is a former Head of the English Department at the Institute of Education, and past Goldsmiths' Professor of Education in the University of London. He is author of *Language and Learning* (Penguin, 1972) and *Prospect and Retrospect: Selected Essays* (edited by G.M. Pradl, Boynton Cook, New Jersey, and Heinemann Educational, London, 1982). He also directed the Schools Council Development of Writing Abilities 11–18 Project.

Tony Burgess is Lecturer in the English Department at the Institute and co-author with Harold Rosen of *Languages and Dialects of London School-children* (Ward Lock, 1980) and co-author of *Understanding Children Writing* (Penguin, 1973).

Phillip Drummond is course tutor for the MA in Film and Television Studies for Education at the Institute of Education. He is a former chairman of the Society for Education in Film and Television, and of the English Film Institute Regional Conference 1980 and 1981. He has been a member of the editorial board of *Screen* and *Screen Education*, and a contributor to both. He is editor of forcoming books on Hitchcock and on French film theory in the 1970s.

Bob Ferguson is Head of Media Studies at the Institute of Education. He is chairman of the University of London Joint Subject Committee in Film and Television and a member of the National Film Archive Science Selection Committee. He is a former editorial board member of and is a contributor to *Screen Education*. His publications include *Group Film-Making* (Studio Vista, 1969).

Judith Graham has been a teacher for over twenty years and a Lecturer in the English Department at the Institute since 1978.

Gerald Gregory is Lecturer in Education at Brunel University and a PhD student at the English Department at the Institute. His special interest is in worker writers and he has contributed a chapter to *Eccentric Propositions: Literature and the curriculum*, edited by Jane Miller (Routledge and Kegan Paul, 1984).

Michael Hamerston was a student of Harold Rosen during 1980–81. He is Senior Lecturer in Education at the Hawthorn Institute of Education in Melbourne.

Heather Kay is a Barrow Poet and Lecturer in the English Department at the Institute of Education.

Keith Kimberley taught for many years in London schools, is a past chairman of the London Association for the Teaching of English (LATE) and a founding editor of *Teaching London Kids*. He is now Lecturer in the English Department at the Institute of Education.

Josie Levine is co-author of *Scope, Stage 2*, language development materials which were an outcome of the early Schools Council English for Immigrant Children Project. She taught English as a second language in Birmingham and is now Lecturer in the English Department at the Institute of Education.

Alex McLeod is Senior Lecturer in the English Department at the Institute of Education. He has taught in New Zealand and London and was a member of the research group which produced *The Development of Writing Abilities 11-18* (Macmillan, 1975). Particular interests are literacy, West Indian students in Britain, media studies in English teaching, campaigning against nuclear weapons, and the rights and wrongs of gay people in education.

Nancy Martin was Head of the English Department before Harold Rosen and directed the Schools Council Writing Across the Curriculum 11–16 Project. She now works as an independent educational consultant, mostly in the USA and in Canada. Her latest publication is *Mostly about Writing* (Boynton Cook, New Jersey, and Heinemann, London, 1983).

Peter Medway, is a former student of Harold Rosen and an English teacher currently researching at the University of Leeds. He is the author of *Finding a Language* (Writers and Readers Publishing Co-operative, 1980) and co-author of *The Climate for Learning* (Ward Lock, 1981).

Margaret Meek (Spencer) is Reader in Education and currently Chairperson of the newly amalgamated Joint Department of English and Media Studies at the Institute of Education. She pursues her particular interests in literacy and literature both in the Department's work and as a critic of books for children. She is joint-editor of *The Cool Web: A pattern of children's reading* (The Bodley Head, 1977) and is author of *Learning to Read* (The Bodley Head, 1982). With colleagues she has also written *Achieving Literacy* (Routledge and Kegan Paul, 1983).

Jane Miller taught English for many years at Holland Park School before becoming Lecturer in the English Department at the Institute of Education. She is the author of *Many Voices: Bilingualism, culture and education* (Routledge and Kegan Paul, 1983) and editor of *Eccentric Propositions: Literature and the curriculum* (Routledge and Kegan Paul, 1984).

Nick Otty is a former student of Harold Rosen and author of *Learner Teacher, Teacher Learner* (Penguin, 1972). He has worked in many areas of education and is now Lecturer at Bristol Polytechnic. A special interest is the concealed politics of education and the efficacy of creative work in enabling students to understand their educational experience.

Martyn Richards was a student of Harold Rosen at Borough Road College and a teaching colleague of Connie Rosen. After teaching in primary schools he became a head teacher and is now a Senior Primary Inspector for Essex.

John Richmond edited and wrote a good deal of *Becoming Our Own Experts* (Talk Workshop Group, 1982). He has taught in London schools for many years and is now an advisory teacher for the Inner London Education Authority.

Betty Rosen is Harold Rosen's wife and Head of the Faculty of Communication at the Somerset Boys' Comprehensive School, Tottenham, London.

Connie Rosen was Senior Lecturer, first at Goldsmiths' College, London, then at Trent Park College (now Middlesex Polytechnic). With her husband Harold Rosen she wrote *The Language of Primary School Children* (Penguin, 1973). She died in 1976 at the age of 56. She sometimes described herself as one of the 'Schiller-types', from the time she attended Christian Schiller's course at the Institute of Education. Many will acknowledge her influence on their way of teaching and remember her personally with great affection.

Michael Rosen is the younger son of Harold and Connie Rosen. He writes children's books, the latest of which is *Quick, Let's Get Out of Here* (Deutsch 1983). He is the author of *I See a Voice* (Thames TV/Hutchinson, 1982) a book about poetry for teachers and secondary-school students. He scripts the Channel Four programme *Everybody Here* and works three days a week in schools.

Margaret Sandra has taught for many years in London schools, has been active in LATE and NATE, and in the *Teaching London Kids* collective. She is at present an advisory teacher in London and a Councillor in the Borough of Lewisham. Margaret Sandra is her formal name, and she has dispensed with a surname and the tradition of women being named by their relationship with fathers or husbands.

Introduction

Margaret Meek

The title of this collection of essays is deliberately ambiguous. The introduction therefore will not reduce to a single theme the resonances of what the writers have to say, but simply make the obvious even more plain: English is changing and being changed. Within the context of studies of language and culture we offer a range of personal perspectives which, by being brought together, reveal more of the nature and complexity of changing English than any one of us might have done alone.

Our common perspective is that of teachers, in the sense that includes poets and other artists as well as those directly concerned with education. Most of us are involved in teaching English so that what we see as our professional commitment necessarily runs through the network of ideas contained in these essays. But what we have to say about changing English is not confined to classroom practices in colleges and schools. Therefore our audience includes all who are conscious of change in the relationship of language and learning at this time of marked and widespread transformations in our societies.

We begin with, and return to, English in history: not simply the traditional study of English as a language, but a conception of the role that language plays in the historical development of individuals and society and of English teachers themselves. This provides a framework for looking at other changes, social and pedagogical. We acknowledge the importance of universal literacy. We include in the range of our concerns the primary child's day in school as well as the significance of the kinds of examinations that influence the prospects of the school leaver. We cannot write about change without confronting the issues of race and class in multicultural societies, so we are bound to consider bilingualism, second and community languages alongside our looking at different ways of preparing young adults for continuing education and work. We confirm the conviction embedded in earlier research that writing is important because everyone should have the power and the means of creating meaning in language. The sooner the young discover the strength of their voices, the greater will be their future involvement in and effect upon both language and literature.

English teachers are immersed in the ways by which the outside world enters their classrooms, whether as a topic like the issue of nuclear war, or by means of electronic media which will eventually change what we mean by reading and writing. We are also caught up in the consequent changes in research and pedagogy. Indeed, teaching and research have become twin aspects of learning; teachers learn as children learn. The classroom is a research workshop. While we must continue to press for properly funded inquiry and the continuing education of teachers, we are now sure that English teaching has changed as the result of teachers responding to the challenge to become their own experts. We can now powerfully demonstrate what counts as evidence in educational research and so we are determined to have a say in how data gathered in our classrooms are to be interpreted and used. We are generating new understandings of the processes of language and thought in society.

These essays demonstrate how language is, for teachers as well as students, the essential zone of proximal development as described by Vygotsky. As we sit at the crossroads of change in the varieties of discourse in which we take part, we also have our own individual preoccupations and our own concern to find a voice. Our writings are brought together so that we may all be more clearly heard as ourselves. Instead of being grouped in topic sections, each chapter is linked to the following one to make a chain of ideas. The key to the overall design is the understanding that English is not just one of a number of curriculum subjects in school, not even 'language across the curriculum', important as that idea has proved to be in discussions of the curriculum itself. Instead, as a language, English is the arena where 'the interaction of language, thought and society is passionately lived out'.

These words are Harold Rosen's. They occur in his inaugural lecture, *Neither Bleak House Nor Liberty Hall*, which formally inducted him as the first occupant of the chair of English in Education with special reference to the Mother Tongue, in the Institute of Education, and from which he now retires. In his long and distinguished career he has been a doughty fighter for social and intellectual regeneration. Every domain represented in this volume has something of his work lurking in it as an influence, an inspiration or even a disagreement, for Harold likes a good argument. The recurrent motifs: what teachers know about language and learning in classroom interaction, the relations of language and class, the challenge of multi-cultural education, the need to challenge the tyranny of the examination system, the ways of poets and the nurture of narrative, all these remind us of the range of Harold's questions. He has been a force in English teaching for the evolution of a deep, systematic understanding of the language itself, its functions and what it creates, and of the ways in which it reflects the human passions that permeate history, language and societies in the process of change.

As he has done many times, Harold has again given his friends and colleagues this opportunity to look to the future of English from within our teaching commitments and beyond them. He has also provided us with a chance to celebrate, in the twin senses of to honour and to make public appreciation of, a distinguished teacher and scholar who has always made all his students active in the belief that the risky business of learning is continuous, lifelong, and essentially collaborative.

*   *   *

The speedy production of this book owes much to the generosity of the Joint Publications Sub-Committee of the Institute of Education and to the confidence of its secretary, Denis Baylis, who trusted us to write it in record time. We thank them all.

The book itself became more than a collection of its working parts as the result of Jane Miller's insights and editorial flair. Her colleagues now wish to acknowledge her contribution as being as significant as anything that appears on the list of contents. Without her maieutic art, *Changing English* would never have appeared.

1.
The Question of English

Tony Burgess

There was a time when teenage revolt was constituted by reading Françoise Sagan after 'lights out' and a tendency towards existentialism. I was then the first person to do English at A level at Winchester College. It was all right because I was also doing history. Perhaps neither fact immediately or obviously carries luminous interest. For me they are reminders of the complex emergence of English as a subject and of the nature of the question this has continuously posed for education and for society at large.

The dilettante joys of 'The Rape of The Lock' might be acquired, it was felt, in the course of a man's normal reading. This was the source of my somewhat easily won novelty. But I was also happily getting grounded in a real subject. Questions formed a big part of the history which we were learning. I rather think that it was Harold Rosen who later displayed to me the significance of these, which I grasped only imperfectly at the time.

Questions came from elsewhere. On the margin of human existence, surveyed from a vantage point I suppose somewhere between the Atheneum and the Palace of Westminster, questions arose. In the Balkans, among the Boers, in India, amongst women. Questions needed to be dealt with. This was one point about them. Another was that their disposal might take time, but was effective. Questions enjoyed a more or less brief existence before they faded into the dark of history. A scratching was heard behind the wainscotting. A man, a gunboat, a solution was despatched. Questions, by the time they reached us, coming along in our studies, were always over. To have felt otherwise we would have needed to feel differently, not just about any of the various issues which passed before us but about our own lives and about history.

Like many readers of this book, I imagine, it was only very much later, when I was becoming a teacher, that I learned that, alongside the others, for more than a hundred years of public education, there had also been an English question. I have sometimes toyed with seeing myself as part of its growth. Didn't I sense something important then? Change might be omitted from the writing of history for schools. It might even be kept successfully from the experience of the ruling class, though less successfully than was implied by its historiography. But, outside the periphery, change was both something to be part of and a part of life. Didn't I see then that I was seeking a place where change *had* to be confronted, as part of the very reason for English as a subject, as I struggled with 'The Rape of The Lock', edited with infinite finesse to appear like a classical text?

I consider now that I was perhaps discovering something about language. Again like many other readers of this book, I imagine, I was discovering a hunger to recognize my own experience not just as whirling infinitely inwards but as attached. Thus I was hungry for ideas made as part of other people's living, which might enter my own. I was trying to do something about this. At the time, however, this was a need I saw only in terms of literature. I did not formulate this as a part of language more generally. Nor of course did I foresee that my concern could ever be connected to a common need; or that the qualities which I attached to literature might be important enough to people at large to have been at the core of the question which English as a subject has raised.

The point which occurs to me now is that if I had been able to foresee much of this I should not have been a part of history, but able to live outside it. I should have been able to predict my life. I should not have had to accommodate changes in my life which derive from living and being joined to the living of others, in a society and in a human world. I should not have needed either the idea which I most powerfully encountered in the work of Britton and Martin and Rosen twenty years ago: that it is because human beings live in history that they have need of language; that if human beings never had to cope with change, which they could not control or predict, they would not need language as their cure or care in the perils and possibilities of living. I want in what follows to recall both some of the strengths and subsequent fortunes of this idea. It is more than an idea now, however. A historical view of language has also become part of history and has been available to us not simply as an abstract theory but as a set of challenges and a many-sided practice.

Unambitious and under-theorized technologies of school English were among the first places where the case for a view of language as lived in history was argued.[1] Here I want to focus on what has seemed to me crucial in this argument. It has been an argument with traditions, not with teachers.

That should be said. The importance of the argument has not been simply for its implications for different practices. Not just the emergence of a different form of English has been sought in its trail. More importantly, a theoretical challenge has been posed, in which teaching itself has been constituted as a form of theoretical enquiry.

English, I may add, was not absent from my education in earlier parts of the school. I should not imply that the subject formed no part of a Public School curriculum at the time. I remember weekly essays. Also there was learning poetry by heart and a certain amount of time given to reading literature. And grammar. This would not be so very different from what must have been available in many other schools. My English, then, was formed by a relatively specific technology, constructed piecemeal from aspirations in a number of different theoretical traditions and from school ways of doing things. It persists. It must be a widely shared memory among most who have begun teaching in any decade in this century.

Perhaps any form of teaching may be conceptualized as a technology. All traditions evolve methods, apparatuses, expertises for making content available to children; and I should not then be scornful of technologies as such. I register the qualification but do not concede the central, critical force of the description. The inherited technologies were powerfully and rightly challenged by a different view of language. This was not just a challenge to ideas. It called in question a reduction of English teaching to methods and procedures of any kind.

Instead, teaching was represented in a cultural and political light, which is not easy to express in a sentence, though I shall attempt to do this. It has to do with the way in which teaching was seen as inserted into processes of cultural making within society at large. Once language is seen as an aspect of people's personal and social practice, as being crucial to their experience in lived and living history, technologies of whatever kind recede. Teaching itself becomes handmaiden or critic to wider processes. The technologies are subordinate to what may be constructed in active, committed and shared classroom encounters and to ways in which these moments in people's lives may be described and theorized.

This must seem very general, as must any attempt to express briefly what has amounted to a transformation of perspective. What follows seems to me, however, doubly important. First, a role is held out for teaching, in which both personal and political dimensions cohere. An advocacy for what children collectively and individually make is not divided from a critical investigation of the cultural processes which they inhabit. It recognizes that children's lives are shaped by these and that, in turn, these may be shaped and changed by them. Second, teaching becomes by this characterization theoretical. That is, of course, always true. Teaching is always theoretical. It is always a practice, containing immanent theory and searching for description. This, however, was a starting point, in which theoretical elaboration was bound to follow. For in this the changing shape of history is made as important as language. The formulation of English teaching's critical and cultural role makes necessary continuing investigation and analysis.

Behind the technologies, there were traditions and beliefs which were bound to be confronted by a view of language in history. Among these, a common thread is the projection of language and literature as something which exists and may be described but has only incidentally been historically made. An historical view of language must counter such theories. It must necessarily reject ways of conceptualizing teaching which are derived from the abstraction of language and literature from social processes, existing in time, by which people's experience is shaped. I apologize again for generality. I am seeking to indicate connections in a range of traditions and beliefs, against which an emphasis on language in history must make its way. I shall become clearer.

Immediately, there was the familiar apparatus, still noted by HM Inspectorate as well-oiled and working in British secondary school: the grammar books, exercises, rhetorical analysis, devices for promoting comprehension and minimal literacy constitute one example. I do not need to recall and labour the point here of the traditions behind this. Abstraction could perhaps go no further. English was projected not merely as a foreign language, but as actually no longer spoken, and surviving, like Latin and Greek, only in written and in school-mediated forms. This was only one stout tethering, nevertheless, of what has remained a persistent belief: that significant learning of a language can take place separately from the practices of which language is part and in which it is pragmatically used.

There is a danger, perhaps, that recent emphases on vocational uses of language may similarly be reduced to an orientation redolent of schoolbook aims. I mention this to illustrate more clearly the central opposition between an abstract and a historical view of language. There is a familiar mix here of intentions and an apparatus. The intentions are important. It is easy to assent to aims of relevance. As importantly, in this newer apparatus of skills and communications, there is a focus on identifiable rather than indefinite goals. A checklist of goals, moreover, does not necessarily produce, any more than did the grammar book, a particular mode of classroom working; and permits a cumulative, profile mode of assessment.

But the abstraction of language as a set of skills is no better than other abstractions, whether they reduce language to a collection of rhetorical devices or to a system of rules and structures. For development in language to be conceived simply as the acquisition of skills language must be severed from its connection with individual intention, with social practice and with wider cultural understandings. At present there is a compound irony. This is reflected in the important intentions which have been channelled into the vocabulary of communications skills, and is balanced by a contrasting fact. Vocational work *is* being undertaken successfully, and where it is, this is from principles about the cultural nature of language, which the conceptual framework of skills is designed specifically to exclude.

It would be wrong to connect every major issue in English teaching to an opposition between an abstract and an historical view. There is enough to the connection, however, for this to serve as a bridge here to other currents, in which an emphasis on language in history has had to make its way. Once language has been abstracted and projected as a system, it is hard to accommodate either different varieties of English or differences which reflect varieties of function within such a conceptual frame. Thus, the recognition of diversity represents a decisive crisis for a fixed and ahistorical view of language. It is not surprising, either, that the challenge to an ahistorical view of standard language should have been paralleled by an equivalent challenge to the assumption of a standard literature.

More has been involved in the challenge presented by cultural and linguistic diversity than recognizing that British education has oddly placed at a disadvantage bilingual and bidialectal children. Entailed within this recognition is more also than the question of relativity, of accommodation to the viability of other dialects and languages. The issue goes further even than the sociolinguists' reminder of the normal heterogeneity of language and languages within national and local speech communities. The issue of diversity and standard language foregrounds inescapably questions of power. In turn, this makes inescapable a view of language as made in history. The logic is inescapable, since the only way of resolving the conflicts presented for teachers by diversity is to move beyond the model of system and of a standard, which has in some way been rendered absolute. The continuing pain in this recognition is the dismantling of an absolute notion of standard. At the same time, there can be no grip for teaching here unless it is recognized that social patterns of language have been constructed and that teaching is inserted into continuing processes, processes about which teaching may seek to make children and students aware and which it may in some measure seek to affect and change.

Alongside the primacy of a single dialect projected as standard, a selective tradition of literature was bound equally to be challenged by an historical and cultural concern. Not only is literature made in language. Both language and literature have common roots in a human necessity to live in history: a necessity to engage with experience which is indefinite until shaped, to feel the impact of other lives and to accommodate to what has been and to what can be made in time. Thus, the challenge to a standard literature parallels the challenge to a standard language. It questions a fixity which has been made as such and in which are evacuated simultaneously the history and above all the relations of power which have attended its making.

Not surprisingly, the force of this challenge has sometimes been seen as an attack on a specific canon. It is easier to limit the challenge of a powerful idea by assigning it specificity than to take on its wholesale implications for reconsidering how culture or language or literature are perceived. But the point of the challenge, for all that, has not been about Shakespeare. It has been about ways in which Shakespeare was read. It has also sought to focus what such ways of reading may serve to *exclude* in people's sense of what counts as literature or of how it may figure along with other forms of making in their lives.

I have been seeking to register, then, the impact of a single, oppositional idea. It has all been rather general. Also, it has been work from my armchair. I will have seemed to have been swivelling in various directions, politely swearing at any belief different from my own. All these issues have a longer and more complex history than I have displayed. The risk is one I must accept. My aim has been to expose a common thread, not to be comprehensive; and in doing this to indicate a connection between powerful traditions and beliefs, against which a theoretical and practical commitment to language in history has to make its way.

However, to impose such a conceptual logic may be to tidy up separate and different engagements a little speciously. I recognize too that so far I have made it all seem too simple. I have smoothed out the ways in which a central challenge has bobbed and ducked and re-emerged, acquiring, in the course of this, increased confidence and resilience. In what follows I shall at any rate turn to face more explicitly some of the theoretical adventures and growth. I shall try to indicate some developments of the central idea and some of its continuities. I will again have to simplify. I will again have to steer a course between a public account and a personal view.

*   *   *

A central continuity has been attention to how thought and language and social processes are interrelated. This needs no initial explanation. An attempt to develop a view of language lived in history must consider *how* language enters people's lives. Also, the way in which the connection between language, thought and society is understood has crucial relevance for an account of teaching and learning. The demanding and continuously exciting challenge in this is nothing less than to describe how consciousness is constructed. That is not one but several questions. If consciousness is socially and culturally created, is this an inexorably determined process? Or if there is no meaning to consciousness outside boundaries of space and time, how is difference possible within these? How is it that created consciousness may also act back on culture and be creative? If human beings speak, as linguists have said, 'an heroic language of our own invention', how is it that language enters inwardly and shapes what can be meant and seen? Questions such as these have commanded attention over centuries. They also figure in a picture of even the minutest moments of teaching and learning.

As the extraordinary work of Vygotsky showed, the force of these questions is not just that they oblige us to grasp that language, thought and history are interrelated, but to find adequately a means of saying how they are.[2] I can remember discovering my own first real meaning in the work of Vygotsky when I went on holiday in Wales with my family. There had been animals in our lives before. For my younger daughter, however, this was a first direct encounter with other than domestic animals. Previously she had known cats and dogs, and by sensible compromise with the outside world and the needs of her own thinking, had used the word 'cat' to refer to both. The holiday added 'sheep' to her vocabulary. She then had two terms. These were linked to normal adult uses but they were not the same. They organized meaning for her, however, in her own thinking. Thus she continued to use 'cat' as she had before, but never to refer to the wide category of animals now known as 'sheep'. The terms were not interchangeable.

There was no simple way of inferring or predicting the meanings within the changing categories of this three-year-old's thought. That independence seems to me as important to mark now as the means of development. The emergent discrimination could have referred to size; to animals encountered at home or away; to those which may enter homes and houses and those which stay outside; to the juxtaposition of different ways of life; to the extent to which different kinds of animals might be approached and known. Any or all of these criteria may be involved. It is only a selection. Others are possible. They are criteria which are perceptual, cognitive, emotional, experiential. I stress the range, because in an interpretation of Vygotsky, the presumption in any human being of a rich and essentially unknowable, a mysterious and personal gathering of experience and meaning is important in the dialectic which he beautifully and lucidly exposed.

Word meaning evolves and interacts with thought. Readers of this book will be familiar enough with the form of the dialectic. It remains for me and I expect many others the most gripping and specific insight within any set of ideas which have borne on teaching and learning. The evolution in word meanings is to be seen, moreover, as an aspect of the general, cultural transformation of mind. In this, children have to construct the meaning of any and all signs, but at the same time signs organize, inwardly, children's thinking. Arriving at word meanings is then a cognitive act. It is not merely given or taken over. The construction of the web of meanings in a language represents a process of development. Also, however, the construction of meaning is organized by signs. Words have to be made to mean in developing personal utterance, while they also anchor within developing thought the meanings which are made.

The insight has been so powerful for so many that perhaps it will not matter devastatingly if the version which I offer is not quite right for some. Here I want to recall especially what has followed from it. The shaping influence of such a rich formulation of the question of development has been of immense importance for teachers drawing together their picture of teaching and learning. Educationally, Vygotsky's thought has posed not simply language or development but language in the development of mind. Generations of teachers have thereby approached language in their classrooms as an instrument of their pupils' learning and development, not just as a set of skills to be trained or of end-products to be achieved.

There has followed from this both the stress on the role of talk in learning and a specific interpretation of the way in which written language may be related to spoken. The routines of centralized teacher instruction followed by a pupil-written response, somewhere between test and memorized record, are decisively rejected by appreciating language's exploratory and constructive role. Vygotsky's description of the cognitive act entailed within language puts pupils' spoken language at the centre of classrooms, but again what is crucial is the way in which this is theorized. The primacy accorded to talk is not simply part of the elaboration of a different methodology. Nor is this advocated just on grounds of language and of language development. It is the complex insight which is distinctive. In exploring and constructing understanding, talk aids learning; and opportunities provided by learning foster language. Both may be conceptualized within development seen as an historical process, mediated by tools and signs.

This redefines the relation between spoken and written language. Certainly, there has been more learned during the Seventies about reading and writing than is fully worked out in Vygotsky's theory. There is, nevertheless, a crucial emphasis in this. This is that literacy is functional in development and should not be theorized separately from the continuing transformation of thinking which is enabled by signs. It becomes necessary to ask for classroom writing, as for all uses of language, that it be considered in connection with its role in learning.

Of course, therefore, the account of writing which was developed from Vygotsky's ideas and from the broader emphasis on language in history sought to centre attention on the role and nature of expressive language. I am not seeking to replicate other accounts of this research in saying this, nor presumptuously offering a different version. I want rather to indicate what have been for me central continuities. The quite specific interpretation of expressive language in the work of the writing research held several theoretical concerns together.[3] The interpretation carries forward the exploratory, heuristic emphases of Vygotsky. Expressive language may be a bridge between speaking and writing; and in that it presupposes an intimate context, expressive language may be closer to inner speech as well, a bridge, therefore, between thought and the public utterance of thought, in fuller and more extended language. Alongside this, expressive language may also be interpreted historically and critically. The language used among one's own people is the site where the import of public, transactional discourses may be re-interpreted, modified, discriminated. There is here an affirmation of the creative power of unmonitored, everyday language and of historically developed vernaculars, and their capacity for resistance. Finally, both heuristic and historical emphases allow for a radical account of the social nature of art. This may begin with reflection on the role of expressive language within gossip, narrative and story.

The powerful programme suggested by the conception of expressive language has still to be fully worked out. It has been kept alive and extended, however, by continuing work on writing. Alongside this, the theorization of expressive language is also extended by the investigation of diversity; especially by focusing on those new vernaculars currently and creatively coming into being in intercultural settings.

*   *   *

I have been seeking, then, a central continuity of ideas. This began from an emphasis on language lived in history and the challenge to approaches which depended on the abstraction of language and literature from wider cultural processes. It was elaborated through the work of Vygotsky. His socio-cultural theory of development focuses on the transforming power of the sign and proposes language as important, not simply in its own right but crucially in the development of mind. The conception of expressive language follows. This carries within it, I argued, both the historical and the inwardly directed aspects of Vygotsky's thought. I have generalized from different educational debates in arguing this, but my promise was to turn towards some theoretical adventures and this seems to me an exciting inheritance of coherent theory.

I want to enlist for this some recent interests in literary and cultural theory, which seem to me powerfully to converge with the central line I have been pursuing. I have in mind directions in the analysis of culture associated with Raymond Williams and the Centre for Contemporary Cultural Studies in Birmingham.[4] The scope of this work has been wide; and some of the widest and most general interests extend the conceptualization of language lived in history, especially the ideas of settlement, cultural dominance and hegemony, within a socio-cultural theory derived from Gramsci. Here I shall focus more narrowly. The immediate convergence derives from a common interest in language, literature and social processes. I want to offer some points at which the theory I have been outlining seems to me to be excitingly taken further.

A redefinition of the sign, through reconsidering the inheritance of Saussurean linguistics, may seem a little abstract as a starting point. It may appear less than breathtaking in its prospective relevance to classrooms or to educational theory. I must ask for a moment's patience. The notion of the sign has had a crucial role in language theory. The extent to which language is theorized as an abstract system or as part of social and cultural practice depends to a considerable extent on the version of the sign which is adopted. The point may be approached by recalling Vygotsky. In his theory of development and its dialectic between thought and language, children achieve word meaning through an intellectual act, while words simultaneously centre and organize the meanings which may be made. There is more to be said about this as a theoretical orientation. Vygotsky's interpretation of the role of signs rules out both mere behavioural association and innate human nature as explanations of development. It is the cornerstone of his argument against behaviourist, idealist and even Piagetian explanations. The effect of the inwardly directed, organizing power of signs is that they transform the biological bases of behaviour into developed human consciousness. For Vygotsky then signs are crucial to an explanation of development when this is seen as a socio-cultural process in which society and individual creativity meet.[5] The importance of this version of the sign will, I hope, be apparent. Different versions may employ the same term but lead in very different directions.

To view language as composed of signs is to propose as central the symbolic nature of language and to link this to a more general awareness of the many ways of symbolizing developed within human societies. Signs allow human beings increasing control over the physical universe and enhanced direction of their own behaviour. They permit *reference* to experience; they allow it to be present in mind when not in fact, and therefore to be independently communicable. This general argument about language, brilliantly explored by Vygotsky with a view to understanding development, has received its fullest treatment in linguistics in the work of Saussure.[6]

Saussure's was a social theory of language, containing, however, a specific version of the 'social' and stressing the relative autonomy of language as a formal, internally self-regulating, structural system composed of signs. In Saussure's famous definition, a sign comprises both form, the signifier, and meaning, the signified. Signs were described as 'arbitrary' by Saussure since it was a purely arbitrary matter that any particular form happened to have been developed, as is shown by the existence of common signifieds related to formally different signifiers in different languages. Language is 'systematic' for Saussure, in that it determines the relations into which signs may enter.

However, in this description of language as a system there are some further points to be noted. The crucial idea carried by 'system' is that of a complex but finite set of elements or structures governed by internal rules about relations into which they are permitted to enter. To describe these relations and rules of relation then becomes the work of the linguist, and it may safely be said that this insight has been of fundamental importance to the development of twentieth-century linguistics. In Saussure, a further distinction follows. If it is asked how this finite system can be known, the answer is through the evidence supplied in everyday speech. However, the idiosyncratic and often less than well-formed utterances of particular speakers can only supply clues to the underlying system, which has to be inferred. A distinction is, therefore, to be drawn between everyday use (*parole*) and the underlying system (*langue*). If it is then asked how this system, which may be inferred but not known, is maintained in being, Saussure's answer is through a collective social agreement, a social contract.

Thus, Saussure's account of the systematic nature of language depends on a specific social theory and renders invisible and unnecessary to theoretical understanding the continuing and actual negotiation of the system within the lived history of social processes. It will be apparent, I hope, that the critique of Saussure which may be made at this point is likely to take forward that central question of language in history, which I have tried to keep before us.

The relevance of such a critique is well illustrated by an example given by Stuart Hall. In an unpublished talk at a recent conference, Stuart Hall indicated the lines of analysis for 'black' which have a bearing on the relationship to be posed between the linguistic and the social. 'Black', Hall argued, represents a concept, whose meaning is currently a site for struggle between different social groupings. As such, its meaning is not simply given within internal linguistic relations, which may be abstracted and projected as pre-existing within an autonomously structured system. Instead, what is exemplified within the contested definitions to be ascribed to 'black' as a sign is the ways in which language is being made through social struggle outside language. The manner in which this relationship between sign and social history is to be defined represents a key theoretical problem.[7]

It would be possible to allow for different meanings to be attached to 'black' within an explanation in which the principle of the autonomy of language was preserved. There would be no difficulty in defining 'black' as semantically ambiguous and indicating for it various (paradigmatic) relations and contrasts. The question is whether by this an important insight about language is not lost. An alternative argument is, rather, that the example of vocabulary where meaning is manifestly related to wider social struggle highlights a general principle, which is lost within Saussure's structuralist emphasis. This is that language is, by its nature, a social practice.

This alternative to Saussurean abstraction may start from Volosinov's revaluing of the sign and, more especially, from Williams's interpretation of this.[8] Williams introduces Volosinov, historically, as polemically engaged with two traditions. On the one hand, there was what he describes as the 'objectivism' of Saussure, modified but continued within traditions of Russian formalism. On the other, there was available an emphasis on language as *activity*, deriving from Vico, Herder and Von Humboldt. In this second tradition, the abstract projection of language as system was avoided. However, the emphasis on activity was associated with a strongly Idealist philosophy. Williams comments, as follows, on this second tradition:

> What happened . . . in Humboldt and especially after him was a projection of this idea of activity into essentially idealist and quasi-social forms: either the 'nation', based on an abstract version of the 'folk-mind' or the (ahistorical) 'collective consciousness'; or the 'collective spirit', the abstract creative capacity — self-creative but prior to and separate from material social practice, as in Hegel; or, persuasively, the 'individual', abstracted and defined as 'creative subjectivity', the starting-point of meaning.

Rejecting but also incorporating something from both these traditions, Volosinov's contribution, Williams suggests, was 'to open the way to a new kind of theory'. This theory retained the strength of Saussurean analysis of the sign, with its representation of the gap between formal element (signifier) and meaning (signified). However, the making and remaking of meaning was also seen as a social and historical process. Williams elaborates this, as follows:

> Volosinov argued that meaning was necessarily a social action, dependent on a social relationship. But to understand this depended on recovering a full sense of 'social', as distinct both from the idealist reduction of the social to an inherited, ready-made product, an 'inert crust', beyond which all creativity was individual, and from the objectivist projection of the social into a formal system, now autonomous and governed only by its internal laws, within which, and solely according to which, meanings were produced. Each sense depends, at root, on the same error: of separating the social from individual meaningful activity (though the rival positions then valued the separated elements differently). Against the psychologism of the idealist emphasis, Volosinov argued that 'consciousness is nurtured on signs; it derives its growth from them; it reflects their logic and laws'.
>
> Normally, it is just as this point (and the danger is always increased by retaining the concept of 'sign', which Volosinov revalued but continued to use) that objectivism finds its entry. 'The material of signs' can be translated as 'system of signs'. This system can then be projected (by some notion of a theoretical 'social contract' as in Saussure, protected from examination by the assumption of the priority of 'synchronic' over 'diachronic' analysis) both beyond history and beyond any active conception of contemporary social life, in which socially related individuals meaningfully participate, as distinct from acting out the laws and codes of an inaccessible linguistic system. Each side of Volosinov's argument has a continuing relevance, but it is in his (incomplete) revaluation of the concept of 'sign' that his contemporary significance is most evident.
>
> Volosinov accepted that a 'sign' in language has indeed a 'binary' character . . . That is to say, he agreed that the verbal sign is not equivalent to, nor simply a reflection of, the object or quality which it indicates or expresses. The relation within the sign between the formal element and the meaning which this element carries is thus inevitably conventional (thus far agreeing with orthodox semiotic theory), but it is *not* arbitrary and, crucially, it is not fixed. On the contrary the fusion of formal element and meaning (and it is this fact of dynamic fusion which makes retention of the 'binary' description misleading) is the result of a real process of social development, in the actual activities of speech and in the continuing development of a language. Indeed signs can exist only when this active social relationship is posited. The usable sign — the fusion of formal element and meaning — is a product of this continuing speech activity between

real individuals who are in some continuing social relationship. The 'sign' is in this sense their product, but not simply their past product, as in the reified accounts of an 'always-given' language system. The real communicative 'products' which are usable signs are, on the contrary, living evidence of a continuing social process, into which individuals are born and within which they are shaped, but to which they then also actively contribute, in a continuing process. This is at once their socialization and their individuation, the connected aspects of a single process which the alternative theories of system and expression had divided and dissociated. We then find not a reified 'language' and 'society' but an active *social language*.

The meaning of the sign in Volosinov's approach is not fixed, as Williams notes. 'The fusion of formal element and meaning . . . is the result of a real process of social development.' In formalizing this position, Volosinov developed an account of the sign as multi-accentual, distinguishing between signs and signals. The signal is invariant, as within a traffic system. The sign, by contrast, has a nucleus of meaning; but, round this, there is an essentially indeterminate and variable range. This variable quality of the sign is perceived as a necessary aspect of relations between language and social practice. The meaning of the sign is negotiated and constructed through practice, conceived as both a group and individual process. As in the earlier example of 'black' within the vocabulary of inter-ethnic relations, meaning is negotiated between groupings. The processes of negotiation and construction, moreover, are also internalized by the individual subject. Volosinov puts it like this, directly quoting Vygotsky:

> Speech had first to come into being and develop in the process of the social intercourse of organisms so that afterward it could enter within the organism and become inner speech.
>   Psychologism is also correct, however. There is no outer sign without an inner sign. An outer sign incapable of entering the context of inner signs, i.e. incapable of being understood and experienced, ceases to be a sign and reverts to the status of a physical object.

Volosinov's account of the sign, therefore, opens the way to a theory in which language is seen in relation to social practice. In this version, moreover, possibilities both of collective and of individual practice are preserved. Williams adds to his account of Volosinov his own distinctive emphasis: that the construction of meaning represents a material process of cultural production qualifying the base/superstructure metaphor in Marxist thought.

★   ★   ★

I have been arguing that the social theory of the sign, developed in post-revolutionary Russian thought, and revived within contemporary cultural studies, offers for English teaching an important extension to a unified theory of language and literature. In this, language is seen as a social and historical practice and is not divided from practices and relations in society more widely. The inwardly transforming power of the sign, the dialectic between thought and language, the human achievement of representations, are similarly theorized as social and cultural processes. In order to complete my argument, I should further note that the sign, or signifying element, represents the minimum unit of language and, as such, the limiting case for the account of language which I have described. If a social conception of language can be demonstrated at the level of signs, all *uses* of language, all extended meanings made within linguistic practices from conversations to treatises, require a similarly social analysis.

From this, it is no more than a step to recognize that language may be conceptualized at a level beyond that of signs. In a manner which is potentially no more than an extension to the argument of Volosinov and Vygotsky, language may be thought of as a set of historically developing and recreated discourses. This conception, altogether different from current linguistic work on discourse analysis, is one which has been associated with the French philosopher Foucault. There are some aspects of Foucault's work which still need careful inspection, from the perspective which I have been describing here. Examples of these are the extent to which discourses are to be regarded as determining and Foucault's novel and specific analysis of power. That said, Foucault's historical analysis of discourse suggests, I believe, a powerful addition to the theory of language; and I shall seek to exemplify this claim by way of completing my account.[9]

Foucault's historical conception of discourse may be illustrated through reference to any of the domains which he has successively analysed. I select sexuality from a catalogue which has included themes ranging from madness and punishment to education. Discourses, Foucault argues, reflect relations of power and the purposes of social control. Developed within specific historical circumstances, they serve to organize and order what it is possible to think. The emergence of new discourses may signal important shifts in social organization and the exercise of power. In a number of texts Foucault returns to the emergence of the mercantile state in the sixteenth and seventeenth centuries as the point of origin of many contemporary discourses. Discourse about sexuality exemplifies this. Since the seventeenth century, in Western societies, the paradox of sexuality has been a simultaneous repressive urging of silence and discretion about its existence, and a huge proliferation of discourses about it, replacing earlier Christian discourse. Foucault's initial questions about this indicate the shape of his specific project and the more general conception of discourse from which this springs:

> Why has sexuality been so widely discussed, and what has been said about it? What were the effects of power generated by what was said? What are the links between these discourses, these effects of power, and the pleasures that were invested by them? What knowledge (*savoir*) was formed as a result of this linkage? The object, in short, is to define the regime of power-knowledge-pleasure that sustains the discourse on human sexuality in our part of the world. The central issue, then (at least in the first instance), is not to determine whether one says yes or no to sex, whether one formulates prohibitions or permissions, whether one asserts its importance or denies its effects, or whether one refines the words one uses to designate it; but to account for the fact that it is spoken about, to discover who does the speaking, the positions and viewpoints from which they speak, the institutions which prompt people to speak about it and which store and distribute the things that are said. What is at issue, briefly, is the over-all 'discursive fact,' the way in which sex is 'put into discourse.' Hence, too, my main concern will be to locate the forms of power, the channels it takes, and the discourses it permeates in order to reach the most tenuous and individual modes of behavior, the paths that give it access to the rare or scarcely perceivable forms of desire, how it penetrates and controls everyday pleasure — all this entailing effects that may be those of refusal, blockage, and invalidation, but also incitement and intensification: in short, the 'polymorphous techniques of power'.

Foucault's subsequent analysis offers an account of one domain. Yet this may be seen as part of a project generalizable towards an overall theoretical study of language in history. It is a project which might have intense relevance for education. Though it would be premature to describe this as existing, some lines along which it might be constructed are, I hope, apparent. Such a study would make central the historical determinations and purposes of different, contemporary discourses. It would also seek to account both for the constitutive powers of discourse in culture and for the possibilities of resistance and change.

I want to conclude by suggesting the relevance of the concept of discourse for understanding classroom processes. Classrooms are related in their objectives to discourses of varying kinds: not only academic discourses, but also politically and educationally oriented discourses, together with the potentially numberless range of discourses through which culture is constituted. In addition, discourses are *created* in classrooms, related to discourses in the culture more widely but constructed by the central participants, pupils and teachers. This suggests a starting point for analysis both of the manner and matter of different classrooms. In an understanding of the discourses which are constructed might lie ways of conceptualizing how different kinds of learning become established and the ways by which pupils are offered opportunities to become learners. I want now to give one example in order to indicate these possibilities more fully.

*   *   *

I select as my example a Humanities classroom in which I worked and observed for a number of years. I should offer a little by way of background. 'Humanities' was then in a relatively early stage of its development in the school. Ways of working were still provisional, and perhaps expectations derived from earlier patterns of subject specialization were proving slow to disappear. There were various reasons behind my presence in this classroom. I had been in the school anyway in connection with a school-based initial training course and had watched Humanities develop. I worked in some classrooms, as my students did, joining Humanities teams. In this particular classroom I was also exploring a number of ideas. I was interested in how patterns of language use became established and I was also trying to watch how different pupil repertoires influenced each other in a linguistically diverse setting. I give these details in order to explain how it was that I came to be helping with teaching and to be in a privileged position to document and observe.

At this relatively early stage of forging new ways of working, drama was of special interest for the teachers in this classroom. It was not their only concern, as I have indicated. Their central task was to evolve curriculum. Within this, however, drama had a new place to find and, potentially, a different and special contribution to make. Quite soon, a pattern began to emerge. Drama was used to extend and vivify learnings which were first approached more conventionally in classroom teaching. For example, alongside the study of the emergence of human societies, a long episodic simulation evolved during one term, which centred in issues and priorities arising for a plane-load of people crashed on a desert island. This was the background to a lesson in the second term of the second year, in which fifteen boys sat for one and a half hours analysing through drama the problems of merchants facing the insecurity of feudal society.[10]

I want now to give some sense of this drama through one illustration of my more general argument. This is that the concept of discourse offers a way of understanding classroom processes within an historical theory of language. The drama began with a role problem, which was introduced by the teacher in the course of a long monologue. It is necessary first to grasp the flavour of this monologue. Here is how it closes:

> Now in this town we have the power, but that power is being threatened. We have a lot of time and effort invested in this town. I myself have worked hard all my life and I believe that I have a good right to my gold and my large house and that no one should take it away from me. But the King's doing nothing about it and I guess you're all suffering the same. Now the town could fall into ruins if those lords are allowed to wander up and down the country fighting each other, threatening the King, threatening us. Those bands of soldiers are dangerous. Now unless there is some peace, there will be no trade. If there is no trade, that's goodbye to us. Now the King doesn't seem to be doing much about it. As far as I can see he's too scared. I think it's up to us, gentlemen. Now although I called this meeting, that doesn't make me any more important than you. We're all the same. We share problems. Can we see if this morning we can share solutions . . .?

Through this monologue the class is turned into a council of merchants and the drama is initiated. Already, certain further terms for the subsequent transaction are being established. Many potential protagonists are ruled off stage and placed as part of the background to the problem. The King is not to be present in what follows, though his ineffectiveness is a key question to be negotiated. Similarly, there are to be present no lords or soldiers or other members of the social hierarchy, though their actions are to figure in the merchants' deliberations. The effect of this is important. Sets of events, a fiction, are made common as a basis for the drama, but the protagonists in these events are to enter only as abstractions. It is a crucial ground rule. As it happens, the convention is demonstrated as such at points later, by the pupils' awkwardnesses in handling it. For example, there will be a difficulty for the pupils about what is meant by the 'weakness' of the King. A number will interpret this as illness. That illustrates one aspect of the discourse which is being initiated. It is to be pitched just at that point of tension between events and generalization of events which is critical in historical narrative.

Relationships, both pupil to teacher and pupil to pupil, are a further aspect of the discourse coming into being in this monologue. Pupil debate and argument, in the context of the teacher's presence, guidance and support, is what is proposed. Clearly, identifying the merchants as the subject of the drama makes plain a central perspective. Behind their roles, pupils are also identified as a working group whose attention is focused, in common, on a central question and activity. The pupil collaboration suggested is that of debate rather than of a more open project.

Meanwhile, the teacher's role is subtle. It is partly integrated with the drama, the teacher as an ordinary participating member of the group, but, also, partly separated. The sources of the separateness lie in the teacher's authority and, in a more complex way, in the terms of the discourse which are being set. It is a given fact at this point that the teacher's command of the abstractions within the initiating fiction is greater, for the drama has been initiated by her. Also, the teacher's presence will monitor and probably be central in shaping what unfolds. It would be wrong to see these relationships, however, as an imposition of authority. Pupil debate and a flexible role for the teacher's authority are, rather, a further constitutive ground rule. The organization of the discourse 'positions' its participants. I shall want to argue for the educational significance of this in terms which go wider than the immediate drama.

Once under way, the gap between pupil and teacher language is immediately striking. The way in which this difference is co-ordinated and used as a central strength is crucial, I believe, to what is achieved. Let me first illustrate the difference, by inviting comparison of the elegant close of the introductory monologue with the staccato suggestions and interpolations of the group as they begin to innovate the drama's momentum.

DL   We could build our own private army.
NM   We need money.
T   We'll we have got money.
NM   We'll we need food.
T   We've got food at the moment but supplies may dry up if we . . .
(confusion of voices)
NM   We could get people working for us.
AW   But who's going to train them, though?
T   Now, gentlemen . . .
DL   We could just have a handful of already trained soldiers and . . . could train them.
PS   But that would be no good.
DL   Why not?
NM   But suppose . . . when we . . .
DL   But then we'll have a chance then, innit.
DL   If we buy our soldiers, right . . .
PS   We should report them to the . . .

Thus the pupil speech is persuasive in mode, pursuing or countering a line, competitive for space, assertive but skilful in turn-taking, confined in length of utterance because of pressure from other speakers in the group. Such pressure entails absolute directness and economy ('We need money' . . . 'Well we need food' . . . 'But who's going to train them, though?').

Qualifications, connectedness between complementary arguments, differences in opinion, have to be left to some extent implicit. So economy is bought perhaps at some cost in explicitness of meaning. The central contrast between pupil and teacher speech is, however, this. Pupil contributions are directed towards particular advocacies. Suggestions are made and countered and particular causes championed or opposed. The teacher's speech is directed towards the group enterprise as a whole. Her interventions maintain the undertaking and influence the range of possible suggestions which can emerge. Thus, a collaborative enterprise is created, not unlike a refereed game. The pupils acknowledge players' rules between themselves. These assert the right to intervene and to be heard and also allow for the possibility of 'taking over' the play for an individual argument. The constitution, the maintenance and the final arbitration of the game are 'given' to the teacher.

There is also being strengthened through this a pervasive and general bond. Classroom drama of this kind supplied the chief experience for pupils of occasions when a teacher worked *with* them. Work on most other occasions in Humanities was done *for* the teacher, the predominant nexus of relationships through the curriculum as a whole. In drama, the common make-believe was mutually ordained and thereafter it brought teacher and pupils collaboratively together in a way which was intrinsic to the work in hand. This may seem too idealistic a formulation. It could be argued that in such a setting, established finally by the teacher's authority, pupil dependency gives to the teacher excessive opportunity for manipulation. I would want to argue, in contrast, that the discourse which was developed in drama was taken on by a number of pupils and put to work more widely in the curriculum; that drama created and released possibilities. To establish this fully I should have to relate discourse in drama to other classroom discourses. This is beyond my scope here, though it is possible to indicate some features of this discourse more precisely and to provide some speculations.

A slightly longer sequence, at a point where the drama is well established, illustrates more exactly the balance between pupil and teacher contributions. For this, we should be aware of features which a transcript does not catch. The pupils' speech is rapid, assertive, bidding to be heard. The teacher's interventions, in contrast, are signalled ahead for her entry. They take up the space which occurs as the group confusion of voices gradually falls silent, recognizing the teacher's intention to intervene. The teacher's contributions synthesize arguments and make explicit principles behind possible courses of action. Through them the pace of the discussion is slowed to allow an interval of reflection.

PB Gordon's the leader right, Gordon should go to the King and ask
. . .

T He's only our chairman — sorry to interrupt.

PB Chairman. He could go to the King and ask the King can he have some of his army . . .

JB But he could . . .

BG Wait Johnny.

PB . . . Could he control his army so we can fight the lords — the lords — and win.

JB But he's too weak to control his army.

PB Gordon will. He's goona to go up to the King and ask him.

JB But we need . . . (?) . . . we need more chairman (?)

(confusion of voices)

OL We can ask him that of his own he wants to get off the throne now and somebody else takes his place. 'Cos he might be tired himself.

BG All right. You're all saying, right, that you need a new King. Who's the King that's got everything . . . soldiers . . . everything . . .

PS Not a King, a man.

— I mean a man.

DL You don't need a King that has soldiers . . . you need a King that's strong enough to control the soldiers.

RN But then again, right, we don't need . . or don't really need a King do we?

— We do.

(confusion of voices)

T The reason why we need a King is that we need peace, we need order. Now if the King can make the laws of the land, most people are loyal, most people will obey the laws. Now it is the lords who are not obeying laws and the lords who are pushing the King to . . . er
. . .

— Punish them.

T . . . forgive them or make laws in their favour. Now if the King can be persuaded to make laws which help us by giving peace and order then we could use the King . . . he's weak at the moment . . . perhaps we could make him stronger.

There are pupil to pupil relations as well as pupil and teacher relations which may be heard within this sequence. Modes of collaborative working, that is, are being negotiated between pupils themselves. The choice of 'Gordon' as chairman has been made by the group earlier in the drama, at the teacher's prodding. This choice merely ceded to him the dominant role which was his anyway. Here, as at other times, the role has to be negotiated with 'Johnny', another strong and trusted personality in the group. Such longer term social relations may need to be inferred. But there is some evidence here of a wider process at work, initiated through the drama. The constitution of the discourse requires pupils to control a group process. The group is itself made central in the conduct of the work and is thus invited into an experience of collaborative discussion. I believe that cumulatively this made a contribution to the classroom climate as a whole.

It will also be clear from the extract that a purpose within the teacher's contributions is to develop more abstract, historical understandings. They seek to open the way to appreciating the adjustment of class interests which may be permitted by law and by control of the process of legislation. This level of abstraction cannot be sustained by the group. The teacher's contributions, however, serve as a marker for the conceptual command which discussion might seek. Thus the pupils are positioned within a discourse in which experience is provided of conducting an argument and of developing a reasoned and persuasive case. Taken with the level of abstraction involved, the experience of negotiating group relations, the collaboration with the teacher in sustaining a common enterprise, there are further points here for speculating on the contribution made by discourse in drama to the development of uses of language more generally.

Educationally, it is worth emphasizing the impetus gained by some pupils from the experience of their own group relations projected into a setting of worthwhile educational endeavour. It was this feature which was made central by a number in the group when they discussed their work in drama later in the term. This is what they had to say

- Like we have Humanities, it teaches us to sit down and discuss, right, so if we do drama, what it teaches is to play together and talk together
- You won't need that when you grow up, will you?
- Yes, you will
- You could be a director
- It doesn't teach you only that, it teaches you to trust your friends — you know who to trust and who to not trust
- You don't need to play together but you need to trust your friends, you need to know who's good and who's bad
- Like Miss P. says that . . . something about trusting friends and making groups between people we haven't been with before . . . making up groups of people.

There are many points which might be noted, even in so truncated a passage of discussion. The pupils have to break through the dominant expectation of drama as theatrical entertainment in order to represent what their experience has been. It is interesting that drama is then linked with learning to 'sit down and discuss'. So also is the consciousness of relationships through which drama is realized. That there are these and wider educational implications in the lesson which I have described I have little doubt. My central interest, though, has been different. I have sought to provide an example, which might be replaced by others, of the theoretical understanding which may be permitted by the notion of discourse.

I find the construction of discourse which takes place in classrooms interesting ultimately because I want to locate the power which is available within education as a socio-cultural site. Among all the bad presses education has had, the most destructive has been to attribute to teachers and children the capacity only to reproduce the ideologies of contemporary ruling classes and dominant cultures. Education cannot change material poverty. That said, a description of social processes which assigns to education only a reproductive role seems utterly wrong. It is false to what happens in classrooms and undermines the work of people who are in a position to care most about the present and future of this society.[11]

As is shown in the work of Volosinov and Vygotsky, language is never simply the dead purveyor of fixed and permanently established meanings. In society, in history, it is always the site of dialectic processes, continuously reconstructed and remade. There are of course, dominant discourses in this, through which the powerful search out consensus and control. Dominant power, however, has always to defend itself and is also always confronted by the power of resistance and critique. Once teaching is seen as inserted into these wider cultural processes, it cannot be right to see classrooms as simply and necessarily the means by which culture is reproduced, though it is a danger that an alternative may be made to look too easy. Classrooms may be part of the *production* of culture; and it becomes possible to see this when notions of language and society as merely fixed and static systems are overturned.

The theoretical notion of discourse, given us by Foucault, may be put to work self-critically in education. There would be no difficulty about this. I could have used as an example a discourse about writing which took place in this classroom and which seemed to me less productive than the drama on which I have concentrated. I had my reasons for not doing this, which partly reflect certain criticisms I have of academic attention to classroom language. Too much of this has been inspired by a technological concentration on teaching or a programmatic sociology or linguistics; though not exclusively.[12] Such criticisms go beyond my purposes here, but partly underlie my choice of example. Mainly, I wanted to illustrate the power which I believe *is* available in classrooms and a self-critical example might have seemed to be part of the widespread denial of this. However, I should protect the interpretative flexibility of discourse as a theoretical notion from seeming to be too tied to a particular illustration.

Power lies in classrooms as a part of the processes of cultural making. This is illustrated in the drama lesson which I have described. The discourse which is coming into being qualifies dominant notions about theatre and behind these a passive and merely receptive awareness of art. The extent to which understandings about literature are here finding a very different orientation should not be underestimated. Equally, and made more central in my description, a mode of historical interpretation and ultimately of intellectual and political analysis is being developed. It is being made available through a discourse in which pupil relations are carried forward; and it rests collaboratively on a teacher's authority, which is retained as support, but is also ceded in order that an invitation may be delivered.

Whatever may have been the misleading theoretical appropriations, the debate about English has always rested on an awareness that language was connected with the experience of power in people's lives. This was understood by Matthew Arnold, when the case for English was first argued, though he was unable to escape either nostalgia for a Platonist oligarchy or the ambiguity in his concern for literature's civilizing mission. Later, the Newbolt Committee thought it a reasonable proposition to alert, for English, the anxieties about national effectiveness in the aftermath of war. It is not difficult to perceive other spectres behind the settlement of the Bullock Committee. If there were no power within English and classrooms there would be no need to talk about them at intervals of fifty years.

I have sought to recall and pay tribute to an idea of language in history. If teachers had not taken this into their special advocacy for children and if they had not found in it a means of becoming theoretical about their work, fewer shadows might have fallen across the Atheneum's sunlit windows. In it, I believe, lies a main hope that the power of English will not be reduced and the necessity that English remain a question.

Notes and References

1. Here and at points immediately following, where I refer to ideas against which an emphasis on language in history has had to make its way, I am recalling debates too numerous to list in full. Harold Rosen writes about language in

history in his essay, 'Out There, or Where the Masons Went' in *English in Education*, vol. 9, no. 1, 1975. The technologies of teaching are a recurrent theme in classroom analysis: see M. Hammersley, 'Classroom Ethnography' in D.H. Hargreaves (ed.), 'Classroom Studies', *Educational Analysis*, vol. 2, no. 2, 1980. There is no single source for the orientation towards skills in vocational education, but the Mansell Report, *A Basis for Choice*, Further Education Curriculum Review and Development Unit, 1979, has been influential in the promotion of this. Debates about language diversity may be approached in H. Rosen and T. Burgess, *The Language and Dialects of London Schoolchildren*, Ward Lock, London, 1980, and in J. Miller, *Many Voices: Bilingualism, culture and education*, Routledge and Kegan Paul, 1983. The challenge to the selective tradition derives from R. Williams, *The Long Revolution*, Penguin, Harmondsworth, 1971, but is joined theoretically by J. Britton, 'The Spectator Role' in M. Meek et al., *The Cool Web*, The Bodley Head, London, 1977.

2. The first work of Vygotsky's available in Britain was L. Vygotsky, *Thought and Language*, MIT Press, 1962. It has since been joined by *Mind in Society*, Harvard University Press, 1978. This has been superbly edited by M. Cole et al. and clarifies Vygotsky's overall project.

3. The main introduction to ten years' research in writing is described in J. Britton et al., *The Development of Writing Abilities, 11–18*, Macmillan, London, 1975. The research was funded by the now dismantled Schools Council and included both a theoretical and a curriculum phase. The latter phase is described in N. Martin et al., *Writing and Learning across the Curriculum, 11–16*, Ward Lock for Schools Council, 1976.

4. Papers from the Centre for Contemporary Cultural Studies, University of Birmingham, have been collected in several volumes published by Hutchinsons. The most relevant here is S. Hall et al., *Culture, Media, Language*, Hutchinson in association CCCS, London, 1980. Raymond Williams's work may be approached through *The Long Revolution*, op. cit. n. 1. This, though, is an early work in what has been a lifelong project. I make most use here of R. Williams, *Marxism and Literature*, Oxford University Press, 1977.

5. See Vygotsky's *Mind in Society*, op cit. n. 2.

6. See F. Saussure, *Course in General Linguistics*, Fontana/Collins, London, 1974, and for commentary, J. Culler, *Saussure*, Fontana, London, 1975.

7. The conference was on 'Language in History' and was organized by the History Workshop in November, 1980.

8. See V.N. Volosinov, *Marxism and the Philosophy of Language*, Seminar Press, New York, 1973; and R. Williams, *Marxism and Literature*, op. cit. n. 4.

9. Among Foucault's many works the following are most relevant to the argument: M. Foucault, *The Order of Things: An archaeology of the human sciences*, Vintage Books, New York, 1973; *Discipline and Punish: The birth of the prison*, Penguin, Harmondsworth, 1977; *The History of Sexuality*, Vol. 1, *An Introduction*, Penguin, London, 1979. For commentary see the essay by C. Weedon et al., 'Introduction to Language Studies' in S. Hall op. cit. n. 4., and

B. Smart, *Foucault, Marxism and Critique*, Routledge and Kegan Paul, London, 1983. I was first alerted to the value of Foucault's work for an understanding of classroom processes by Valerie Walkerdine's work in the teaching of mathematics. See V. Walkerdine, 'From Context to Text: A psychosomatic approach to abstract thought' in M. Beveridge (ed.), *Children Thinking Through Language*, Arnold, London, 1982.

10. I should like to thank Frances Magee for a long classroom collaboration which underlies the arguments here and more specifically for permission to use the example.

11. The sources of the view of education as merely reproductive are widespread. Primogeniture is usually attributed to L. Althusser for his account of ideological state apparatuses. Althusser's works are many. The easiest access to the educational relevance of his arguments is in L. Althusser, 'Education and Ideological State Apparatuses' in B. Cosin, *Education: Structure and society*, Penguin and Open University, Harmondsworth, 1972. Among other difficulties, different versions of 'reproduction' locate the part played by education quite differently. Althusser's emphasis on ideology is utterly different from the direct reproduction of labour relations described in S. Bowles and H. Gintis, *Schooling in Capitalist America*, Routledge and Kegan Paul, London 1976. For Harold Rosen's critique of the new 'dismal science', see H. Rosen, *Neither Bleak House Nor Liberty Hall: English in the curriculum*, an inaugural lecture, University of London Institute of Education, 1981.

12. The work of Douglas Barnes is the exception I have in mind. See D. Barnes and F. Todd, *Communication and Learning in Small Groups*, Routledge and Kegan Paul, London, 1977. But see also A. Edwards and J. Furlong, *The Language of Teaching*, Heinemann, London, 1978, for a similar interest in learning, unusual in this literature.

2.
Story-time, and Beyond

Betty Rosen

> So happy was the beautiful Yasmin as her wedding day drew nigh that she cried
> aloud, 'I am afraid of nothing and no one, not even of Death!'
> Death chuckled to himself. 'I'll get her when she least expects me!'

At this point I paused in my story-telling and suggested the boys split up into
twos or threes to work out what might happen next. This is a fairly unusual
move in the story-telling session: generally tales are told without any inter-
ruption. After lunch every Friday afternoon normal timetable ceases for all
first- and second-year pupils at the Somerset Comprehensive School for
Boys in Tottenham, and Leisure Pursuits take over. Groups of about two
dozen pupils go sailing, play guitars, hoist garden forks, pull out the mats for
yoga, etc., and one lot comes to me for story-telling. Stories are told, never
read out.

Each week I prepare a story for the group, usually a fantasy story, and, like
Viola, I 'have ta'en great pains to con it'. Often this comes during the last
thirty minutes of the eighty-minute session, but sometimes I can't fit it in.
The boys are themselves full of stories. Some they have heard, some they
have read but most come from their own everyday lives. 'Has anyone got a
scar? How did you get it?' or 'What was the best present you ever got?' or
'Were you ever scared in the middle of the night?' or Labov's 'Did you ever
think you were about to die?' Such questions elicit story upon story, stories
within stories and stories which beget stories in others. No one is left out
because each child is subject to the narrative of his own living. I see six different second-year groups, as there is a general swop around each half-term.
Occasionally a group throws up a really talented performer who can hold
everyone's breath; it is not necessary, though, for a boy to be exceptional in
the telling for every listener to hold his tongue. And it makes no difference if
a tale is second-hand as long as it is not told as such: the rule is to re-vision it

so that it becomes the property of the teller. These have been my happiest Friday afternoons in many years of teaching.

But what happened to Yasmin? You wouldn't know, would you? On the other hand, you may well know that a skeleton in bridal robes was discovered inside an old oak chest long years after that fateful Christmas wedding feast in Minster Lovell in oldenday Oxfordshire. While the mistletoe withered on the castle wall, 'they searched all day and they searched all night' for the bride who was lost forever in an innocent game of hide-and-seek. That was the story I was telling. I saw it all in my head as I told it. It lacked a peaches-and-cream English maiden with golden tresses — we'd had one of them a week or so before — so it was time for Eastern dark eyes and long black silken locks. I can't recall now how I explained the fact that the village beauty who entranced young Lord Lovell had originated from India but she had, much to the satisfaction of the several pupils of Asian origin in my story group.

Many stories told on Friday afternoons had very precise ethnic locations, such as Anansi stories or the story of Gelert, the faithful Welsh dog buried at Beddgelert in north Wales. It is enough in some cases just to state that, like older members of my pupils' families, the story had travelled from Greece or Italy or Nigeria or wherever. And there are those stories we know travel everywhere: Abit, a non-English speaking Turkish-Cypriot pupil in my first-year English class, is quite convinced that the story he wrote of the boy who cried 'Wolf!' is about Ali who lived and tricked and came to his ugly end in a Cypriot village. Once, well on in her story, a princess escapes from her tower to seek out the distant land where her wounded prince dwelt. At last she reaches the edge of his kingdom. If, gazing out towards the high spires of the alien city where her love lies bleeding, she happens to have hidden herself in the dark cedar tree under which the witches of the four corners of the earth have chosen to meet and gossip, be sure she will hear of the amazing wonders of each country of my current pupils' origin, which I have swotted up beforehand. Sometimes I will stay close to the exact words of the story I have prepared to tell:

> And all the while Sadko played cunningly on the dulcimer. 'Play on', said the Tsar of the Sea, and he strode through the gates. The sturgeons guarding the gates stirred the water with their tails.
>
> And if the Tsar of the Sea was huge in his hall, he was huger still when he stood outside on the bottom of the sea. He grew taller and taller, towering like a mountain. His feet were like small hills. His blue hair hung down to his waist, and he was covered with green scales. And he began to dance on the bottom of the sea.

Great was that dancing. The sea boiled, and the ships went down. The waves rolled as big as houses. The sea overflowed its shores and whole towns were under water as the Tsar danced mightily on the bottom of the sea. Hither and thither rushed the waves, and the very earth shook at the dancing of that tremendous Tsar.

He danced till he was tired . . .

Other times I will deliberately avoid the words I've read. When, for instance, the luckless prince Ivan's newly born sister turns out to be a witch baby with iron teeth I cut at least one word of their father's: 'See, you have a little sister; a fine girl she is, too. She has teeth already. It's a pity they are black, but time will put that right . . .' In this group, a third of whom are West Indian in origin, black is beautiful, so I take no risks, even with teeth.

The story group takes much planning in spite of a predominance of spontaneity. Every half-term I arrange to have an outsider come as a visiting story-teller. As yet there has been no offer from a relative, friend or neighbour of one of the pupils, even though there is a written invitation which goes out with each boy at the start of the half-term. Do these letters slink out of the plastic bags? Do they get shoved down a grid or chewed by the dog? Perhaps my letter is wrongly worded or, more likely, secondary schools are not very attractive places to venture into. The story of Minster Lovell — or, rather, my version of it containing the figure of Death, determinedly stalking the ill-fated heroine, whose loving selflessness had so often cheated him out of the life of some trapped animal or lonely outcast — was in fact a preparation for the following week. John Richmond was due to come. He would be telling his version of *The Pardoner's Tale*. I hoped my pupils would thus be made ready for the three drunken youths, busily tracking down that perpetrator of the Plague, Death himself.

The 'outsiders' have always turned up trumps. Renrick Henry from St Vincent proved a second Alex Pascall as an Anansi story-teller. My husband so enjoyed the experience of revealing his sins in school detention when Hoffman set off the fire extinguisher that later he wrote down the whole story— and the pen transformed it into a tale of a very different order. On other occasions we heard of sparrows from up north, alias dunnocks, and an old auntie's expertise in lip reading, deafened as she was by long years in a cotton mill's din; and of a blizzard which forced Tony Lenney, years before he became Haringey's CEO, to spend an unplanned night on a bare mountain. When we talked about him the following week, one child said, 'He talked good, Miss, not all soppy like we were little kids but as if he was talking to adults like he was talking to you, Miss.' I wonder how many chief education officers would even *want* to spend 80 minutes with a class of kids, let alone know how to talk to them.

But to return to Yasmin. What would you have done with her? You will remember the boys went off to work out their own notions of how Death might entrap her. No earthly need to remind them that she must not be run over by a bus or burnt alive by a faulty electric blanket. Each group had its spokesman who became story-teller. Here, in brief, is what emerged.

Hitesh   In the castle grounds a cat climbed to the top of the tallest tree and could not get down. Yasmin went up to rescue it and when she was up 'Death created a great wind and she fell to her death.'

Berkand   Yasmin heard the squalling of a rabbit in a snare. Death had disguised himself as the rabbit and as she reached down he rose up and took her away.

Zahid   The wedding feast is in full swing and a young man appears with a fine wedding cake. He invites Yasmin to take and eat the first slice. She does and she dies. The man recedes into a mist. The man is Death.

Jason   The wedding service takes place and at the very moment the ring is slipped on to her finger they turn towards each other. Yasmin sees into the eyes of . . . Death and falls to the floor. Death is Lord Lovell.

Kevin   Yasmin drinks from the wedding goblet. She dies and Lord Lovell looks into the wine and faintly sees in it the form of Death with his scythe.

So much for Yasmin.

Each version was delivered with serious intensity, as is fitting. Such is the idiom of the story. Such is its symbolism. It drew boys eagerly to my room at the weary end of the week. It stilled their truanting spirits. Discipline came in the shape of expectation. Ex- or non-members of the group would be attracted, little begging waifs and strays, so the circle of chairs would shuffle larger to make room for them.

★   ★   ★

But Yasmin did not end there. Stories like hers, spoken, become magnetic, too powerful to be confined to an end of the week slot. It seemed high time to put the telling of such stories centrally on the agenda of mainstream English lessons. This was easier said than done. Telling a tale can take three-quarters of an hour or more. In 1U, my first-year class, was Abit (remember Abit?)

recently of Cyprus, speaker of Turkish, speaker of Greek, total non-speaker of English. What happens to him if I switch to make story-telling the focus of a whole term's English lessons?

Abit was lucky. He had two props, Erkan, an extraordinarily sociable Turkish speaker, fluently bilingual, and Peter Whetman, the ESL specialist, who joins Abit and 1U for a double lesson of English once a week. Abit had arrived in December and it was now almost Easter time. He had got used to being included, occasionally being the star turn even. Not so long ago I had decided to use a dual text worksheet about grandparents from the ILEA's second language learner's pack *The World in a City*, so the whole class could see what Turkish looked like in print. Abit had often read to me in Turkish (all double Dutch to me, of course) but with this sheet he could read to everyone. He would be chief reader followed by others reading aloud the translations. By the end of the lesson Abit was the centre of a busy group wanting to know which word in Turkish said *family, daughter, friends, lonely* . . . Listening to Abit reading aloud must have given his classmates a taste of the patience of this shy little stranger who sat silent through hours of alien gabble delivered almost exclusively by teachers. Even on this topic, selected particularly because of the Turkish/English worksheet, he had to suffer my serialized reading of 'Granny Reardun' from *The Stone Book* by Alan Garner. It caught up these pupils, though distant from them in time, place, dialect and pace, but meant nothing to Abit — Erkan was listening too hard to think about transmitting the gist of it to his undemanding protégé. My story-telling would have to coincide with Pete Whetman's visits.

It takes a lot of work to prepare a story so that the telling sounds effortless. While I smiled, gestured and goggle-eyed my way through 'Prince Ivan, the Witch Baby and the Little Sister of the Sun', a long and complex narration, Pete Whetman sweated over his note-taking. During the last twenty minutes of the lesson, Pete, Erkan the interpreter and Abit went off in a little huddle to piece it all together. The story had gone down a treat. By the time it reached my story group I knew it would become a party piece. It had its young hero, Prince Ivan, rejected by his parents, cared for by a wise and loving groom and eventually forced to ride to the End of the World alone on a black stallion the very day his evil little sister was born — with those unmentionable teeth. It has a giant who tears up trees by the roots and an even bigger one who hurls mountains. Two old crones sit sewing in the middle of a vast plain, sewing, sewing until death becomes due when the last silk thread is in place and the last needle breaks. Happy is the day when Ivan joins the little sister of the sun in her gleaming castle of clouds. They play hide-and-seek within the wispy turrets, pluck down stars to toss to each other and have lots more larks . . . but that's only part way through the tale. Ideal for dramatization, by which time Abit was thoroughly *au fait* with the situation and performed a very creditable Giant Tree-rooter. 'Can we do it in assembly, Miss?' So they did, with Dennis, the most unpredictable, ingenious and stentorian-voiced member of 1U taking the key role of narrator.

Next time I felt I could do better for Abit. It was to be an Italian tale of yet another princess confined to a tower who eventually saves her lover from death thanks to information gleaned from one of those witches I referred to earlier under the cedar tree. I drew a series of pictures to help Abit follow the story. It was something of a disappointment to learn from Erkan that he had only managed to follow as far as the third drawing: I had painfully produced about twenty! The time was certainly ripe to put Abit at the centre of the lesson again.

Which brings me near to the end of my story. That is, as far as you are concerned. Stories, like English lessons, flow on. There are no real endings. Perhaps there are no beginnings either.

Together, the whole class looked again at the simple tale of Ali who, in Turkish, had cried 'Wolf!' We considered the facts as translated a term or more ago by Erkan with assistance from Pete. A good deal of time was spent discussing how this sequence of events might have affected individual members of the village community. Then the whole class wrote new versions from the point of view of any villager. Had I taught them theoretically about the structure of *the story* the results would have been very different. Dennis, for one, would have written absolutely nothing.

Their stories were remarkable. Many stories were exceptionally well done, and every child in this mixed-ability class produced something of real interest. 1U believed their success was due to Abit, the 'originator' of the story. I knew it was the result of magic, the magic of narrative itself — the telling, more telling, the talking about, the dramatizing of, the reflection upon . . . a *gestalt* of story.

Here are some tasters of what was entitled 'Abit's Story'. Nicholas began with,

The sun rose over the trees and the flowers seemed to come alive . . .

Nobody had instructed him in the craft of story openings. For Chris it was a different sort of day:

It was a cold, chilly day. I was mending shoes in the shop. I worked as a cobbler, fixing shoes, putting new soles on, fixing heels. Normally it's not a busy day but today was very busy, people coming in and out, until about 3 p.m. I heard 'Wolf! Wolf!' . . .

He follows the crowd, armed with his cobbler's hammer and,

> . . . tried to get to the front. I heard Ali's voice. He said 'I've tricked you! You all came thinking there was a wolf but there isn't really.' The villagers all came back, mumbling to themselves . . .

Che, like one or two others, responded to my throw-away line, 'Remember the blacksmith's shop in *Granny Reardun?*' This is how he wrote:

> 'Everybody get your sticks and guns. I'll get my forge hammer and batter or destroy the vermins . . .'

> Soon after I was back at work.
> The clang of metal against metal is like music to my ears — steam, smoke, sweat, the bellows are puffing. Four more horse shoes and then today I'm finished . . .

> ''Tis I — Ali!'
> 'Everybody get him! Let him be beaten with a hand as rough as coal yet as hard as steel!' . . .

Che shouldn't be writing like that without a lesson on similes, should he? I wonder how the APU would set about assessing him. Presumably he has a Reading Age. I wonder what a standardized test would tell? Its tongue would not be as sweet as the tongue of Che's own story, that's for sure.

*   *   *

It is fitting to end with a complete story. An international story, written down by Abit in Turkish, translated into English by Erkan (born in England) and transformed in Tottenham by Dennis Humphrey, aged twelve, who is Jamaican in origin. After a few paragraphs Dennis establishes himself as Ali's father who, like any fond parent, refuses to countenance a tragic ending for his child. In real life, Dennis too has reason to hope for salvation rather than retribution. Here it is, the only doctorings being my addition of many of the full stops and all of the inverted commas for your convenience.

Abit's Story or The Boy That Always Lied

Ali was a boy aged about ten. He was a bad boy who never stopped telling lies. He had a job of looking after the sheep.

One day Ali's mum was going into the village.

'May I come, please?' said Ali.

'No,' said his mother. 'You have been a bad boy lately and as a result you will not go into the village for a week.' And with that she stomped out of the house.

Ali went up the hill to the sheep. Ali's dad was with the sheep, stick in one hand, gun in the other.

'May I look after the sheep now?' said Ali.

'You may look after the sheep', I said.

'Thank you, father', said Ali to me.

I said nothing but walked down the hill leaving Ali sitting under a tree watching the sheep in the blazing hot sun. As I walked down the hill I thought to myself, Ali will have to stop lying because one day something very bad will happen to him.

It was four o'clock in the evening. Ali sat there watching the sun set. As Ali done this he became bored. 'I'm bored', said Ali to himself. 'I wish I could do something to liven things things up a bit.' Well, as Ali thought about this he had an idea. He would go to the top of the hill and shout 'Wolf! Wolf!' That should liven things up a bit. And so Ali put his ideas into action and so he ran to the very top of the hill and shouted 'There's a wolf! There's a wolf!'

Some farmers came out carrying guns and sticks. 'Where is the wolf? Where is it?' But as we know there was not a wolf in sight for miles around. All there was was the trees whistling in the wind and the bright red sunset and of course there was Ali laughing his head off.

'Ali, you are a liar and one day a pack of wolves will come but we won't believe you for all liars must come to a bad end.'

'No, no!' shouted Ali. 'Nothing can happen to me and nothing never will!' he said in his stubborn way.

But, alas, Ali was wrong as you will see later in the story. The people said nothing but went back in their huts. The next morning all the farmers that had fallen for Ali's trick the night before came to complain to me about Ali.

'You are Ali's father, aren't you? Can't you keep the boy under control?' said a farmer to me. 'One day something is going to happen to Ali when he is least expecting it.'

'Well, I have thought about that', I said, 'and if anything does happen to him it will be his own fault. There's only one thing for it — leave him to learn the hard way.'

All the farmers turned away and went home. Secretly I was very very angry with Ali so I went up to the foot of the hill where I kept the sheep. 'Ali!' I shouted up. 'I want to see you about something' I shouted up but there was no answer. I walked up the hill and when I got to the top Ali was sitting under the shade of a tree near to where the sheep were. Ali seemed to be sleeping. I was just going to leave Ali and see if the sheep were all right when Ali sneezed. 'I thought you were meant to be asleep. You were pretending, weren't you? Well, you can't fool me. I want a word with you.' But Ali ran down the hill, leaving me behind. 'That boy!' I said to myself, 'That Boy!'

As the sun started to set Ali ran to the hill and started to hunt for his dad. Good. He wasn't there. Ali kept watch on the sheep. Nearby a traveller had stopped to camp near where the hill was. Ali did not know this. Meanwhile Ali was watching the sheep and the sun set. It started to go dark but it was bright enough to see the sheep.

Ali then heard a howling sort of noise. It was nearby but Ali took no notice of it. And then something caught his eye. It was a brown slinky figure. Ali had seen that figure somewhere before. Now what was it? Then he remembered that howling noise he had heard and all at once a wolf jumped out of one of the bushes nearby and started to attack the sheep. He shouted 'Wolf! Wolf!' But of course nobody heard him. They didn't want to hear because they considered him a liar.

But also somebody heard his shouts and cries. Somebody ran up the hill with a gun in his hand, somebody who didn't know Ali was a liar, somebody who did not ignore his shouts and cries. Somebody shot at the wolf who turned and ran away. It was the traveller, you see. The traveller had not been there the night before when Ali had told the lie about the wolf so instead of ignoring the shouts and cries he reacted quickly.

'Thank you!' cried Ali. 'You . . . you saved my life. But who are you and why did you come to my aid?'

'I came to your aid because I heard you shouting, "Wolf! Wolf!". You see I am a traveller and I stopped here to camp the night.'

3.
'You Liar, Miss'

Josie Levine

It is Friday afternoon a little way into the Autumn term. Ours is the reception class for immigrant children, non-English speaking immigrant children, at the local secy mod in Handsworth, Birmingham, parliamentary constituency of Sir Edward Boyle, Secretary of State for Education. Boys and girls, only one of them more than a year in the country, all of them from Jullunder District in the Punjab, are sitting comfortably together. It is 1964 and we are an unusual group of people.

Until this time, the handful of non-English speaking children who had come into schools had, apparently, just picked up the language. In our school there were four or five outstanding boys, bilingual, high-fliers, confident. One, who acted as our interpreter, had, in the space of a few short years, taken hold of opportunities for qualification for apprenticeship, and also had so become 'one of us' that the remarkable thing about his speech, so I discovered from what the newly arrived children said, was not so much that he spoke English with a Birmingham accent, but that he spoke Punjabi with a Birmingham accent. Teachers were as pleased and proud of boys like Rupinder as they were of their successful indigenous pupils. Certainly, teaching them had not threatened their expertise nor created in them a need for change.

It came as a shock, therefore, to find that Rupinder's pattern of progress was not to be general. As numbers increased and children no longer came into classes singly, the concept of mixed-ability teaching hardly having been aired yet, teachers found themselves increasingly at a loss as to what to do and correspondingly resentful of the fact that the sort of teaching they ordinarily did reached fewer and fewer children in their classes. Non-English speaking children, now in classes in fives and sixes, found themselves, literally, sitting on the edges of the class, given things to keep them occupied. (Over time, some tens of thousands of houses must have been drawn, coloured and labelled for want of knowledge of something better to give them to do.)

With teachers so anxious and uncertain then, it was apparent that something had to be done to preserve 'normality'. Nationally, the debate on this issue centred on numbers: what percentage of immigrant children, culturally and linguistically different from the indigenous population, could be tolerated in a school before the school must necessarily cease to function in its usual ways? Thirty per cent was suggested as the crucial figure in a parliamentary speech of Sir Edward Boyle's (27 November, 1963).[1] Where this figure was reached, he suggested, immigrant children should cease going to their neighbourhood schools and, instead, be dispersed among other schools. The other proposal for a speedy return to normality was for the non-English speaking children to be taught English on a withdrawal basis, so that when they knew enough English, as received opinion had it, they would be able to take their rightful places in ordinary classes and schools.

Withdrawal teaching of English gained ground. Our school went along with this. Even those of us who some 15 or 20 years later argue for a very different provision for the needs of developing bilingual pupils in our education system could at that time see no other way of fulfilling the obligation to provide all children with an education according to their needs. At that time, we were probably correct in thinking that unless the non-English speaking children were removed from the mainstream in some way, they could only go on being the 'non-learners' they appeared to so many to be, and would increasingly gain the disrespect of their peers and teachers. Certainly, they had to be sheltered from that. With hindsight it is easy to see that our good intentions can also be labelled institutional racism, but the experience and the analysis which now enables us to do so had not yet been developed.

The usual way of organizing ESL (English as a Second Language) teaching was for peripatetic teachers to visit about three schools a week and withdraw children for special English lessons. On average, children would attend three lessons a week, for about an hour each lesson. The classes were often made up of children of all ages, with the children put with others from classes different from their own, who were estimated to be at about the same level of English.

We did not do this in our school. I was not a peripatetic teacher but a full-time member of the school's staff. Nor did we withdraw children randomly from different subject lessons, the usual way in which the specialist classes were composed. Ours was a full-time, all-age reception class. All newly arrived non-English speaking immigrant children came into it. There certainly were advantages in this. We were able to get to know each other, develop, as in all other classes our group dynamics, lay down our own class-room culture, and also have some feeling — small though one has to recognize it was with hindsight — of belonging to the school.

The Head had acted with pragmatism and a certain caring. By now his school had well over 30 per cent immigrant children on roll. If he acted on the recommendation about dispersal his numbers would fall (for no one, of course, spoke of bussing white children to replace the dispersed immigrants). He preferred that his school remain a neighbourhood school, and so it was the impracticality of bussing in Birmingham, if not the outright rejection of the principle, which provided us with some stability. The setting up of our reception class increased that sense of stability.

The children certainly needed it. And so did the teachers. Like almost everyone else in the country doing this work at the time, I was not trained for it. Because mine was a full-time class of mixed ages I was quickly forced to acknowledge that it was not pedagogically possible to do English language lessons all day every day; you don't learn a language *first* before starting to use it. For my first two weeks I tried it — from a highly unsuitable book written for adults that required the teacher to drill the students in sentence patterns. It drove the light out of the children's eyes. Moreover, if the children were supposed to go back into ordinary classes as soon as possible, hadn't they better get to know what they could of some of the subjects taught there? From then on, as far as was possible, we tried to follow a timetable of curriculum subjects in learning English — some parts of which also took in the standard specialist practice of teaching language structures. The children responded to doing school learning and, like all children, to being able to give voice to what they thought and felt, and to the opportunity to ask real questions.

Our group was significantly different, then, both in the way it was organized and in the way it worked, from most other groups constituted for the purpose of learning English as a second language. I did not know enough then about learning or about language learning, or about how to analyse the educational system in which I was working to be theoretical about any of it. I was simply responding to the children's disappointment and to my bright-eyed belief that schools could be enjoyable places to be in if your mind is actively engaged. It was an exploration in communication, accommodation, construing, de-centring, indeed mixed-ability teaching (although, of course, I did not know those words then), an exploration which quite often faltered at the level of initial comprehension, but was seldom characterized by intention to misunderstand.

This Friday afternoon, as always, Santokh Singh and Jai Singh sit side by side in the double desk near the door. Jai, silent, shy, contained, is often the butt of offensive racial and sexist remarks from his fellow Punjabis, because, unusually in their experience, his hair grows in tight curls. Santokh, at thirteen, is small, tough, streetwise; a foot shorter than Jai and two years younger; outgoing, daring, the class spokesman. The class looks to him for the otherwise unthinkable — to challenge the teacher.

Sarwan Singh is there. He had arrived one day with Santokh ('Miss, Miss, new boy. He very clever. Know English very good. You teach him') but was, nevertheless, unable to respond to my basic questions. 'No, Miss, not talk, write. You write, Miss. He know writing' Santokh instructs. So I write *What is your name?* The boy, understanding instantly, takes the chalk and writes beneath my words on the blackboard, swiftly and fluently, *Sarwan Singh*. The whole class smiles with pride and Tarlojhan takes him under his wing, for Tarlojhan — whose name was constantly mispronounced by his teachers — was the guardian of names, insisting, when others of his peers gave up, on respectful attempts by foreigners to say them correctly. Indeed, one of my colleagues considered him an awkward customer on the grounds that he refused her the license to call him Tommy when she suggested it as a solution to *her* difficulties. 'No, Miss, everyone must have right name. No good change.'

This Friday afternoon, Sarwan and Tarlojhan sit together in another double desk, two back from the front against the high-windowed wall. Biro Kaur sits in front of them, next to no one — Kuldip is away today. Biro is supposed to be eleven; more likely she is eight or nine. Everything she does suggests this. She skips and plays round the classroom, distracting the others until they must appeal for help. 'Miss, tell her be quiet. We want work.' Today though, she, like the rest, is sitting quietly, ready to begin.

Besides, Kabel, too, is sitting quietly, at a desk in the centre of the room next to Gurnak. Unusually, Kabel has returned from lunch untroubled by the length of the school day. The calm around him suggests that we shall escape his song of disaffection and, therefore, Biro's dancing accompaniment to it — for Kabel, at twelve years of age, is expert in rhythm and finger drumming, highly skilled in it, and with an evident ability to weld new experience and words into his songs. Endlessly, unstoppable, he sings this song, until his feelings are spent: 'Tk, tk, no good; Tk, tk, no good; Fuck, fuck, no good . . .'

Gurnak is one of those who call for quiet when Biro and Kabel tell their troubles in this way. He is more explicit about what is going on inside and outside the classroom. The windows of his house brick-broken for the second time, he asks bitter questions. 'What for they do this thing, Miss? My father good man, my mother good woman. Work hard. No make trouble.' And on another day, when I am lecturing them about how they should behave, he challenges me. 'Miss, why you tell us be good all the time? I *am* good boy, Miss. Why I must be gooder than English boy? Why you tell me this, Miss? Where is fair?' I cannot answer. I am shocked to discover how much of what I resented as a kid, but could not articulate, I am unquestioningly asking of them. ('Don't do your homework in the kitchen', my mother once said. 'You'll get grease on the paper, and they'll say "Those Jews are dirty".') Gurnak's question reveals to me that I do not know what to do to act against the racism on the streets, despite the fact that some twenty years before we too had hate and stones thrown at us by other children as we left our (Jewish) school for home each day.

In front of Gurnak, in a desk by himself, sits Dara Singh, tiny, chirpy, namesake of a renowned Punjabi heavyweight wrestler, his hero. Tiny Dara, his desk festooned with posters of Dara Singh, all biceps, torso and thighs, has appointed himself my guardian.

Elsewhere, behind Tarlojhan, Dara's elder sister, Monahan, sits, also by herself, but sullen, forced by English law to be there (glad of it I discover months later but then so split by the disparity between wanting to be in school and another felt knowledge, deeper for having been grown up with and still constantly reinforced, that education is not for girls, that even depressive inactivity comes to look like a major achievement on her part).

Jasbir Kaur and Ranjit Singh, sister and brother, newly arrived, sit together, quiet, courteous, watching, alert; no 'Pinished, Miss' from them. Exquisitely trained, they put down their pens, close their books, fold their arms and wait calmly for the next assignment. They do not address me except to answer a question directly put, and then, monosyllabically. But they are not silent children. Anyone can see that from watching their conversations and interchanges in Punjabi. Nor does their 'goodness' and refinement of manners estrange them from the rest of the class, as one might be forgiven for anticipating. However, it becomes increasingly and worryingly clear to me that such exquisitely dutiful behaviour, applauded and approved by almost every teacher, is in effect a barrier to what Ranjit and Jasbir want to learn. Of course, they need time just to become acclimatized and also to grow accustomed to the sound of a new language. But how on earth, I ask myself, can they learn to *speak* English if the 'correct' way to behave in class is *not* to talk? I go along with them, though. Shamefacedly, ambivalently, I offer Ranjit *Ladybird Book 6a*, and with the irony that often accompanies these events, he initiates for the first time a dialogue with me.

Handling the book like an insulted expert, he says 'OK, Miss, I understand. I learn read this book (he meant learn to read English by using the book; after all, he is already a reader in Punjabi) . . . then you give me good book.'

Finally, sitting across the gangway from Jasbir and Ranjit, is Dalbir Kaur, artist and only friend of the silent Monahan. Some months earlier, before she could write English, Dalbir had started to draw marvellous, colourful, descriptive pages. We would sit together as she pointed at the things in her drawings which she wanted named. Little by little stories emerged. I wrote a sentence or two. She copied. Then she began to write her own sentences for the continuing flow of pictures. By the time Jasbir and Ranjit had joined the class, through Dalbir's talents we had found a classroom enterprise that gave us all great pleasure, one worthy of sustained attention. It was our communicative currency, the way in which real incidents and imagined stories, episodes and events from the past were shared; the way we came, in fact, to know each other. It never occurred to me to encourage the use of Punjabi as a learning medium. It was taken for granted that English was the language one had to use in the classroom. After all, I could speak only English, and English was the task in hand: mine to teach and theirs to learn it.

Normally on a Friday afternoon we would be in the gym, dancing and playing games, activities much looked forward to. This was our time for relaxation, a fitting end to the tensions of the week. But this Friday we have a job to do. The children's personal details have to be checked. The Head needs them — at the last moment, of course — and no, Monday, when Rupinder, who translates for us, will be back at school, won't do. The returns have to be made by four o'clock *today* or the school won't qualify for the special government assistance available to schools with immigrant children. I decide not to mind, and rationalize it as a chance to do the sort of English work that will always be useful in the outside world — form filling.

I explain that we have a job to do for the Head, that it shouldn't take long, that after that we can go to the gym. On the blackboard I have drawn a simplified form.

Name _____

Address _____

Age _____ Date of birth _____

Time in UK _____

I ask them to copy the form on to their pieces of paper. This they do. They are attentive.

We do 'Name' first, which is easy. Some *can* read it, of course, and others take the meaning from the *shape* of the written word. Furthermore, they can all *write* their names. Then we do 'Address'. Again, everyone can either read it or knows the shape; they can all *recite* their addresses, too. Unfortunately (for speedy delivery from this task), they cannot all *write* their addresses. It doesn't matter, though. It's all good practice. I go round helping, and today, such is our rapport, they give the task their full concentration. Today, too, for the first time, Dara is able to ask for help.

'Miss, show me, Miss. You write. I write same.'

'Copy', I say. 'I'll write it first and you copy.'

'Yes, Miss. You write. I write same.'

I walk round, back bent. Many tongues are caught between lips in concentration. I see Jasbir helping Monahan.

'Age' is easy. They all know the numbers. Biro, too, can write 11, even if she can't read 'Age'. But I write it down for her because everyone else has finished. Sailing along now, relaxed, confident, happy. Soon we'll be finished.

'Right', I say. 'Date of birth.' I look round for someone I think will know. 'What's your date of birth, Ranjit?'

'Don't know, Miss.'

I try Jasbir. Same answer. Tarlojhan. The same.

It must be they don't know the *phrase* 'date of birth'. I turn to Santokh. After all, he is not only *their* spokesman. He is mine, too. He is sure to know, and then he can translate, and Gurnak will get it, too, and then we'll be finished.

'Santokh, what's your date of birth?'

'Don't know, Miss. What means date of birth?'

Ah! so that *is* it. They haven't met the phrase before. Our time in the gym recedes. But never mind. I turn to the blackboard, and as an example start to fill in the form with my own details. Name. Address. Age. They become extra attentive and polite when I fill in my age.

'Now, *date of birth*', I say, writing down the year, 1964. 'This is how you work out your date of birth', I say. 'I am 28, so to get the year I take 28 from 1964 and the answer is 1936.' I put 1936 at the end of the 'date of birth' line on the blackboard.

'Now', I say, again, 'my birth *day* is on the fifth of May. That's the fifth day of the fifth month', and as I say it, I write 5 for the day and 5 for the month in front of the previously written 1936 on the 'date of birth' line. 'You understand?' I ask, 'My date of birth is 5:5:1936.'

They smile comprehendingly, for in so far as I have performed for them the meaning of the phrase 'date of birth', they *do* understand. We are all extremely warm and pleased with each other. Delighted, I rush straight to the follow-up. 'OK, so now you all understand *date of birth*?'

'Yes, Miss.' A chorus and more smiles.

'Good, so all of you write down your . . .' The smiles evaporate. '. . . date of . . .' They shuffle, their attention flying elsewhere. '. . . your date of birth', I finish, lamely.

They look at each other in consternation.

'Come on', I say. 'It will only take a minute. What's the matter with you?'

'No, Miss. Not understand.' Not understand! What do they mean, not understand! They've just said they *do* understand. Silence. They look down. I look at Santokh.

'Santokh,' and I am speaking harshly, separating the words. 'Do you understand *date of birth*?'

'Yes, Miss.'

'OK, Santokh,' I say, measuring my speech still. 'Then please tell the others so we can write everything down and finish and go to the gym.'

'No, Miss.' What?! 'No, Miss. You liar, Miss.'

Anger flashes, and hurt as well. A liar! How dare he! Is there a child who can call his teacher a liar and think he can get away with it? Well, Santokh is one such, obviously. I can hardly breathe, but he, seemingly careless of the effect of his 'insolence', continues in his role of spokesman.

'True, Miss. We not got date of birth like you got date of birth. We can't write answer for you. We not know.'

I breathe deeply. 'But you know how old you are, right?'

'Yes, Miss.'

'So how do you know how old you are if you don't know your date of birth?'

'My mother know. She tell me how old I am. But I not know date of birth.'

I am mystified. I cannot see how anyone can know their age *without* knowing their date of birth. Nor, if I am to be honest, how anyone cannot know their own date of birth. It's *natural* to know one's date of birth. Everyone does, Why are they being so stupid? I try again. 'But you have a passport. What's written in your passport? Your date of birth must be written in your passport.'

'Yes, Miss, but not like for you date of birth.' Santokh sighs patiently. 'You not understand, Miss. Nobody writing like here, Miss, when baby is born. When we come England, my mother say my son born when this happen or that happen. High Commission man in India listen, then he write in passport date of birth number.'

I get it. At last I get it. And it is I who feel stupid. It is my misunderstanding, my lack of cultural understanding, not theirs, which is blocking the progress of this lesson. Somehow Santokh must have understood this and decided to get the matter cleared up instead of being resigned to an impasse. Why else would he have called me a liar? He could have said I was wrong. He knows that word, But they had already told me earlier in the exchange with that 'No, Miss. Not understand', that it was *I* who did not understand. Only I had assumed they were telling me that *they* still didn't understand — easily done when the frame you are working in allows you to assume that in the relation between those who know a language and those who are learning it it is always the learners who have to do all the understanding. Locked in my own way of thinking, taking for granted the 'naturalness' of 'date of birth', it must have seemed as though I was *deliberately* not understanding the truth as they knew it to be. Puzzling, too. If they could understand my truth, how come I could not understand theirs? I was their teacher, after all. So, to Santokh, I wasn't just wrong, since you can't be wilfully wrong. He needed something else to convince me that I was in error. 'Liar', when you look at it from his point of view, isn't such a bad try. It has in it the sense of deliberateness he must have been looking for. That he did not yet know that the word 'liar' is specific to *telling* an untruth and not generalizable to *failing to understand* the truth or that he didn't seem to know the force of the common effect of uttering the word, was the result of inexperience in the language, not wilful ignorance, contempt or abuse on his part.

Everyone learning a language, whether it is the first or a subsequent one, takes time to get to know the range of particular words and the limits on their use in that language. Everyone makes 'mistakes' in trying words out, and the more daring you are in these attempts the more you are open to other people's mirth and anger. This kind of risk-taking is much to be encouraged. Sometimes this exploratory use of language creates a poetic phrase like 'Miss, I like best lion's jungle room', following a visit to a zoo, or a classic howler like 'The shits on the bed', in describing a picture in an English language lesson, but it also produces phrases like 'You liar, Miss'. Because of the different, indeed hurtful, ways in which such attempts at communication are often received many second-language learners never take the risk, preferring to stay within the safety of what they know they know. It need hardly be emphasized that this is a constraint on their learning. Inexperienced users of language, almost more than anyone else, although that, of course, is arguable, need teachers who will both encourage this risk-taking and be willing to go for the intentions behind their words.

Chastened, I continue. 'Good, so you *can* write for me. You can write the date of birth number in your passport.'

'Yes, Miss . . . er . . . no, Miss . . .'

My consternation returns. 'But I thought . . .'

'Yes, Miss, but we not have it except for passport, so we not know it, Miss.'

Kabel, ever alert, responds. 'Miss, passport number in register'.

And I laugh. For so it is.

If those of us in education in the 1960s, who questioned its provision for newcomers to this country then, could have been transported to the 1980s we would have been astonished to find how much progress had been made:

- comprehensivization
- mixed-ability grouping
- mixed-ability teaching
- knowledge about the relationship between talk and learning, based on interactional learning theory and communicative theories of language learning
- ever-increasing knowledge about first- and second-language development
- mother-tongue teaching and maintenance
- bibliographies and suitable books of fiction
- documentation and analysis of racism, classism and gender in education
- anti-racist teaching and multicultural curricula being developed by teachers
- equal opportunities policies introduced in some LEAs, with timetables for schools to begin implementing them.

In the area of teacher training we would have found students on initial courses of training calling for proper integration of multicultural issues into their education courses, and — at last — being taken seriously; the same students, our next generation of teachers, calling for their subject methods course to prepare them for working with the developing bilinguals they will undoubtedly have in their classes rather than — their words — always leaving the work to specialists. In schools we would also have found teachers, often in partnership with ESL specialists, asking questions about their own curricula and teaching methods, and finding ways and means of changing and developing so that second-language learners can *usefully* learn where they ought to learn best — in the mainstream classroom; and crucial to much of this development we would have found teachers undertaking investigations through which they are not only learning better how to respond to diversity, but also making significant contributions to curriculum development — in fact, becoming their own experts. We would have found too, the concept of everyone, not only those in urban, multiracial settings, receiving an education fitting them for living and working in a multicultural society, and the equating of such education with that of a good, i.e. normal, education.

Achievement indeed. So it would come as a shock to learn that, despite all this, children in the 1980s still and daily experience racism, lack of opportunity and an inappropriate education. Gurnak's cry of 'Where is fair?' reverberates across the years. While the concepts for it are firmly with us, fair curricula which grant to all members of a school community equal access to learning are still to be fought for and made real.

Surely, we could reasonably ask, more should have been achieved than this? Why does it take so long to begin to institute educational changes, the changes in training, curricula and pedagogy which are necessary if we really do aspire to a fair society? First, it is because most initiatives are made in the teeth of an established opposition, which works equally hard and with an equal commitment to maintaining the status quo. Second, initiators work from positions of powerlessness *vis-à-vis* the administering of changes.

A short-term view of the amount of conflict and energy necessary for change in education leads to despair, and every day without change works against people's life chances. It is monstrous that the 'fair' changes we argue for are still so hard to bring about.

An oppositional posture is bound to increase the time that is ordinarily needed for ideas to be developed and for the practice that stems from the theory to be developed. Change does not happen by virtue of one insightful theoretical leap nor by the spread of theoretical ideas alone. Individual teachers have to learn and think about theory, take steps to implement it, reflect upon their practice and develop it. Moreover, each new generation of teachers has this learning to do and needs a climate which encourages it.

The best thing about the present time, despite government policies and economic hardships is that change *is* being initiated. Some local education authorities even support it. This certainly helps creative, committed teachers. It improves the climate in which they work and encourages a growth in confidence among them as practitioners. They have made and can continue to make a unique contribution to the development of curriculum and teaching styles suitable for a multicultural, multilingual society.

The development of new pedagogies for mixed-ability teaching — coming out of theories about the relationship between talk and learning, which have been around for some time; and theories of second-language development, which are less well-known in the mainstream of our education system — is an area of curriculum innovation which needs to be strengthened. By putting these ideas into practice on behalf of second-language learners, language specialists and mainstream teachers, working together, have developed both their strategies for supporting second-language learning and better learning environments for everyone. Importantly, groups of teachers are discovering for themselves that talk helps learning and that children becoming bilingual need support across the curriculum (also what that support might be). This learning anew what is already known by some is an important step in teachers' learning about teaching. To be able to state that this will involve both the taking on of collaborative roles between pupils, between pupils and teachers and between teachers, and also in some sense a negotiated curriculum, and then be able to describe how, over time, these conclusions and practices are reached, takes this learning further. It is also, and significantly, a contribution to the *theory* as well as the practice of teaching.

If the insights and practices of this current generation of 'learning' teachers are to take hold we have to continue the fight for conditions that will foster them. Our present ground-base offers hope. We can now say that there is a greater recognition that diversity of need is the norm rather than one standard all-purpose curriculum. But best of all is the fact that teachers are seeing themselves as active participants in the making of curriculum and classroom methodology rather than accepting without question a role as transmitters of received 'wisdom'.

Reference

1. Sir Edward Boyle, House of Commons, 27 November 1963, *Hansard*, vol. 685, cols. 433–44. Quoted in E.J.B. Rose et al. *Colour and Citizenship*, Oxford University Press for the Institute of Race Relations, 1969, p. 268.

4.
Researchers and Learners
Some changes in the direction of research in English

Nancy Martin

Of course research of any magnitude needs special arrangements and the funding that such arrangements demand, but in recent years a different kind of research has been developing within the field of education. This is a grass roots kind of research concerned with classroom enquiry, wherein research assistants don't have to be appointed and the 'raw data' as well as the enquirer is at hand; a class and a teacher. Of course, classes and their teachers have always been there, but the potential for teachers of conducting their own enquiries based on their own classes or their own schools is now becoming a reality.

Certain changes, in part social and political, have altered the focus of much educational research in Britain and North America, both the kind of questions that are being asked and many of the procedures of enquiry. These changes are associated with changes in teacher-student relationships and the perceptions each has of their respective roles. Since I am concerned here to direct attention to the status of classroom enquiry as a valid form of research, which carries with it implications about the status of the enquirers (classroom teachers), I want to refer particularly to three shifts of focus within the educational scenario.

First, there is the shift of focus from teaching to learning. People are asking not so much, 'How do I teach?' as, 'How do my pupils learn?' Learning is a process which takes place over time, and in studying how people learn, as distinct from what has been learned, all kinds of contextual features become relevant. Student-teacher relationships are seen as highly significant; students' past experiences of lessons, schools and teachers all figure; and the intellectual and social climate of classroom and school as it affects both teacher and student is considered important. The view of learning as a process — an interactive process — means that there must be some shift of focus from the class as a whole to individuals within the class; one child responds differently from another, and differently, maybe, this week from last week, so we begin to look for other models of research than those taken from the physical sciences, with repeatable experiments using large numbers and with results generalizable across classes and across schools.

My second point concerns this shift of focus in research procedures. Educational research has been, and still is, much concerned with the control of variables; variations of teachers, teaching methods, schools, and the past histories of individuals — all those features which form the learning environment, and which are now recognized as playing a significant part in learning. But in order to study learning processes which take place within the network of human relationships and institutional behaviours which constitute a school different procedures are needed, procedures based on observation, documentation of environments and classroom events, analysis of work products and of language samples, and on the keeping of records and personal journals. Any or all of these may be used. Sometimes such case studies will be concerned with individual pupils over periods of time, sometimes with the interactions of small groups. The models are there in other social sciences. Anthropologists, clinical psychologists and social workers, for instance, have always been concerned with case studies. Their validity in these fields is unquestioned, yet educational research has for too long been strait-jacketed by procedures (and philosophies) derived from technological models, and the weight of the educational establishment is still behind them. The mould, though, is beginning to crack, and it is important that educationists — teachers, administrators and researchers — recognize that case studies are respectable and valid procedures in their field.

The third shift of focus that I want to draw attention to is in the attitude of many teachers to themselves as enquirers. Classroom experiment, which many teachers do continually, and observation of individual pupils over periods of time, together with the dissemination of their studies in one form or another have put classroom enquiry as a recognized form of research not only within the reach of all teachers, but right into their court. They can now see themselves as able to contribute to educational knowledge from the work they do every day. To make such contributions is a powerful incentive to question and explore further, much more influential than hearing about the results of research carried out by people far from the classroom. Classroom enquiry carries with it the notion that teachers are learners too, and this is a big shift from the stereotype of teachers as people who know the answers to most things. In a recent article in the American *English Journal* called 'A Quiet Form of Research'[1] James Britton wrote,

If research is seen primarily as a process of discovery, then the day to day work of teachers comes under the term, *teachers as researchers*. Teaching consists of inter-active behaviour and in the course of interacting with individuals and classes, a teacher must make a hundred and one decisions in every session — off the cuff decisions that can only reliably come from inner conviction, that is to say by con-sistently applying an ever-developing rationale. Every lesson is an enquiry, a further discovery, in short, a quiet form of research.

This 'ever-developing rationale' is the other face of classroom enquiry and carries with it the need for further education for the enquirer. These two closely-linked directions, classroom research and a developing self-education, represent the vanguard of current educational thinking about research in English teaching, and the implications go far.

I have used the term case studies to cover many forms of classroom enquiry and have suggested that this is a developing form of research, but case studies are not entirely new, even in the field of English teaching. In the past, for instance, many teachers have recorded samples of children's writing over periods of time, and what may be seen from these writings is a progress towards mastery. Because nothing was shown of the contexts, though, we can learn little from them. Contrast, for instance, those collec-tions of children's writings, usually printed without context or comment, with the records kept by Donald Graves[2] and his helpers at the Atkinson Elementary School in New Hampshire, where the teachers have steadily documented their 'conferences' with beginning writers as they talk to their teachers about their revisions and re-writing. Both the interviews and the re-writes are recorded in the many work-in-progress papers produced by the team, and from these accounts appears a tapestry of conversations and writing through which both the teachers' influence and the changes in the writing may be traced. Not everyone agrees with Donald Graves about the value of multiple revision in such young writers (six to ten years) but this is not the occasion to argue about pedagogy. The point being made is the value of documentation, which enables teachers and parents to see children engaged in these processes.

The range of possible classroom enquiry is enormous, but the conditions for success would seem to be a measure of collaboration among at least some of the teachers in a school, and some support from school or local admin-istration for dissemination of ideas and findings. Present-day concern over literacy has meant that in most schools where enquiry is going on some teachers will be working on language-based studies, studies of reading, writing and talking, yet each study is as different as the teachers who made it, the pupils whose work it describes, and the schools and the neighbourhoods where the children live. This range is well illustrated by the studies carried out by a group of teachers in one multiracial Inner London Education Authority secondary school. The titles of just four out of the 15 case studies which were made demonstrate this range, and the way in which these studies came into being and were developed as part of day-to-day teaching is described and discussed by John Richmond in the following chapter.

- An account of some of the languages spoken at the school (25 languages or well-defined dialects).
- Reading development in a fifth-year girl.
- Five girls: classroom interaction and informal speech. (Observations of in-school and out of school speech, and the demands of the former.)
- Talking in class: language activity in four subjects.

Such richness of studies from one school is unusual, and in this case its production in book form was made possible by a grant from the Schools Council.[3]

In other places subject advisers, with the help of their local education authorities, have given support to their teachers by publishing studies they have made as pamphlets of 24 to 36 pages. These are written by individual teachers and describe various classroom enquiries. They are written, in the first instance, for teachers in the writer's school and for others in the neighbourhood who are associated in a continuing pattern of in-service education. It is this last feature of the situation which makes the Wiltshire work initiated by Pat Darcy of particular interest. The dozen or so pamphlets, under the general heading of 'Learning about Learning' are part of a project which links the ongoing education of the teachers with their classroom enquiries. Each summer a different group of primary and secondary teachers attends an intensive residential course in which the teachers present most of the material themselves, and they write. There are follow-up sessions during the year to maintain contact and give support. A growing series of pamphlets has been the outcome. The project has the purpose of learning about learning. Comparable projects have now been set going in counties adjacent to Wiltshire, where classroom enquiries are linked to study and discussion groups for the teachers concerned.

It is, perhaps, important to make clear the distinction between written accounts of classroom enquiries and reports of good practice. What distinguishes them is the difference between uncertainty and certainty. Enquiries originate in questions. The exploratory nature of the Wiltshire pamphlets is illustrated by some of the titles:

- Experimenting with learning logs in physics. (Learning about Learning, No. 5)

- Five-year-olds talking: how five children interacted in talk together. (No. 5)
- Shaping and re-shaping meaning: a teacher explores her own writing. (No. 14)
- An evaluation of the use of diaries with a tutor group. (No. 10)

These pamphlets are based on patient long-term documentation which includes relevant samples of student work, teachers' logs and records of conversations, and they are presented through careful selection and with interpretive comments. Moreover, the comments have a proper tentativeness as they enquire into particular aspects of work with particular children, and they report in reflective journal form both the teachers' and the pupils' part in the learning operations. They are unlike textbooks or pedagogic writing in that they are mostly unprescriptive. For example, the physics teacher concluded his pamphlet as follows:

> I am hoping that responding to their entries in a helpful, informative and conversational way will instigate further dialogue between us about the learning processes needed for the work my students undertake in Physics lessons . . . and they may develop in other directions, which at present I know nothing about. It is this 'not knowing' which makes learning logs and their possibilities a new and exciting adventure.[4]

The enquiries so far described are grass roots studies and are important because their scope and authorship are so wide. There are, of course, other forms of ethnographic study. For instance, a case study of English in a school requires further data than teachers' logs and records of students' work. It needs to develop procedures which become tools of analysis. In 1980 I was able to base a report[5] on the teaching of English in Government High Schools in Western Australia on case studies of nine schools. We used an in-depth interview with the two teachers in each school who volunteered to work closely with us and (among other procedures) the documentation of environments, an analysis of work products and descriptions of particular lessons as they were perceived by the teacher, by samples of the students and by an observer. To these strategies we added some documentation of how students, parents and teachers saw the teaching and learning of English. The study was not only concerned with English lessons but also with the learning environments of the English lessons in the nine schools, and it enabled us to make some estimate of the conditions (the features and contexts) which appeared to foster or inhibit the learning and teaching of English.

In the USA the move towards ethnographic studies in education is much more developed than in Britain. One of the most seminal of these studies was *Beyond Surface Curriculum: An interview study of teachers' understandings*,[6] published in 1976 for the Ford Foundation. The book offers an important theoretical framework for educational research based on case studies. The authors suggest that case studies demand a different methodological paradigm from that most generally used in educational research. Such a paradigm, they say, 'would be based on an interactive notion of education and a view of persons other than that portrayed by behaviourism and technology . . . It would have to be as much concerned with the quality of experience and meaning of behaviour as with the occurrence of behaviour . . .' They suggest a number of strategies 'aimed at eliciting meaning and uncovering various qualities of experiences, thought and production.'

There are two further American case studies I want to refer to. First, a study of a freshman writing course from Nancy Jones[7] in the University of Iowa, and second, a study by Marie Nelson[8] of the ways of teaching writing used by teachers who are all published writers themselves. The former is concerned 'with the ways in which student writing developed under the impress of assignments, responses and class sessions, that is, within the texture of relationships which constitute a course.' It focuses on the writing produced throughout the course by eight representative students, writing seen in relationship to the course assignments, the instructor's written comments, and the written log of class sessions. It borrows from the approaches of literary criticism and ethnography. 'As a case study it conforms to ethnographic definition: it is interpretive; and it is interpretive of a large number of selected linguistic interactions among selected members of a class community, as seen through the inscriptions which they left.'

The second study set out to explore the extent to which teachers who were themselves writers drew upon their own processes of writing in their teaching of writing. What is interesting about this case study is the divergence that appeared within a group that had in common their experience as writers. Some of them taught from their own experience of writing and chiefly without precept; others worked from the precepts of textbooks and made little or no reference to their own experience of writing. This raises an interesting point — the extent to which we are socialized by our early experience of instruction in school, and the extreme tenacity of this socialization into stereotyped patterns — the topic sentence for example, or the five-paragraph essay, the writing of detailed plans, etc. The strength of this early socialization is indicated by the way in which the influence of ideas and work at in-service courses, highly acceptable at the time, tends to fade when teachers resume work in familiar contexts.

The relative failure of research findings to influence practice in schools may be seen as the result of a closely knit community, with highly institutionalized procedures, resisting, consciously or unconsciously, the infiltrations of outsiders. And even when outsiders are insiders, that is to say when they are the teachers who come back from courses with different ideas, they still need support. They need approbation from someone, an audience of some sort, some recognition of their new directions: social sanction for what they are trying to do. This is the function of the support systems (described earlier) provided by local Education Authorities for teachers engaged in classroom enquiries. In some places they have given support for regular meetings, have encouraged the teachers to write and have disseminated what has been written. The Wiltshire English Adviser says she sees the function of the pamphlets as helping teachers to clarify what they are doing for *themselves*, and to share tentative thoughts about new ventures with *as many other* teachers as possible. I would add to this that to have work published is among the most powerful forms of social recognition.

American rural teachers in recurrent summer schools in the Program in Writing at the Bread Loaf School of English in Vermont have begun to take account of this fact. Each teacher plans and sets up a self-chosen classroom enquiry for the following year, but also includes in the design the building of a support system within the school, or with teachers in neighbouring schools, or, where facilities exist, with local administrators. Two enquiries from this group will illustrate the possibilities: one teacher will compare the work his students do on assigned and unassigned topics, assigned themes being the pillars of American high school writing courses. He will keep a log of all his writing lessons and record all the writings of ten students, together with interviews and written comments by them about their attitudes to assigned and unassigned themes, and estimations of their own work. For support he has got two colleagues to agree to keep journals of their lessons with one class and to discuss these with each other.

A second teacher believes that familiar contexts often anaesthetize students' capacity to observe, respond and write. His previous experience of taking students on field trips in order to write will be developed and documented during the coming year. He has found three other rural teachers who are also willing to try out what he is doing and to document it, and to maintain contact with each other.

I have attempted to show the scope of case studies as a method of enquiry in the field of English teaching and learning. They range from studies of the development of particular children as readers and writers to studies of groups of children talking together, of courses and of schools. I could not conclude, however, without reference to Shirley Brice Heath's immensely rich case study of three communities, *Ways with Words: Language, life and work in communities and classrooms*.[9] She sets out to record the natural flow of community and classroom life, with a focus on what she calls 'literacy events'. She traces the fortunes of children from three different communities as they move into school. The different patterns of socialization into language use go some way towards explaining the varying success of the children from these different groups when they go to school. She also has a section on what teachers might do to help the children for whom school proves to be a very different kind of social and language community. The picture given here of the whole lives of children — in school and out — is immensely valuable, and reminds us of what we know but often forget — how truncated a view of children we get when we know only their classroom selves.

Most of the studies described here are, however, being undertaken in a time of shrinking educational perspectives. It has become fashionable to regard changes in education as just swings of a pendulum or the whims of fashion, yet enlightened, or progressive, education has long roots, as any history of education will reveal. As James Britton has written, 'It is a slowly growing movement with philosophical roots way back in the past, and pragmatic roots deep in the intuitive wisdom of the most successful teachers today.'[10] The methods of enquiry discussed in this article would seem to demonstrate that the way is open for these same successful teachers to be, in addition, the researchers of the future.

Notes and References

1. J.N. Britton, 'A Quiet Form of Research' in *The English Journal*, vol. 72, no. 4, 1983.
2. D. Graves, *Writing: Children and teachers at work*, Heinemann, London, 1983.
3. *Becoming Our Own Experts*. Studies in language and learning made by the Talk Workshop Group at Vauxhall Manor School 1974–79, 1982, available from the ILEA English Centre, Sutherland Street, London, S.W.1.
4. G. Jones, *Learning to Think in Science Lessons, Learning about Learning*, no. 6 Pat Darcy, County Hall, Trowbridge, Wilts.
5. N. Martin, *Case Studies from Government High Schools in Western Australia*. Education Department, Western Australia, 1980.
6. A. Bussis, E. Chittenden and M. Amarel, *Beyond Surface Curriculum*, Westview Press, Boulder, Colorado, 1976.
7. N.L. Jones, 'Design, Discovery and Development in a Freshman Writing Course', unpublished thesis, University of Iowa, 1982.

8. M. Nelson, 'Writers Training Writers: Models for their students and their peers,' unpublished thesis, George Mason University, Virginia, 1982.
9. S. Brice Heath, *Ways with Words: Language, life and work in communities and classrooms*, Cambridge University Press, 1983.
10. J.N. Britton, Foreword to F.R.A. Davis and R.P. Parker (eds.), *Teaching for Literacy: Reflections on the Bullock Report*, Ward Lock, London, 1978.

5.
Setting up for Learning in a Cold Climate

John Richmond

The word 'language' and its related phrases, 'language policy', 'language and learning' and 'language across the curriculum', have a mixed ring to them in the mid-1980s. For many, they represent yesterday's idea. Some time in the last decade there was a flurry of interest in language. The origin of the flurry was obscure to most teachers then, and is even obscurer now. Other pressing concerns have since pursued it down the long slide of haste and anxiety which is teachers' working lives.

For a group of us working at Vauxhall Manor School, a girls' comprehensive in south London, in the second half of the 1970s, the phrases meant asking each other critical questions in a spirit of trust. I don't intend to report here in detail on the activities of the Talk Workshop Group, as we called ourselves. That report exists elsewhere.[1] I do want to try to draw some lessons from our experience which might be useful to other teachers now.

Our group of about eight people, representing nearly all the areas of the secondary academic curriculum, spent five years looking at the language of each other's classrooms. We used sound tape, videotape, transcripts of talk and drama, examples of children's writing and reading. We visited each other, watched each other teaching. We met weekly after school to discuss the accumulating evidence, and as a result of becoming learners in our own classrooms we produced a body of writing about language and learning. The whole process made us better teachers, and was an implicit though largely unsuccessful suggestion to the school where we worked that it needed to examine, as a whole, how well it was providing for the children's learning.

Looking critically at our own classrooms involved a great amount of self-exposure and vulnerability. You had to be prepared to admit that you had done something wrong, had missed opportunities; you had to be prepared to reveal the things which embarrassed you about your classroom, as well as the things you were proud of. So trust was the crucial thing in the first place.

It may sound mundane, but meeting regularly was important too. Quite frequently our weekly meetings had no prepared agenda. People would read, or transcribe tape, or write. The fact that we were doing it together gave coherence to the enterprise, which it wouldn't have had if we had met more occasionally, and we would share things that we'd got back from our classrooms, even if they were in a rough-and-ready state. A lot of the sessions we had were inconclusive. We spent a whole term, right at the beginning, just looking at video of each other's lessons, which one or other of us had made on the school's Portapak. Often our reactions to what we saw were vague. We didn't really know, early on, what we were looking at.

The broad range of the curriculum represented in the group was an enormous bonus. Some of the most instructive extended talk that we studied came from chemistry and commerce. So we didn't have that problem about English teachers telling the others what to do. And we engaged straight away with questions which English teachers are apt to avoid, like: how do you square the central hole of talk in learning with the requirements of fact-dominated subjects?

We used to have a phrase, 'We must become our own experts', which eventually gave itself to the title of our book. It sounds rather cocky. We didn't mean that everything that had ever been written about education or language or learning was no use to us. Nor were we all planning to become academics. We meant that the process of understanding about language and its role in learning needs to start from the needs that teachers themselves perceive. If teachers perceive a need, sense a problem, get excited about a possible way forward, they've made a start. It may be that books and research ideas will be useful in helping to confirm and generalize what the teachers are discovering already. That discovery starts with the pupils.

Our relationship with the pupils, what we were doing with them in the classroom, and what we were finding out for ourselves every Thursday afternoon after school, were intimately connected. Conventional research involves a long, high parabola, which goes from the place where the research was done, through time and space a long distance to the place where the research has some effect. The kind of research that we were doing involved short, local hops, frequent meetings between ourselves the teachers and ourselves the researchers. When I say ourselves the teachers, I should add that in the most successful moments of our group's work, the children always taught us more than we taught them. I'll give two examples of the connection between teacher and researcher.

In 1976 we spent several weeks studying the transcript of a lengthy group discussion in a third-year chemistry lesson. The discussion, and the experiment on which it was based, concerned endothermic and exothermic reactions (reactions in which heat energy is taken in and given out, respectively). The two-part experiment, involving the heating, cooling and re-heating of copper sulphate, was designed to bring pupils to the understanding that the heating of the chemical was an endothermic reaction, and the adding of two drops of cold water to the cooled copper sulphate, causing it to become hot again, was an exothermic reaction. After repeated playing of the tape, reading aloud and discussion of the transcript, we realized that at the two significant moments of the experiment the children were aware that the reaction could be described as both endothermic and exothermic, depending on how you looked at it. The chemistry teacher confirmed the validity of the children's understanding, and admitted that on both occasions when he had intervened in the group to push them towards the answers he wanted he had been unaware of the complexity of what they were trying to say. The realization that the pupils were using talk to struggle with an abstract reality more subtle than the teacher at the time was even aware of was a piece of knowledge with impetus in it. It rebounded directly into the chemistry teacher's assumptions and practice, and, by analogy, into the classrooms of all of us. The thinking and the doing were near neighbours.

Later the same year, a third-year English class of mine performed an improvised play which relied very heavily on Jamaican Creole speech forms. That play taught me a lot about Jamaican Creole, and made me think about the relationship between non-standard dialects of English and the language demands of the school. I could have gone to certain Creole linguists, had I known they existed in 1976, and found out from them that Creoles are well-formed, rule-governed linguistic systems. But finding it out for myself made it a different kind of knowledge, not just an amateur version of what I could have read in the books. Later on, the Cassidy and LePage *Dictionary of Jamaican English* was very useful in giving me linguistic detail which I needed, but because the pupils had taught me something before the linguists, I had, again, knowledge with impetus in it. About two months after the play was performed, the girl who was the main character in it, one of the most troublesome and talented children I've ever met, came into an English lesson at the head of the class, sat me down and informed me that the class were about to teach each other to read, or help each other to become better readers, because, she said, 'There's some of us in this class who can't read very well, and there's only one of you and thirty of us.' For several weeks after that, until the girl was removed from the school as being too disruptive for the institution to handle, I had the astonishing sight, for an hour and a half a week, of seeing fifteen pairs of heads, perfectly matched socially and academically, teaching each other to read. There's no doubt that the play, in preparation and performance, was a great collective challenge for most of the class. The two-month job of transcribing it from video-tape after the performance was, for its main character (who did the transcribing with one other girl), an additional rare episode of constructive and enjoyable learning in a largely negative school experience. The enthusiasm for reading led straight on from it. Something which might be called research (though of course I didn't think of it as such at the time), which brought about the work I subsequently did on Jamaican Creole and the relationship between non-standard dialects and the school curriculum, was handed back to me before I had even written anything down, in the shape of a transformed attitude on the pupils' part to the content and purpose of their English lessons. The teaching and the research, the learners and the teachers, made a kind of inter-penetrating whole, where things changed because things belonged to each other.

Let me temper the optimism of recent paragraphs by pointing out some of the hazards which may await anybody who tries to investigate the language of their own classrooms. In the first year or two of our group's work, it was amazing how many people advised us to stop what we were doing and try something else. Some of those people were frankly our enemies, and their intentions were destructive. So as soon as we called ourselves the Talk Workshop Group, a name which reflected our particular concern with oral language, we were told we needed writing workshops too. When, in a moment of self-criticism, we said our work lacked a linguistic dimension, it was reported that we were at last admitting our mistake in not teaching punctuation. But there were people who were our allies, too, who tried to make us adjust our activities to fit into moulds which they found more convenient or immediately comprehensible.

Another hazard comes when you have been working for a while, and people get to hear about you. Some of them then start to try to assign you your place in the academic constellation, as a minor star, of course. They say, approvingly, 'In fact, what you've really done here is what so-and-so has been working on in such-and-such a place.' And you nod weakly. There is nothing wrong with drawing connections. But connections are often drawn which try to make you safe territory, and in that process the texture of the experience from which you come is lost.

The worst hazards, however, are in yourself. There are times when you stare at video, or at transcripts, or at writing, and you ask yourself, 'Well, is there anything here at all?' and for a while you lose your nerve. Or there are periods of impatience for answers, when there may be no answers. In any case, sometimes questions are more useful than answers. You can go straight from some questions to action, without a need for answers, because the identification of the right questions carries within it implications for your behaviour as a teacher, which will change you more effectively than answers will. Answers are limited, change from time to time and circumstance to circumstance, but some questions are permanent.

We should not get too dispirited when our theory and our practice don't exactly match. The Talk Workshop Group spent much of its energy trying to get those two things somewhere near to each other, like magnets with the same orientation. When it does happen it's a golden moment. But we are not failures if it doesn't happen all the time. Getting them close to each other is the hardest and most worthwhile struggle.

I said earlier that our group largely failed to influence the school where we were working. There were local reasons for that failure, which are not of interest here. What is of interest is the intersection, or rather non-intersection, between the messages our group was putting out about language and learning and the school's official behaviour on the subject. For the school had its language policy, and a recently devised one too. Let us investigate for a moment how that came about.

Between 1968 and 1975, language had a brilliant career. It went from being a word on the lips of innovators to the official prose of the Bullock Report. The word in this context has two important dimensions of meaning, both associated with dissatisfaction with the way schools are now. The first dimension is psychological. Language and learning in schools are utterly intertwined, and the more we know about how language processes work the more we shall understand about how learning takes place, and how to help it to take place more effectively. We know the negative truth that teaching, in the sense of the supply of information, is no guarantee of learning; for knowledge to leave our mouths, or the blackboard, or the overhead projector, and be transferred into children's ears and folders, where it waits until called for, is not adequate as a description of the learning process. Put as crudely as that, and of course we know it. But many schools and teachers have behaved, and still behave, as if that were, only and always, how learning happens. The second dimension is organizational. Many schools, particularly secondary schools, offer their pupils a quite incoherent set of values and classroom approaches to language and learning. On the one hand, for instance, subject teachers' ways of responding to children's writing may be completely at variance with each other, while a deadening monochrome may prevail in other respects: a pupil's day, at worst, may be a procession of five or six passage-plus-ten-comprehension-questions worksheets. Teachers may be completely oblivious of the contradictions and the repetitions which confuse and alienate the pupils. Such a situation requires urgent remedies.

That might be a summary of part of the influential opinion which saw to it that the Bullock Report did not come out as the Black Paper which Mrs Thatcher presumably intended when she commissioned it. Weighty to carry, dull to read, tentatively progressive, hedged about with qualifications and reservations, it was of course the prime mover of all the meetings, workshops, committees, policy-making, books, packs and reports of the period between 1975 and 1978. The Chief Inspector of the Inner London Education Authority wrote to all schools asking them to describe their language policies for him within a few months of his letter; the Bullock Report had said that every school should have one. Our school, like hundreds of others, hastily convened a committee, produced a statement, sent it off, filed a copy and forgot about the matter. We were, I should think, unusual at the time in having some idea in advance about what 'language policy' might mean. Most schools had never heard of the phrase, and there was much telephoning between perplexed head teachers. Some schools borrowed a language policy which a diligent neighbour had already done, changed the letterheading and sent off the scissors-and-paste job with a token change here and there to make it look different.

The way it was handled, in the ILEA and elsewhere, the sense advisers and in-service workers had that this was an operation — whether military or surgical — that needed to be carried out, the sense many classroom teachers had that this peculiar-looking new item on the staff meeting agenda was another burden to add to their back-breaking load, are reasons why, in all but a small minority of schools (10 per cent would be an optimistic estimate), language policy across the curriculum has not meant a change for the better in the lives of teachers and learners.

There are other reasons. Before you even get to page 1 of the Bullock Report, there are three brief paragraphs signed by Mr Prentice, the middle one of which made it quite clear in 1975 that teachers could go away and be as busy as they liked with the report's recommendations, there would be no financial involvement on the part of the government: 'action . . . which would involve additional resources must be postponed'. Then, within months of the report's publication (£100,000 worth of the collective wisdom of the country's most experienced educators), the tide began to turn and soon the Great Debate was upon us and the Assessment of Performance Unit was set up. Hand-in-hand with plans for the biggest-ever education cuts came the unmistakable message that teachers had been given too much rope for too long, that the simple task of teaching children to read, write and reckon was being compromised by a mixture of soft methods and dubious political motives.

The Bullock Report is an honourable document. It scotched the myth about a drastic fall in reading standards and went on from there to put its weight behind things like talk, group work, the need for children to learn by doing as well as by receiving. Some of HMI's productions since have carried forward the best of Bullock, pointing out, for instance, the enormous amount of tedious and repetitive copying demanded of pupils. These have, quite properly, contributed to a contradictory government influence, in which enlightment has shone intermittently from one door of Elizabeth House while vandalism and reaction have gone forth in tandem from the other. In most education authorities economy, whether understood as a painful necessity or a moral crusade, and more fashionable and manageable activities like measurement of skills, have made language and learning remote in the memory. The moment, officially at least, has passed.

Fortunately, what happens officially is only a small part of any story. Language and learning remain on the permanent agenda for schools, even if most schools are not paying attention to that agenda item at the moment. Schools should be places which are set up for learning. If they are to be that or become that, rather than remain as sites of disintegration, gossip and routine, it is necessary that a continuing critical process is at work in them, in which the success or otherwise of structures, curriculum and pedagogy in promoting learning is under constant review. Language remains a primary perspective of that review, a review which must be liberating and developing, not a strait-jacket of obligation.

How do we make that happen? One way, and I don't know a better, is to go back to the group of teachers in the school. As it should have done the first time the group must represent all areas of the curriculum and all levels of seniority. Only this time they're not in a hurry to get a document out (though, who knows, documents do have a way of coming out). They can be called the 'Language and Learning Working Party' or the 'Learning Review Group' or the 'Curriculum and Language Committee'. The group needs, first, foremost and indispensably, long-term, slow-burning energy and a sense that there's something in it for them. Then they need what the Talk Workshop Group did not have; the support of the school's senior management and the informed interest of a majority of the staff. They should not, this time, be a group of zealots walking round an ink duplicator late at night, for a purpose inspiring to them but obscure to most. The purpose this time is to make sure, in an open and agreed way, that the school is set up for learning.

What should they do? There is absolutely no shortage of things to do. Here are four possibilities. They could look at the way writing is initiated, organized and responded to by teachers throughout the curriculum, bearing in mind two key questions: how does children's writing develop? and how do we help it to develop most effectively? They could examine the way children are asked to read information texts throughout the curriculum, and they could see if there is enough variety, depth and satisfaction to that process. If there isn't, they could develop ways of improving the variety, depth and satisfaction of reading for information, all of which qualities, in many places, are in short supply. They could investigate how pupil talk is regarded throughout the curriculum, and develop strategies for supporting purposeful and extensive pupil talk in conditions which minimize palpitations and paranoia for the teacher. They could look in detail at all the language activities in which one pupil (or one pupil in each class in a year, or one pupil in each year) is engaged in the course of a week. How coherent is the total effect of a week of schooling? The work must be construction as well as criticism, construction emerging from criticism, depending on it.

What outside factors would be helpful? A feeling that the school is paying attention, not because paying attention is good manners, but because attention will bring benefits. Head teachers need to recognize that there isn't much that is more important than whether or not their school is set up for learning, and so money needs to go in this direction as a priority, both to lighten teaching loads (perhaps on a rotating basis) and to disseminate. Dissemination doesn't just mean amongst teachers. One of the reasons why the lies about state schools, and about comprehensives in particular, in most of the newspapers and some of the television networks, have been so effective is that they have entered an information vacuum. Those of us who believe in popular education have not been very populist about it. We need to say what we are doing in plain language, so that parents and other lay people will understand. Besides, the attempt to say something simple but not simplistic about a complex activity is an excellent way of making what we are doing clearer to ourselves.

Local authorities, in the persons of their advisers, teachers' centre staff and other in-service workers, need to see that autonomous, critical attention to the learning process in schools on the part of teachers is the best possible sort of staff development. They should support it by helping to bring groups into existence where the will is there and the moment right, by putting like-minded people in different schools in touch with each other, by offering financial support, reprographic services and, most of all, their own ideas and presence.

It would be immensely helpful to groups like ours if universities would begin to democratize research. They need to put their energies into partnerships with groups of teachers in schools, working on negotiated areas of useful enquiry. Structures must be changed so that such partnerships become normal rather than eccentric frameworks for research. The 'Language in Inner-City Schools' network, based at the English Department of the Institute of Education, has, over the last eight years, been an imperfect and totally unfunded sketch for what collaboration between schools and universities might look like, and it has had its successes. At the same time, there is the constant sensation, working within it, of the old·categories trying to reassert themselves. Those categories, that old division of labour between thinkers and doers, are dead but not buried. The corpse still looms large in our view.

Should the group, the staff, the school, be aiming to produce policy? Well, policies are often useful milestones. But let them be milestones, not millstones. The learning that happens along the way is usually more extensive and deeper than whatever change in behaviour occurs once the policy is arrived at.

What, in a word, is the point of it all? The point is to see that schools are places where growth happens. Is that not a very difficult undertaking in a climate where survival, let along growth, is a struggle? We take it for granted that it is difficult. But for those of us who believe in growth, who see that looking at language and learning in our classrooms is a prime way to foster it, there is (to use a slogan employed recently by the enemy) 'no alternative'.

Reference

1. Stephen Eyers and John Richmond (eds), *Becoming Our Own Experts*, Talk Workshop Group, 1982, ILEA English Centre, Sutherland Street, London S.W.1.

6.
Jenny's Thursday

Martyn Richards

Jenny is nine, and she's in school early today. Slim and fair-haired, she's lying on a cushion in the quiet corner deep in a story. One or two other children are also in the room at 8.30, well before the teacher, talking or carrying on with unfinished work. There's a serenity about the place. Partly it's the morning sunlight pouring it, but the colours of the room, with its displays of plants, children's batiks and embroideries, give extra depth and warmth and welcome to the children. This is an urban school in a tough neighbourhood and many of the children need the sanctuary it offers from a stressed and tense existence outside. In here it's calm, and every child, however uncomfortable he may be, is acknowledged and liked, and has his place. But in some ways Jenny's an exception. She's the youngest of four and Dad has a regular job as a skip driver for the local Council, while Mum works at home. Jenny's in the room early to get away from her older brother who's still in the playground. She puts her book down and wanders over to a display of exotic seed-pods which children have been handling and painting. In fact she's not really very interested in them, and after a moment's desultory fondling, confides that she 'can't wait until music time'; and goes back to her book.

Most children are in by now, chatting, or getting on. Why, after such a hot summer, are the mohican heads, the skins and the crewcuts so pallid?

The teacher arrives, hardly noticed by anyone, and over a period of ten minutes or so has a word with most of the children. There is no sense of an abrupt start to the day. The calm continues. They all seem to know what's to be done, and chat or joke quietly as they do it. Some are writing, some reading, some painting. Three drift into the corridor where a volunteer Mum is going to help them bake cakes.

Now it's music time. Off goes Jenny with three friends to a little carpeted room where the percussion and pitched instruments are set out. There's no teacher and no explicit briefing, but the conventions of the occasion are appreciated by all four. Jonathan suggests they play 'Jenny's Tune' again, and they each select an instrument. There is no written music, simply a well-practised ostinato from Jenny to which the others add delicate and harmonious improvisations. To show that it's more than a fortunate accident, they perform the identical piece again, hoping, they say, to make it good enough for assembly. But this is clearly revision, and today it's Jason's turn to set the pattern for a new piece, to lead the discussion about which instruments to use, about how to begin. Concentration is intense. Each suggestion is quietly considered. There's little heat of argument since today Jason has the whip-hand. Jenny's eyes are excited. She tries what Jason suggests, on a metallophone, alters it and tries it again. The others join in. A piece begins to take shape. They watch their hands intently, listen with absorption to each other's phrases, deciding when and how to collaborate; and they talk, changing entries, rhythms, volume. Teacher comes in, and they play it for her. She listens but doesn't comment on the tune. They tell her what improvements they have in mind, and she encourages them to continue. Their success, negotiated in talk, is underpinned by trust and mutual acceptance. How well the teacher models this!

But it's time to go back. They can't believe they've had three-quarters of an hour. Outside the music room they smell the cooked cakes and anticipate their turn, although it won't be today. In the classroom most children have moved on to some maths work, though two or three are making beautiful machine-embroidered observational pictures with the help of a parent. Still the teacher is unobtrusive, moving about the room to where children need her or where she wishes to intervene. She has no desk. The room has no front. She encourages several children who are finding the work hard, questions others on their activities, draws out with individual children the implications of their work.

Jenny has three pages of maths to do. It's the price of spending the previous two days working on a string collage picture. Maths comes at a page a day. Jenny is calmly resigned, opens her books at a seat near the window and begins her work.

Difficulties arise pretty soon. She has to construct shapes of a variety of given areas on squared paper. She's done the first two, but feels uneasy. The third one won't work properly. A word of explanation from the teacher, and she realises she has misread the task and substitutes 'perimeter' for 'area' and so, back to work. Two minutes later she comes again to the teacher. The required areas are in cm^2, while her exercise book pages are ruled in 7 mm squares. A piece of centimetre-ruled graph paper is found, and with good grace she repeats the shapes, cuts them out and sticks them in her exercise book. No great sign of boredom, but no interest either, just a tell-tale slackening of the shoulders.

Playtime arrives, unnoticed by most children. Although it's a fine morning, few go outside. Jenny begins her next maths page, knowing that after the break she'll have half an hour in a small group, trying out a micro-computer under the eye of an expert from the local FE college. The school's own machine is due to arrive next week.

The computer activity consists of feeding data into a programme in such a way as to create a file of 'criminal identities'. All the children are keen to join, but with six of them waiting, and with the data input a slow, letter-by-letter process, their attention wanders. It takes half an hour to file the total data from this group. The demonstrator then shows them the capacity of the machine to sample the data at speed. They watch with interest rather than excitement, hands on hips, and then go back while another group comes to feed its data in. While an outsider might question the effort needed for fairly trivial results, the children show no sense of anticlimax.

Jenny goes back to the classroom, back to her three pages of maths. She doesn't need to be told. There is a lot of varied acitivity in the room now, and one or two children are clearly feeling restless. Jenny finds her window seat and starts work. Although she can manage the task with little difficulty now, time is beginning to drag, and the pace of her work is desultory. Her pencil lead keeps breaking. She chats with her neighbour, looks dreamily out of the window, and works intermittently. A lot of sustained concentration has gone into her morning so far and now there seems to be a reaction. 'Use squared paper and string to draw and measure the area and perimeter of a leaf.' She picks up a leaf from the classroom display and draws around it. She counts the whole centimetre squares, but has forgotten how to handle the fractional parts. A quick enquiry and this part of the task is over. Finding the peri-meter, however, is more of a problem. Winding a length of string accurately round the perimeter of a lobed and serrated leaf requires superhuman dexterity. Jenny grins at the absurdity of the activity, and has another word with the teacher, who directs her to a more purposeful task, requiring the maintenance of a given perimeter, while the shape itself is changed.

Jenny barely has time to start before lunchtime arrives and her books are put away. She takes the visitor to see the string collage pictures of an Afghan Hound she and Sally had constructed together, clearly very proud of the result and of the lengthy period of time taken to achieve it. It's a beautiful, large piece of work on a delicately printed background, mounted by the girls on a neutral sugar paper, and displayed on a prominent part of the wall. It is part of Sally's project on dogs but was clearly a two-handed job. Other children come over. They seem proud of it too. Jenny glows.

The teacher asks Jenny, after lunch, to continue with her topic. It, too, is about dogs. Jenny has a Jack Russell at home, and seems to know a lot about animal welfare. She has planned, and negotiated with the teacher, an index of 'chapters' for her topic book, and she is beginning with a small needle-work picture of an Old English Sheepdog. Later activities involve the monitoring and cooking of the dog's diet, looking at hair under a microscope, and using reference books to 'get extra information'. Not all of these plans are in the written index. She takes her work to the quiet corner and sits on a cushion, her sewing on her knee. Jason is beside her, struggling with a particularly difficult wooden construction puzzle. Every few minutes they exchange a desultory word or two but Jason is concentrating too hard to say anything much, and Jenny seems sunk in daydreams. Anthony appears and finishes Jason's puzzle. They wander off to some other work. Jenny continues unmoved. All around the room, and in the spaces outside it, children are working at their varied tasks — maths and writing, reading, sewing, painting.

After twenty minutes of single-minded work, Jenny feels like trying a different part of her project. She will carry on with the sewing tomorrow. She wants to collect data for a graph about dog ownership. However, the familiar problem of suitably-sized squared paper arises again. After a few minutes she admits defeat and asks the teacher. She takes her paper and, helped by a book of dog breeds, sets about producing a comprehensive taxonomy, which she will use as a tick-list when she conducts her survey. But it becomes a very long list, with some unlikely varieties. Sally asks her why she does not just go round and list the dogs children *do* possess, rather than spend ages on a list of scores of breeds which will not feature. A pause. The logic of the suggestion is clear to Jenny. However, she has spent a long time producing a list of which she is quite proud; she does not want to scrap it. Anyway, she says, she likes making lists, and continues to augment it. The list completed, Jenny plans to go around all the classes collecting data but the teacher feels the moment is not right and Jenny is temporarily satisfied with surveying her own class. Having collected the information, and created a category for mongrels, she starts to write a few notes on her findings. But the flesh is weakening by a quarter to three. She feels the list, the graph and the notes are too scruffy to feature in her hand-made book. She will put them into final form tomorrow.

Jenny takes a spelling puzzle from a tray, and begins it in a tired way, with long breaks for conversations with Sally. But there's not long to go.

Everyone packs away, and they gather in their quiet area, each reading his or her own book. Jenny has a comforting 'Milly-Molly-Mandy' story, and plans to carry on with it in bed — but first she has the after-school table tennis club to look forward to. The school day ends as gradually as it began, tailors itself slowly back into the world outside.

So much of Jenny is accommodated in the school. The lack of haste, of anxiety to 'cover the ground', matches her calm pace of activity. There is time to reflect on what's been done, and to daydream of other possibilities, to pace the work and change activity when it feels appropriate. Yet internalized disciplines exercise their control. Work has to be finished, and to be presented well, but it doesn't have to be completed in a single session, or in pristine first drafts. There is time to do it well, and to become proud of it.

And as the pace of school matches Jenny's pace, so the activities it presents or facilitates, are not foreign to her personal needs and interests. She loves dogs and knows a lot about them. Her expertise is extended and validated in the classroom. She not only has knowledge but learns that further insights can be gained through her own efforts, that learning can be active and investigatory rather than passive and receptive and that mistakes can be productive. She learns too that, as with her music, some activities are only fully satisfying when they involve shared effort and collaboration. There is no great fear of individual failure, and the success of each child is a cause of corporate pride.

The school is not monolithic, presenting itself to the children as unchanging and predetermined. Instead, it adapts itself to meet the needs of each of its children, to acknowledge their individuality and the unique pattern of each one's growth. Jenny is busy coming to know herself and her world, learning to perceive its patterns and causations and to predict and control experiences, to be master rather than victim. Her primary schooling supports her efforts, encourages her when the task is difficult, offers audiences and resources for the reshaping, refinement and sharing of her perceptions. It takes sensitive and determined teachers to lay the foundations for a community such as this, especially today, when the purposes of education are so commonly identified with economic and commercial requirements, with mechanical monitoring and output control. But the principles of individual worth and potential, of growth through security and success, and of educational quality residing in a quality of present experience rather than in preparation for some anticipated future, inspired a generation of fine primary schools. These principles are alive and well down Jenny's way.

7.
Knowing by Becoming

Developments in writing and in art

Myra Barrs

Very young children's stories can have a particular quality, a quality that is not always present in the writing of children who are only a little older. Children as young as six or seven are capable of composing brief and satisfying narratives, stories which are complete in themselves. Although their narrative means may be very slender, they often use them with a remarkable sense of economy. In older children's stories this sense of shapeliness is not always so apparent, and there is often a feeling that the construction of a narrative has been a laborious process.

When I have interviewed young writers I have found a distinct difference between younger and older ones as far as this kind of confidence and sureness of touch is concerned. The younger writers (top infants and lower juniors — 6, 7, 8) were generally confident and untroubled about their writing, which often seemed to 'come to them' in one piece. Older writers (top juniors — 9, 10, 11) were more inclined to admit to problems of composition, and had begun to make changes in their stories in order to solve some of the narrative problems that they perceived.

Typical of the younger writers was Alison, whose recollection of writing her story was that she had thought of the whole story right at the outset of writing. Her teacher had put the first sentence of the story on the blackboard. I asked her whether she had had the idea for the story all at once.

Alison	Yes. When Mrs D. started two lines I thought of it.
MB	The *whole* story.
Alison	Yes.
MB	When you wrote this down did you change anything?
Alison	No.
MB	Nothing at all?
Alison	No.

MB   So the idea you had at first, you just wrote it all down?
Alison Yes.
MB   Aha.
Alison Only took me a little, about three or five minutes. Didn't take
        me ever s — at all long.

Similarly, Angela (7) stressed that she never made changes in her
stories, remaining true to her original story-plan throughout the
composition process.

MB   Now did you change anything in this story? Did you change
        your mind?
Angela No.
MB   Not at all? Do you ever do that? Do you ever change your mind
        and decide to put something else?
Angela No I never do that.
MB   You never do that. Is that 'cos you're always quite happy with
        the ideas you have?
Angela Mm. Because I always get the right idea and then start going on
        with it but I don't change it.
MB   You don't change it?
Angela I start with a good idea and then . . . so's I don't have to change
        my mind.

What these transcripts fail to convey is the extremely confident and
assured tone of the children in these conversations, a tone which makes it
clear that their sense of their own competence as writers is highly developed,
and that they equate competence with 'having a good idea so that I don't
have to change my mind'. These young children have all the high-handed
confidence of experts; they are perfectly at home in the medium and are
delighted with their sense of their own command over it.

But children who were only a little older often seemed less confident and
decided about their own writing performance. They were of course often
writing at more length, and they seemed more aware of the problems of
managing a story line. They were more likely to get stuck, more likely to
make changes, and more likely to worry about the narrative problems that
they perceived in their stories. When they talked about process they were
more likely to emphasize that they were composing as they went along.
Darren, aged nine, explained:

D   When I write I think of what I'm going to do after it as well — while
        I'm writing.
MB   While you're writing . . . you don't think of it all before you start?

D   No.
MB Right.

The most striking illustrations of an older writer's concerns emerged in my interview with Pritesh, aged nine. When I interviewed him Pritesh was in the middle of writing a story with a title supplied by his teacher, 'The Rusty Key'. I asked him what he had done when he had been given the title first of all.

P   Well I started, sat there and thinking, and I just came up with an idea.
MB Right, what was your idea, what was the first idea that came to you?
P   Boy going into a castle. But I, you know, made it a more adventurous. Put it, a boy finding a key. Seaside.
MB Yes. So the first thing that came into your head was this castle. Did you start to write then? Or . . .
P   No.
MB No, why not?
P   Well, I wanted to make it look like a big adventure.
MB Right.
P   Like, we'd go under the water or something. Like that.

The opening paragraph of Pritesh's story is printed here for reference purposes since it will be discussed in detail in the pages that follow.

One day a boy called Peter was walking along the sandy beach in Blackpool. He decided to go for a swim. He went home and got his costume and he was going to wear his swimming costume on the beach because nobody goes there often. People say there is a curse on the beach. He was just about to go into the sea when he felt a piece of metal under his left foot. He bent down and lifted up a rusty key. He was puzzled. He took it home and he thought it was the key to a house, but he realised it was the key to a treasure chest.

Adventure stories hold a special interest for children of about this age. One of Pritesh's own favourite writers was Enid Blyton. It is clear from his account of his own preliminaries that one of Pritesh's main concerns from the outset was to construct a satisfying narrative, with strong elements of adventure and mystery in it.

In structuring such a narrative Pritesh will be making use of what Barthes, in *S/Z*,[1] termed the hermeneutic code. It will be important for a successful narrative that the final resolution of the story be concealed until the last pages, and that it should only be hinted at until that moment. Writing a narrative of this kind might be described as *making a secret*. Pritesh has a strong tacit awareness of the conventions of such stories, and the transcript shows his struggle with the problems that he faced in trying to manipulate them.

In parenthesis I should like to remark that some of the most popular genres in literature are centrally concerned with this fundamental appeal of narrative, that it offers a secret to be uncovered. Spy stories and detective stories exemplify this basic shape most clearly. Most experienced readers have felt the need to finish a book, even a bad book, in order to 'see how it ends'. In *S/Z*, Barthes, by choosing *Sarrasine* as his basic text, was choosing a story which arouses this deep curiosity most dramatically. It is interesting that Barthes made no attempt to explain his choice of this text in the early pages of *S/Z*.

> The text I have chosen (Why? All I know is that for some time I have wanted to make a complete analysis of a short text and that the Balzac story was brought to my attention by Jean Reboul, who in turn is supposed to have been inspired by Georges Bataille's reference; and thus I was caught up in this 'series' whose scope I was to discover by means of the text itself) is Balzac's *Sarrasine*. (p. 16)

This may be disingenuousness. What is apparent immediately is that the secret of this text, prolonged and preserved until the last page — for after the disclosure of la Zambinella's sexual nature, there is to come the revelation of M.de Lanty's sexual identity — is the secret of sexuality itself, the subject which arouses our earliest curiosity. The symbolic power of the secret in narrative could be said to have its roots in our most primitive desire for knowledge.

In certain kinds of narrative, then, the genre of a story with a secret and the nature of narrative itself are closely allied. Enid Blyton's adventure stories, which lay very strong clues for the young reader, are for many children a good way of 'learning the rules' of narrative. It is these rules that Pritesh is trying to apply when he sets out to make his story 'look like a big adventure'.

But Pritesh also had other considerations in mind. He is concerned about realism, and he wants the details of his story to be convincing. This is most clearly demonstrated in the following extract from the interview.

P   . . . And this all happened in Blackpool.
MB   Yes.
P   I've been there.
MB   You've been there.
P   Yes.

MB Do you think it's important to write about places where you've been?

P Well . . . let 'em know, people know about it.

MB Which people?

P Mm . . . When I read it out the class . . .

MB Yes.

P . . . When it's finished. They'll all know about Blackpool now, it's got sandy beaches not like Brighton. Brighton's got pebbles.

This is characteristic of Pritesh's intentness on realism. The sandy beach actually does figure in the story itself, as we shall see, and Pritesh is aware when he is making narrative choices that details like this can add realism and credibility to his tale.

Another example from a later point in the interview illustrates the same kind of concern:

MB (reading) 'He went home and got his costume and he was going to wear his swimming costume on the beach because nobody goes there often. People say there is a curse on the beach.'

P Yes. But he doesn't believe in it.

MB Why did you introduce that, 'People say there is a curse on the beach.'

P Make it . . . 'Cos when he was swimming thing, costume, 'cos 'no one often goes there', no one often goes there. So if there weren't a curse on the beach in summer everyone would be going there . . .

MB Right.

P And it is summer there.

MB It's a reason why the beach is empty.

P Yes.

Obviously the 'curse on the beach' has another function too, in that it helps to build an atmosphere at the start of the story. But Pritesh, interestingly, only picks out the point about it that matters most to him. His narrative depends on Peter being alone on the beach and finding the key, and so the fact that the beach is so conveniently empty must be explained. The need to explain, to build the realistic foundations of the story strongly, is very marked throughout Pritesh's interview. The bringing out of a sledgehammer to crack a narrative nut, as in this example, is characteristic of his approach and, I suggest, of that of many children of his age. It argues a highly developed sense of an audience, and a concern for realism and narrative 'rules'.

One later extract will illustrate this same tendency, as well as Pritesh's overriding desire to 'make a big adventure'. I asked Pritesh to go back over the story he had written so far and tell me if he had made any changes.

MB OK, what else did you change?

P Changed that too, I writ 'suddenly'. I was going to change the whole story then.

MB Oh were you? Why?

P Yes, but I didn't. I writ 'decided'.

MB You had 'suddenly'. 'He suddenly'?

P Um, put his left foot on a piece of metal, but I wanted to make it right down there.

MB I see, so you were going to bring the key in in the third line . . .

P Yes.

MB And then you decided against it . . .

P Yes.

MB And you made Peter decide to go for a swim. Now why did you choose to leave the key out until right down here.

P 'Cos he would have been wearing his shoes on the beach and he wouldn't have felt it.

MB Oh I see! So it was when you realised that if he was dressed up walking on the beach that he just wouldn't feel the key under his foot that you had to make him go home, get his costume, come back . . .

P Get his shoes off and put the costume on.

MB Good Lord above! That's very extraordinary. Well, why didn't you just have him taking his shoes off?

P I dunno really.

MB Did you think it would be *better* if you left it to later?

P Yeh.

MB Why?

P Well, I just felt like it.

MB Yeh.

P Because it'd be a really short story, it wouldn't make that much se . . . wouldn't be that *interesting*.

MB So . . .

P The longer the story, the more interesting it is.

Here are two of Pritesh's main preoccupations, clearly demonstrated. On the one hand is realism. So close is Pritesh's attention to detail and so determined is he to make the story life-like, that he writes another page (the intervening text takes up almost a page of his handwriting) rather than contravene the rules of realism. Peter is going to step on the key just as he is about to go in the sea. He has unfortunately come out without his swimming costume, so he has to be sent all the way home to get it — no other solution occurs to Pritesh. But it can also be seen that Pritesh quickly turns his 'mistake' to good account. He sees that it actually helps the story to delay the introduction of the key until later. 'I wanted to make it right down there,' he says, pointing down the page. The finding of the key is an exciting narrative movement for him and he chooses to build up to it, to defer the pleasure of it deliberately.

Pritesh is obviously a writer who is writing with a reader's eye and his awareness of internal discrepancies is well developed. He is liable to worry about detail and when he meets a narrative hurdle he may go round a very long way to avoid it. In all these ways he is a more anxious and a more self-conscious writer than the younger writers I interviewed. Older writers seem to have more choices than younger writers but they also experience more constraints.

The differences that I have noted between younger and older writers are very similiar to the differences between children as artists that are documented in Howard Gardner's book *Artful Scribbles*[2]. Gardner has two very interesting chapters. In Chapter Five, 'Children's Drawings as Works of Art', he attempts to account for the flowering of children's art between the ages of five and seven. In Chapter Six, which he entitles 'The Reach Toward Realism' he describes the way in which, as children grow older, their drawing gains in accuracy and technical competence but becomes less artistically satisfying. He quotes his daughter, aged nine, as saying 'I used to draw much better. My drawings were more interesting. But my perspective is 3000 times better now.'

Gardner has carried out a survey in which he and some colleagues have studied drawings made by the same children as they proceeded from kindergarten through the early years of schooling.

> Time and again we find the drawings by the older children increasingly regular, increasingly neatly coloured in. But by the same token the sense of life, power and vitality and the delight in colour and form for their own sake, which are so characteristic of the drawings by the younger children, also wane. Indeed this finding has been captured in a rating scale: while *technical competence* is found to improve steadily with age, *flavourfulness* — the extent to which drawings incorporate individualising features — reaches its apogee in first grade and then steadily recedes thereafter. (p. 148)

Gardner then attempts to account systematically for this change. Although one of his points is that drawing and writing are not absolutely parallel modes, in that writing is tending during this period of childhood to take over from drawing, much of what he says about the 'reach towards realism' in drawing can be generalized to writing. He sees older children as becoming acutely aware of accuracy and realism, and describes their increased preoccupation with the mastery of conventions, the learning of notations and the practising of skills and techniques. The pressure for this development comes, he thinks, from the culture itself and the kinds of graphic representation it values, from the peer group and their pre-occupation at this stage with rules and conventions, and from school, where a general premium on 'getting things right' is clearly conveyed to children.

Much of what has been written about children's play would confirm this sense of an increased concern among older children for doing things properly, conventionally and like other people. Piaget's study *The Rules of the Game of Marbles*[3] delineates three stages in rule-consciousness. In the third stage, which Piaget sees as beginning at age nine to ten, children are shown as being as concerned with the observance of correct rules as with the outcome of the game.

> The child's chief interest is no longer psycho-motor, it is social. In other words, to dislodge a marble from a square by manual dexterity is no longer an aim in itself. The thing now is not only to fight the other boys but also and primarily to regulate the game with a whole set of systematic rules which will ensure the most complete reciprocity in the methods used. The game therefore has become social.

But although it is possible to explain the development towards a more convention-bound, rule-conscious and realistic stage of representation in older juniors by reference to other aspects of child development, it is quite impossible to account for the peculiar power and artistry of younger children's stories and fantasies by any such scheme. The kind of freedom, freshness and energy that very young children bring to their writing and drawing cannot be categorized any more than the qualities of art in general can be categorized. Bruner described the hallmark of a creative enterprise as 'an act that produces *effective surprise*'[4] and that is surely an excellent description of the kind of delight that is kindled by young children's paintings and stories. Gardner describes the expressive power of children in this period very sensitively.

> This eruption of artistry at the threshold of school represents for me the central fact — and the central enigma — of artistic development. One can speak without exaggeration of a flowering of capacities during this period. The expressive

forms, lively colours and stunning compositions bespeak a consciousness that is heightened if not inspired. (p. 94)

He also notices the parallel developments in singing, construction, movement and poetic expression at this period and concludes, 'even as the child appears at this time to be a youthful artist, he also may lay claim to be a young musician, dancer, or story teller.'

Gardner is concerned not to lapse into a simple Rousseauism at this point in his argument, and indicates the role of the accidental in children's productions, as well as the importance of the role of the observer — what the adult reader or viewer brings to the children's stories or paintings. But he allows the enigma of this phase of artistic development to remain an enigma. Two very useful concepts seem to me to emerge from his balanced discussion of this complex question. One is encapsulated in a phrase, 'first draft artistry', and the other is his reference to young children's intuitive 'sense of the whole' of an organized picture.

'First draft artistry' is Gardner's useful way of defining the particular strengths and limitations of young children's creative power. Gardner sees a child as having undoubted gifts, of which he or she is in only partial control,

> partial both in the sense that he can sometimes (but not always) achieve what he wants and in the sense that he sometimes (but not always) is actually pursuing explicit ends.

The feeling that children in this age group have powers that they cannot control and are not conscious of is supported by conversations with infant teachers. Two infant teachers told me recently that they often take paintings away from children at the point when they, the teachers, sense the children have accomplished something really special. If children are left to continue painting for as long as they like they will often 'spoil' the picture; they are not always aware of the aesthetic effect of what they have made.

The 'sense of the whole' is in Gardner's view something that is lost in middle childhood, when children become preoccupied with detail.

> Whereas the literally oriented child is intent on getting every detail correct and will therefore dispense with a 'sense of the whole', the child of five or six has an intuitive sense of what an organised picture should be like — a sense which is, at the very least, submerged during the subsequent periods. (p. 148)

Both these concepts can clearly be used for thinking about young children's writing. I should like now to concentrate on the 'sense of the whole' and to discuss how children develop the remarkable feeling for whole form which we are aware of in their paintings and in their early stories. Quite clearly this has nothing to do with analysis, or the application of rules, William Stafford parodies such a suggestion effectively in *Writing the Australian Crawl*.[5]

> Practical people assume that creating in art takes place in a mechanical manner. For example, some complex form in poetry — say, a sonnet — is analyzed. A person studies and learns that sonnets are fourteen lines long; so he counts down fourteen when he writes one. And he learns that a sonnet has five stresses in each line; so he counts five across. And he may go on to learn intricacies — a sonnet breaks between lines eight and nine; so he chops his poem decisively in that place, amid the fourteen lines. Then, putting together the successive moves he has learned, he writes a sonnet. No.

Stafford is writing about creative art in general but his rejection of the 'mechanical manner' must be even truer of young children, who would not be capable of articulating the stylistic rules that they nevertheless follow in their own story-writing. Polanyi's chapter on skills in *Personal Knowledge*[6] is fundamentally concerned with this kind of phenomenon, with the fact that

> the aim of a skilful performance is achieved by the observance of a set of rules which are not known as such to the person following them.

But it is to a later chapter in Polanyi's book that I wish to turn in an attempt to examine how it is that young children come to feel a 'sense of the whole' in art, music or literature. In the chapter on 'Intellectual Passions' Polanyi writes about contemplation as a way of knowing, and describes the experience of 'losing oneself' in this process:

> The impersonality of intense contemplation consists in a *complete participation of the person in that which he contemplates* and not in his complete detachment from it, as would be the case in an ideally objective observation.

In other places Polanyi refers to this process as 'in-dwelling'. He sees it as a *bodily* process in which, by attending to experience, we come to 'incorporate it in our being — or extend, our body to include it — so that we come to dwell in it'.[7]

Polanyi sees the 'intelligent contemplation of music and dramatic art' as the *end* of education. But it is clear that what he calls contemplation, even if it is not 'intelligent' contemplation, is a means of understanding the world that is available to us from infancy. As small animals we experience form, colour and rhythm in physical ways. Recently I was reading from a poetry book to a five-year-old girl. She had very little experience of hearing poetry apart from nursery rhymes, and I was reading to her as a 'bedtime story', so she was in bed. As I read each poem she moved about in time with the rhythm, feeling it through her whole body quite spontaneously, a perfect example of bodily contemplation.

It seems to me very probable that young children experience the tunes of stories and the shapeliness of story forms in almost as physical a way as this and that, from repeated readings of favourite stories, and from growing acquaintance with a range of literary models, they derive a strong, unconscious 'sense of the whole' which they can later draw on in their own creations.

But the kinds of 'in-dwelling' that are observable in young children's story-making go beyond an intuited sense of form. The young writers that I interviewed often expressed a strong sense of *inhabiting* the worlds they were creating. They seemed to live their own stories and to be aware of them from the inside. One very obvious example was that of a child whose visualizations were particularly full and vivid. Angela, aged seven, was explaining to me that the king and queen in her story, who had shut the princess in a 'big, big box', had a key to the box:

A   But they hid it, but the prince found the key 'cos it was behind the curtain.

MB   Was it? Oh, you didn't say that in the story, I don't think.

A   'Cos I didn't have enough time to say all that.

MB   'Cos you didn't have enough time so you had to make it very much faster. But was that in your head, that the key was behind the curtain? When you were writing the story you were thinking . . .

A   Mmm.

MB   When you're writing a story, do you have pictures in your head?

A   Some . . . Yes, I do have pictures in my head but I don't write . . . I don't draw them.

MB   Can you remember any of the pictures that you had in your head when you were writing this? Could you tell me about them?

A   Yes.

MB   Go on.

A   One was, I, a princess with a blue skirt and a yellow jumper, with silver and gold bits of jewels on her things and a necklace and jewelleries, and the prince was wearing a gold jacket thing and blue trousers.

MB   Mmm.

A   And then I've got the curt . . . there was a big, y'know, it wasn't, it was a wooden box, a wooden kind of box.

MB   That she was in.

A   Yes, and with a door on it, and the key was behind the curtains, and the curtains were, have got flowers on them in all kinds of different colours and the door was next, just next, the *back* door was just next to the curtains.

This is a form of eidetic imagery and suggests that the story takes place in a kind of internal theatre. Angela is playwright, producer and designer, and one may guess that she is also involved in the action, most probably in the role of the princess whose costume she describes in such detail.

Other children have told me about a sense of being 'in the story'. The most striking description was given me by an eight-year-old boy, John, who said, 'It's just as if I was one of those persons, I'd be there. Like I'm imagining myself in a dream being there.'

Probably most writers of fiction experience this strong sense of imaginative participation in their own creations to some degree. Young children, with their remarkable capacity for projective identification, may find it particularly easy to create and enter new worlds in this way.

In order to appreciate young children's predisposition towards this kind of world-making one has only to consider dramatic play. Edith Cobb, in her strange and interesting book *The Ecology of Imagination in Childhood*,[8] notes that the essential distinction between the play of small animals and small children lies in this habit of imaginative identification.

> The important distinction, however, is that while other animals do play, the human child's play includes the effort to be something other than what he actually is, to 'act out' and to dramatize speculation. Practice play and even 'pretense' of a sort are to be found in animal play — as, for example, when dogs pretend to fight yet are prevented by 'social inhibition' from serious biting. But a dog never tries to become a horse, a train, a bird, or a tree, while a child may imagine himself to be any one of these organisms or things at will. Unless the child (or the adult) is emotionally ill or schizophrenic and cannot, therefore, establish boundaries to his own body image, the gift of early plasticity in human nature inlcudes the ability to resume the role of selfhood at will.

It seems likely that for young children all forms of creation partake of the nature of dramatic play, in which the child *enacts* the experiences that he or she is representing, sometimes physically and vocally, and sometimes in a purely interior fashion. A particularly striking example of this kind of fusion of dramatic play with picture-making is given in Sylvia Feinburg's study of 'Combat in Child Art', a study of her five-year-old son's pictures of battles.[9]

> What was notable about these productions was the specific approach to the 'making' process. Battle pictures were not so much akin to picture-making in its traditional sense as they were to the activity of dramatic play. Initially, Douglas

Norman, London, 1980.
3. J. Piaget, 'The Rules of the Game of Marbles' (1965) in J. Bruner et al., *Play*, Penguin, Harmondsworth, 1976.
4. J. Bruner, *On Knowing*, Harvard University Press, 1979.
5. W. Stafford, *Writing the Australian Crawl*, University of Michigan Press, ed. D. Hall.
6. M. Polanyi, *Personal Knowledge*, Routledge and Kegan Paul, London, 1958.
7. M. Polanyi, *The Tacit Dimension*, Routledge and Kegan Paul, London, 1966.
8. E. Cobb, *The Ecology of Imagination in Childhood*, Routledge and Kegan Paul, London, 1977.
9. S. Feinburg, 'Combat in Child Art' in J. Bruner, op. cit. n. 3.
10. D. Heathcote, *Drama as Context*, National Association for the Teaching of English, 1980.
11. 'There Was a Child Went Forth', *Walt Whitman: The Complete Poems*, ed. F. Murphy, Penguin, Harmondsworth, 1975, p. 386.
12. B. Berenson, 'Sketch for a Self-Portrait', quoted in Cobb, op. cit. n. 8.

One Day

Michael Rosen

It was long after the time of family holidays:
all four of us, two tents
on farms and campsites
in places like the New Forest or the Welsh Borders.

Brian was away on field trips and expeditions
with geological maps and specimen boxes.

Mum was on a course, giving a course?
preparing a course? recovering from a course?

I was old enough to go hitching
to Leeds or Paris or Watford.

Somehow
one Whitsun
there was just the two of us.
Harold and me.
I think it was Harold who said
'Why don't we spend the week
camping at Skenfrith?'

Yes — I remembered —
on Fidler's Farm
on the banks of the River Monow —
there was a red sand beach
red earth hills, badger-woods
trout . . .

I'd spent weeks of summer
making sand-dams, milking cows
and climbing the Sugar Loaf mountain.

One thing though
we'd never done
was put a boat on the river.
So I said to Harold
'Why don't we hire a canoe for Whit week?'
'No', he said.

Maybe he thought we wouldn't use it
maybe he thought we couldn't use it
maybe he thought we could but we wouldn't.

So I rang PGL Holidays
they'd deliver one evening, collect the next
at Fidler's Farm.

They did.
It was pouring. Straight down.
They delivered the canoe to the farm
and we tobogganed it down the hillside
to the tent.
All night it filled up with rain.

In the morning
Harold said
'You're not going out in that thing, are you?'
'Yeah', I said
'Do you want to have a go?'
'Might as well', he says.

We got into big plastic bags
and shorts and plimsolls
and we spent a whole day
in the pouring rain
canoeing up the Monow
and back again.

We ran rapids
we slid under trees
we rested in the curves of meanders
we paddled past Hereford cows
we beached on sand banks
and it poured with rain on our plastic bags
we lugged the canoe through shallows
we imagined Amazons and Colorados
and Norwegian kayak champions.

Mind you,
it was the first time either of us had ever done it.

That evening
we lugged the canoe back up the hillside
and PGL came to collect
at Fidler's Farm.

It was one day
squeezed into a holiday
that was itself
squeezed in between
college and teaching and study.

One day.

8.
Training Teenage Teachers

Judith Graham

The English department at the Institute of Education has for many years now run a course for Postgraduate Certificate of Education students on the teaching of reading. This puts at its centre the practical experience of helping a struggling reader with the business of learning to read and write. With Margaret Spencer as my tutor I followed the course myself shortly after its inauguration and now with Margaret as colleague I help in the teaching of it. I believe it remains an important and exciting aspect of the training year.[1] Indeed, so rich are the possibilities in this sort of work that I began to wonder whether students still at school might not benefit from a similar programme. When I joined the staff of the Institute of Education I continued to teach part-time at Clissold Park School in Hackney, so I had the opportunity to set up, with sixth-formers as 'teachers' and first-formers as 'pupils', a course on the teaching of reading which borrowed much from the course at the Institute. I shall try here to capture some of its flavour.

A dozen sixth-formers, all taking the CEE exam in English, were each invited to help a first-former and to keep a written record of what happened which, when written up, would fulfil the exam requirement for a 2,000-word essay on a subject studied 'in depth'. The sixth-formers jumped at the practical element in the work and envisaged the final essay almost writing itself. Other 'depth study' choices looked formidable by comparison. The appeal of the research element and a more original end product was powerful. I hoped that less tangible results might be increased awareness of how they themselves learn and even eventually a sharpened insight into their own children's learning. For the first-formers the hope was that the additional help and attention from an interested, albeit non-professional, adult in a relaxed atmosphere might result in improved self-image and consequently in more fluent reading and writing.

From the beginning I emphasized that careful observation and detailed documentation were more important than teaching techniques. I wanted them to see themselves as a sympathetic and encouraging audience for their first-formers' anecdotes, comments, confidences and anxieties, and to understand that a growth in self-confidence is often accompanied or followed by an improved attitude to and facility in reading, even if no formal instruction takes place. The research findings documented in Denis Lawrence's book, *Improved Reading Through Counselling*, were helpful here[2]. I discovered that this provided an important reassurance for several sixth-formers, who were initially fearful of failing ('What if he still can't read at the end of six months?'). In my underplaying of teaching techniques, however, I had reckoned without the fixed models the sixth-formers had in their heads. Many of them rejoiced in the opportunity to play teacher and visited on their pupils much overt instruction, harsh homework and even punishment for what was interpreted as laziness or forgetfulness. On the whole, however, they gradually got the hang of noting and responding to what their pupils were trying to do, and their log-books reflect this sensitivity.

Just as at the Institute, where we have a few sessions with our students while a pupil is found for them, so I had three double lessons with my sixth-formers while I was making arrangements with first-form teachers to find likely pupils. Looking back now I seem to have crammed a great deal into those lessons. We discussed first of all how we learnt to read ourselves. Many remembered that the purpose of reading only became clear when we began to read real books rather than meaningless reading schemes. Already some were realising that controlled vocabulary doesn't mean an easier read. We discovered how flash cards were hard work and how isolated words in meaningful contexts were not necessarily difficult. They came up with Police, Squeezy, Marmite, Woolworths and Exit. They recalled how sound/symbol relationships were taught and realized how many exceptions to the 'rules' there were.

From these personal memories we went on to games designed to convince ourselves that reading is only 'incidently visual'. Is reading 'decoding' from symbol to sound or do we sample print to confirm expectations? My debt to Frank Smith is clear.[3] We unscrambled texts like:

Nomral reding is a knid of hgih-speed gessuing game, wihch explians why we find it difficult to proof-raed. The raeding porcess is incredibly flexilbe and can cope with all kinds of worng infromation, such as revresed lettres, missprimts, punchuation errers and chainges in tiep font, eny of witch wood compeltely fox a comutre. But so long as sence is comming over the i bounds on. What does hold up the porcess are unfmeilar langauge consturctions, so a when of juggled the about are all sentence words the brian gets into an awful staet tyring to recnocile a snesible antiiciptaed messaeg and nonsesnical messaeg which was actaully recieved.

Interestingly, when we tried to read texts written backwards memories came back of the shame and terror of having incompetence exposed in public. Athough we knew what the name of the game was, it was still very difficult to remember to read 'no' as 'on', 'was' as 'saw', 'god' as 'dog' and not to see and want to say the word 'depart' in the written 'deppart' rather than the correct 'trapped'. At this stage one of the girls was so discomfited that she asked to be moved to a different option. Of all the dozen she turned out to have had the greatest initial difficulty in learning to read, and the 'games' we were playing were just too painful for her. However, I persuaded her to stay the course and she became finally the most thoughtful and caring of 'teachers'.[4] Part of my aim had been, I suppose, to show how powerfully feelings are involved in the reading process. The students also discovered that we bring an amazing amount of knowledge about language (word order, sentence construction, etc.) and about life to our reading, that to read well we often need to ignore the cues in words, that proper names require most letter-cues, that understanding meaning comes before pronouncing correctly, and that you almost certainly don't look at every word when you're reading.

Then we looked at some of the obstacles to learning to read. The sixth-formers offered ones like long absences from school, neglect in school, misguided teaching (and the thought that some pupils learn despite the method), boring books and, again, fear of ridicule from classmates and teacher. We wanted to put the emphasis on external reasons so that there would be less temptation to subscribe to views of their pupil as stupid or lazy or of themselves as inadequate. I referred them to the findings of Margaret Clark in her book *Young Fluent Readers*.[5] She discovered that questions of socio/economic background, IQ, personality, auditory, visual or manual/motor skills, health or oral development had far less bearing on a child's early reading ability than might be expected. She found that good experience of playing, an interested, relaxed adult and a ticket to the local library were far more critical. One major difference, worth mentioning at this stage, between the sixth-formers and postgraduate students is that the sixth-formers (with one exception) could not be persuaded to go to the literature, though over the year they both generated and assimilated many complex ideas.

As their first encounter with a pupil approached the students focused on how to handle the first session and what they should record in their logs. They were anxious not to pressurize their pupils by any sort of reading-for-testing and some of them went so far as to compile a list of questions: What are your hobbies? What do you think of your new school? In nearly all cases the first sessions were somewhat awkward, and many fell gratefully back on the books I'd supplied, *Hackney Half-Term Adventure, My Life, Sinbad the Sailor*. Second and subsequent sessions were always more spontaneous. We agreed that any of the following would be promising signs of progress and worth recording:

- coming readily to the lesson
- volunteering remarks about why reading is difficult
- bringing something themselves to read
- remembering what happened in the previous lesson, finding the right page, etc.
- exercising choice in what they do (i.e. not just submitting passively)
- making deductions about likely contents from book cover, etc.
- predicting how a story is going to develop or end
- self-correcting
- criticizing weaknesses of plot or discrepancies in illustration or text
- using pictures, common sense, linguistic clues to get at meaning
- willingness to take risks
- relating text to their own experience of life

We also looked at some of the common 'miscues' in reading (this is Kenneth Goodman's term and more useful than 'mistakes'[6]) and discussed their relative importance. For instance, do you stop to correct when a child reads 'father' as 'dad'? Later we spent much longer on 'miscue analysis', which proved to be a turning point in the students' understanding of the reading process.

During these three weeks of discussion I was busy selecting pupils from the first year. The London Reading Test threw up fifty children as 'at risk', so I consulted form teachers, English teachers and year heads and drew up a short list of possible children. Their scores on the LRT ranged from 0 to 33, some were ESL learners and all were thought likely to respond to help from a sixth-former. Sixth-formers and first-formers were then roughly matched. Certain preferences were expressed by the sixth-formers, but not necessarily met. The biggest mistake I made was to accede to one boy's request to be given the 'really hopeless case', 'the worst of the lot', without realizing that he would be violently disillusioned and frustrated when he failed to work an instant miracle cure. Meeting times and places were arranged (twice or thrice weekly in the library during registration), letters written home and introductions effected. The whole project was under way.

At every stage I emphasized the nature of the commitment involved in helping a child to read. After a history of failure, hopes which are raised by a bright optimistic newcomer should not be lightly dashed. We had also discussed the nature, likelihood and problems of dependency. It seemed that most sixth-formers were aware of the seriousness of what they were taking on. With the exception of the boy quoted above all of them turned out to be reliable, usually enthusiastic and occasionally jubilant. Once launched, the pairs evolved a way of working together which suited them, and I was occasionally able to join them and analyse the sessions later with the students. All of them made tape-recordings of one or more sessions and after listening to these I sent back written comments, which were not always quite as dauntingly comprehensive as this example to Sema, who taught her fellow Turkish pupil in a mixture of Turkish and English to very fine effect.

Sema, I have listened to your tape and think that you and Yulmaz are doing marvellously! Yulmaz is obviously improving and your commitment and thoughtfulness come through at every point.
I would see the signs of *strength* in her reading as:
1. relatively few mistakes (day/way, coming/going, that/what)
2. the mistakes she makes often make sense (e.g. 'What a life it was' for 'What a life this is')
3. she self-corrects (e.g. 'because he was, *has* never liked to cry in front of any friend')
4. she uses the knowledge she has of how words are made up to help her with long words (e.g. 'education')
5. she has great stamina (she keeps going and doesn't avoid the task in hand)
6. she doesn't wait for you to help her or appeal to you.
7. she is able to identify where she might have made mistakes (on your invitation, she points to the 'that/what' confusion)
8. she makes sense of what she is reading (she would not have emphasized the word 'you' in 'It's *you* that's going abroad' unless she understood the text).
The most obvious weaknesses are:
1. she reads slowly, appearing to tackle words one at a time or in rather short phrases. She often pauses for several seconds. (What do you think she's doing in these pauses?)
2. she doesn't volunteer much comment on the text (maybe this is because you were using the tape-recorder)
3. she doesn't *risk* much — she doesn't guess and then correct if necessary
These are the things that I think you are doing which are helping Yulmaz enormously:
1. asking her to point to where her mistakes have been

2. ignoring the occasions where her mistakes don't alter the sense of the passage.
3. suggesting that she use *sense* as a criterion for working out what a word is (e.g. going/coming)
4. pointing out that words read correctly once hold the same meaning when they come up again (e.g. the word 'religion')
5. giving good advice (e.g. look ahead, go back over muddles, make it make sense)

Keep doing all that and Yulmaz will get better and better.

But, here are three things I want you to think about:

1. Do you really think Yulmaz needs to look carefully at words one by one? You see, I think trying to follow that advice slows her up, which then makes *predicting* what could come next more difficult.
2. Give her an opportunity to comment more on what she's reading and you comment yourself to show her that having *reactions* to books is permissible!
3. Give her a little more praise — after all she gets an awful lot right! Especially congratulate her efforts to self-correct.

It is obvious from your tape that you have built up a relationship with Yulmaz based on respect and a joint sense of purpose and I think you should be very proud of your achievement. Well done.

Mrs Graham

It is time to give the sixth-formers a chance to speak for themselves and so, in conclusion and by using selections from the final essays, I shall try to suggest the rewards and the hazards, the felicities and the shocks that this project produced for me. The problems for the most part could have been ironed out with closer supervision and more time for group discussion (though I know the sixth-formers discussed their pupils together endlessly). One joyful aspect for me was reading essays which were unusually committed, written with a real sense of purpose and recording very real achievements. Another was noting the delight, faith and loyalty that the first-formers had for their pupil-teachers. I regret that I did not more formally interview the first-formers at the end of the project but it seemed obvious that they were all gaining in confidence and facility.

Let's hear first from the sixth-former who needed longer than this year to eradicate from his mind the image of teacher as tester and detector of cheating:

I asked him to answer the questions as homework so tomorrow I shall have some proof that he actually read the story again and understood it enough to answer the questions . . . he read clearly and correctly into the tape without any mistakes. It seems to me that he had been practising this before he turned up today but this is not for me to say. Let's get back to what happened.

And the student who was perhaps recognizing something of herself in her mischievous pupil:

> Today I found out that she isn't as quiet and good as she appears to be. There's a lot more to her than her sweet little innocent face lets on. First, thinking she could copy out of a book and get away with it, even get credit for it. Then writing on the palm of her hand the hardest words in the test or the words she thought she might have trouble with . . . Today's session made me realize what sort of person I'm dealing with. Just because she's learning to read doesn't mean that she isn't just as cunning, crafty and intelligent as the next child.

These extracts make us smile as well as gasp. More frustrating because they were more accessible to pushing towards valuable insights, if there had been time, are the numerous detailed observations which hang in the air:

> The book he chose was Sinbad. He read for a while. He seems to be enjoying himself. He kept telling me what was going to happen before he read it.

(What a breakthrough it is when children start to predict in this way. No wonder he's enjoying himself.)

> When I tried to take away the sheet of paper which I'd marked 'very good' she was keen to keep it herself.

> I asked him to look through the book and choose one of the short stories he'd like to read. He chose one called 'The Undersea Bells'. This time he read with much more confidence.

> One word that she couldn't read was 'awfully' so I put my fingers over 'aw' and 'y' [*sic*] and said, 'what's that?' and she read it right and after that she still didn't seem to know what the word said, not that she should mind you. But I told her it anyway.

(Well, she was lucky, she got her information eventually.)

Most of the children were lucky, and these final extracts show the quality of response that these new 'teachers', still only 16 years old, were making to their pupils. How about this for resourcefulness?:

> We had five minutes left so we looked at the map of Hackney on the back of his folder and he showed me where he lived and I showed him where I lived. Then we found his dad's work place and where his Nan lives.

or this:

> I asked him if he'd ever done a project before. He said no. I told him I had

but that I'd forgotten how to start it. He then pointed out to me how it
should be started and we were off.

or this:

She didn't understand the meaning of 'describe'. She said simply, 'I don't
describe' so I gave her a description of her jacket and then she understood
what it meant.

And this seems to me to show a splendid instinct:

I had some time left so in that time I wrote my diary. When I finished I
read it over for him so that he wouldn't think anything suspicious.

Here is one boy evolving his working method. Slightly pompous perhaps
but what control!

The words he found hard to pronounce were 'geometrical', 'precision',
'spectacle', 'athletics', 'unaccustomed'. [!] I didn't expect him to be able
to read these words because I felt they were hard for him. At first I told
him to guess at the words. If he was getting close to them, I would cheer
him on but if he just could not pronounce them I would tell him. This
way we both learn a bit about each other's way. Within no time of that the
pips went and we departed.

And:

Today we read another book about the Roman Empire. We read through
the first two pages and he kept crashing up on words such as Octavia,
Caesar, Cleopatra. The first time he read them wrong I corrected him.
Then if he read it wrong again I would ask him to think about the way
that I'd pronounced it before. Sometimes I'd just leave him because I
knew the words would come up again.

There are acute observations like this:

She doesn't appear to have an inferiority complex or feel shy at the fact
that she comes to me for reading. She has the usual shyness anyone would
have when meeting someone for the first time

And:

Sometimes she says she knows things when perhaps she doesn't. I don't
want to underestimate her by explaining something which she says she
knows as it might make her feel small.

And there is sensitivity in:

I haven't set her any homework as I don't think she'd be able to do it which might make her think she's off to a bad start if she can't finish it.

and in:

When I went to mark it wrong she said, 'no, it's right', so not to disappoint her, I left it.

Even if we disagree with the pedagogy the instincts seem sound.

I'll finish with a piece from the student who was herself a slow reader but whose pupil perhaps made the most progress. She expresses herself more simply than her fellow sixth-formers, certainly more simply than our postgraduates, and many would want to draw clever conclusions from this recorded moment. As an example of pleasure and learning on both sides merging and shining I find it very powerful and it will certainly do to justify my trying out the Institute's reading course on my sixth-form pupils.

I could hardly believe this piece of well-presented work with her name, the title, the date all in the right place and with what appeared to be excellent punctuation. I asked her whether it was for English or could I keep it. She said I could keep it, that she just did it last night and off the top of her head. She just sat down and did it and I could have it if I wanted it. I read it and said it was very good. This compliment pleased her like it would anyone. She had a great big smile right across her face at the success of her work.

Notes and references

1. Further description of this course can be found in Margaret Meek's contribution to H. Rosen (ed.), *Language and Literacy in our Schools: Some appraisals of the Bullock Report*, Studies in Education 1, University of London Institute of Education, 1975.
2. D. Lawrence, *Improved Reading Through Counselling*, Ward Lock, London, 1973.
3. F. Smith, *Understanding Reading*, Holt, Rinehart and Winston, New York, 1971.
4. This girl wrote movingly in her final essay on her own early reading experiences:
    Reading for me was a subject I wanted to run away from. I was always making some sort of excuse not to read because I was frightened of making a fool of myself and being laughed at. I thought if my friends knew they wouldn't be friendly with me anymore. I didn't even want to go to school sometimes, because I was so scared of being asked to read. I used to become very nervous when I was told to read by a teacher at my junior school or come to that, even

people outside school, my parents' friends for example and my friends.

I remember when I was out shopping one day with my mum and an old lady asked me to read a birthday card, she had forgotten her glasses. I turned away from her because I was scared yet again of making a fool of myself. I passed the card over to my mum to read and I later discovered I could read the card. Then I said to myself why was I so nervous? It's just that I kept telling myself I couldn't read.

The only person I would read to is my mother but even then I lacked a little confidence. Learning to read came gradually I don't know how but it just came to me. One day I picked a book up after a very long time and I could just about read it.

5. M. Clark, *Young Fluent Readers*, Heinemann, London, 1976.
6. K. Goodman, 'Learning about Psychological Processes by Analyzing Oral Reading', *Harvard Educational Review*, vol 47, no 3, 1977.

9.
'Epic' Education

Some suggestions about the implications of Brecht's dramatic
theory in the sphere of education

Nick Otty

> What we must learn above all is consent.
>
> Many say yes and there is no consent.
> Many are not asked.
> And many consent to wrong things.
> Therefore: what we must learn above all is consent.
>
> As to the old great custom I see no rhyme or reason in it.
> What we need is a new great custom to be introduced at once —
> To wit: the custom of re-thinking every new situation.
> Bertolt Brecht, *He Who Says Yes; He Who Says No*[1]

The BA Humanities at Bristol Polytechnic is one of those courses which
came into being as an indirect result of the student ferment of the late Sixties. In particular, it represents a response to (and, necessarily, a reactionary
accommodation of) the demands made at that time for more student choice.
It is a modular degree — a module being a third of a year's work for a
student — and the students can pick and choose amongst the modules and
half-modules available in English Studies, Historical Studies, Communications Studies and Geography and Urban Studies. So, far more than was once
the case, these students can shape their own course to their own needs and
interests. Since the course first started in 1974 the choices have, for all sorts
of highly respected academic reasons, been limited by prerequisites, and in
talk of the degree's future there is fairly constant canvassing of the advis-
ability of further restricting choices by means of gates and quotas and so
forth. In any case, even in the early days there was widespread agreement
that the students' active choice should be made *before* the year's courses
began. Student choice ends with the first seminar in most of the modules.
The subject matter, the order, the teaching methods, the approaches and

emphases (again for 'excellent' academic reasons) were from the start decided by the tutors.

This is what I mean by 'a reactionary accommodation'. I do think that the Bristol BA Humanities is an excellent and interesting course. I do think that it is well taught, by committed and well-qualified teachers. But while it offers choice at one level, it avoids the more radical implications of the idea of student choice in education. Students, as used to be said, always did have choice; the choice (subject to certain constraints and prerequisites: the right A levels, but also the right manner at interview) of institution and, within the institution, the choice of the degree for which they wished to study. Now, in courses like the BA Humanities, they can choose from a variety of options *within* the degree. But these new choices, being structurally identical with the old ones, do not necessarily open up fruitful and creative educational relationships. The educational transaction is still mediated by power expressed through assessment and course validation, for instance. It is therefore oppressive of the learner in that, whatever the subject matter of the course, from post-structuralist criticism through imperial history to Anglo-Saxon, the structural levels remain unchallenged. And it is these levels that transmit our society's models of knowledge and their relation to political power.

Within the Bristol Humanities degree there is now a course which in some ways manages to avoid this oppressiveness. Here is the course description as it appears in the handbook.

EPIC AND ENSEMBLE DRAMA
Prerequisites: None
Epic theatre and ensemble drama, with reference to some of the work and ideas of ARTAUD, BRECHT, GROTOWSKI, ARDEN, BECK, BOAL and others.

Aims
1. To explore the ideas in some of the books and plays listed below.
2. To work in groups at ensemble techniques of play-making, rehearsal, improvisation, etc.
3. To use the dramatic process as a way of deepening understanding in and synthesising material from other areas of the degree (e.g. Sociology, History, Politics, Anthropology, etc.).

NB. Following the logic of ensemble work, *the actual sequence and balance of the work will be decided by the group and the tutor as the course proceeds*. For example, a term's work in the course *might* follow some such pattern as the following:

Activities	**Possible Reading**
Week 1 Interaction games, theatre games, discussion.	BRECHT *Der Ya Sager: Der Nein Sager.*

Week 2	Talk about the plays. Rehearse parts of them. Choose one. Start work on it in detail.	ARDEN and DARCY *Ars Longa Vita Brevis.* SPOLIN *Improvisation for the theatre.* Introduction.
Week 3	Continue work on the play, using improvisation.	
Week 4	Perform the play to an audience. Production to be absolutely 'minimal' in terms of set, costume, lighting, etc.	BRECHT 'The Street Scene.' (*Brecht on Theatre*, ed. Willett. From page 121.)
Week 5	Discuss Brecht essay and 'epic' theatre. Work at exercises in *Brecht on Theatre*, p. 129.	
Week 6	Confer about the work so far. Two issues likely to arise: 1. What material would the group like to use as a basis for drama? 2. What kinds of action, spatial relationships of actors/audience etc.	BROOK and others. Introduction to *US* ALBERT HUNT *Hopes for Great Happenings.*
Week 7	Start improvising and writing/notating around Week 6.	ARTAUD 'Production and Metaphysics' from *The Theatre and its Double.*
Week 8	Discuss the ARTAUD essay in relation to Week 6. item 2. and the 'concrete physical language of the stage.'	Mummers plays and Miracle plays.
Week 9	Choose a mummers play and work up an elaborated version of it so as to explore the possibilities of the ARTAUD essay.	
Week 10	Perform the mummers play in a number of different contexts: in a lecture, at a party, in different schools, etc. Discuss it with the different audiences and discuss reactions in the group.	

Pick up from weeks 6 and 7 in the following term and go on to make and perform the group's own drama.

Assessment

To be in the following form:

1. *Course work* (to be completed during the year in which the course is taken).
   (a) A diary relating to practical work done during the year so as to give the

      student credit for that work in terms of the understanding that came from
      it. 10 per cent.
    (b) An essay on any topic agreed with the tutor. 20 per cent.
  2. *Project* (which need not be completed during the year in which the course is
     taken).
     This could be on any topic agreed with the tutor.
     (E.g. A comparison of *Mother Courage* and *Sergeant Musgrave's Dance* as ways
     of using theatre to analyse the logic of war, OR an account of the ways in
     which the practical use of drama illuminated the student's understanding of
     some text or texts (not necessarily dramatic) OR an exploration of the rela-
     tionship between story-telling and dramatic representation.) 70 per cent.
    Total = 100 per cent.
    NB. Since the point of the course is to achieve a certain kind of understanding
    and since much understanding can come from a theatrical production which is a
    failure, the direct results of the practical work are not assessed.

While the above description may well be seen as unusual for course hand-
books in general, the reader might be forgiven for thinking that it was not
particularly radical in its effects. In order to try to indicate why I think it *is*
actually rather deeply different from other courses I have taught on I would
like to give an account of some of the experiences which led to the course
being set up in the first place.

In 1975 I was teaching a first-year poetry course on the Humanities
degree. The aim of the course was to enable the students to perform competent critical analyses of poems in the first-year English exams, and the
course took the form of weekly hour-long seminars. My group was unusual
in that it contained two people who were not officially studying English at
all. They were only there out of an interest in poetry; they did not have to
learn to be competent literary critics. One was a technician at the Art
College, who wrote his own poetry. The other was a mature student on the
degree course, who was specializing in History. For the first term our work
was centred mainly in writing, reading and discussing our own poetry.
When, towards Christmas, I mentioned the fact that the course required us
to look at the work of at least one twentieth-century poet, it emerged that
several of the group were very interested in D.H. Lawrence. As a group decision, which included *some* of my ideas, it was agreed that we would concentrate on Lawrence's poetry in the Spring term, that we would go on a trip
to Nottingham and Eastwood as part of our study of the poet, and that we
would put together a poetry-reading or lecture or drama-show or event by
Easter which would be a way of focusing our work and our discoveries.

Well, we went to Nottingham and Eastwood. We certainly did learn quite
a lot about Lawrence. But we learned even more about the differences

between University and Polytechnic, about campus police, student politics, the Nottingham bus service, the public library in Eastwood, the laws of copyright, Lawrence's literary agent, T.S. Eliot's (unpublished) contribution to the Lady Chatterley controversy, and, of course, about ourselves and each other. We put on a rather chaotic show about it all. No one failed the poetry question in the exam, though one student did raise blood pressure in the department by doing his practical criticism of a Larkin poem entirely in the vocative: 'Ah! Philip, do I detect a note of fastidious snobbery in the words "a cut-price crowd"? I don't like that, Mr Larkin, you are talking about my family.'

Most of all we were struck by the way in which inventing and notating the show affected our understanding of what had occurred. The exacting requirements involved in assenting to a single, concrete re-presentation of events, clarified, deepened and articulated our communications. I remember dreaming wildly of institutions in which everything was taught through drama. Romantic Poetry would one year produce shows about the lives of Shelley and Byron, and the next year do dramatizations of 'Christabel' with alternative endings. There would be Brechtian cabarets in which Leavis and Empson sang of their contradictions, while Roland Barthes juggled with semes and signs and lexias. But as the Seventies progressed and the Sixties receded and as I no longer had freebooting, outside elements in my seminar groups, the students were more and more unwilling (as they saw it) to waste time on activities which did not seem to lead directly to the achievement of educational goals defined in terms of assessment. Honouring the practice of student choice, I could not but go along with them in tame neither-nor discussions of Ted Hughes and the War poets.

The next real step forward occurred in a corner of the degree known as the 'Open Seminars'. These are unassessed, voluntary seminars, which are intended to allow students to consider the interdisciplinary implications of their studies. With a small band of volunteers, some of whom had been on the trip to Nottingham, we set about presenting the original Grimms' version of *Little Red Riding Hood* as a parable about education.

This story, well known to every child, bears one obvious meaning about education:

> 'Walk nicely and quietly and do not run off the path', says Little Red Riding Hood's mother, 'and when you get to your Grandmother's room don't forget to say "Good morning" and don't go peeping into every corner before you do it.'

Good children (and good students) do not branch out on their own or they come to sticky ends from which only timely (male) intervention can save them. But our group quickly became interested in what the wolf had to say:

> 'Turn aside from the path. Look at the flowers, the birds, the sunlight under the trees. Pick some flowers for your Grandmother.'

In educational terms: you'll never learn anything unless you go your own way. Without labouring the point, the two contradictory meanings of the story set up a rich dialectic, well known to anyone interested in education:

authority/autonomy
male/female
adult/child
human/natural
social/natural
duty/pleasure

The Huntsman, who nearly shoots the wolf and 'saves' Little Red Riding Hood, is immensely male. The wolf is male too — a seducer — but dresses up in the Grandmother's nightgown to get at the girl. After *he* has eaten them, both Grandmother and Red Riding Hood are born or re-born from his belly. When they have been freed in this way Little Red Riding Hood sews stones inside the wolf's belly, which cause his death. When the wolf is dead the Huntsman dons his skin, just as the wolf wore the Grandmother's nightgown and just as the girl at the beginning of the story dons the red cape as a sign of her Grandmother's approval.

The further opposition of the Mother, Grandmother and Huntsman as human, set against the wolf as animal, makes for further contrasts between the rational and the social as against the passionate and the wild/the natural. This is reinforced with a slightly altered emphasis in the opposition between the humanly ordered path/life between the two houses, Little Red Riding Hood's house of childhood (her Mother's) and the house of her old age (her Grandmother's), for the ordered path is surrounded by, embedded in and gains its meaning from, the *natural* forest which surrounds it.

We had to work towards a model of performance which would allow us to express and explore these oppositions and also relate them to familiar present-day educational practice. The narrative was something we could rely on the audience knowing before we started, so we were freed to represent the oppositions in terms of a series of disjointed literal contexts. Little Red Riding Hood was not just one character — principal girl, heroine — instead a number of different actors represented her; as a young child, as a school pupil, as a male undergraduate, the identity of each new incumbent being indicated by the donning of the red cloak of approval. The mother-grandmother-huntsman-father principle emerged as parent, but also as teacher, lecturer, judge, bank manager. As the performance progressed it moved at one level through the narrative from the beginning of Red Riding Hood's journey to the end; at another level it followed the chronology of any life through the educative functions working on that life; and at a third level it was intended to provoke critical thought and debate about the educational practices of our culture. Furthermore, this attempt led our thinking into a consideration of the contradictions which impel and inform individual behaviour rather than seeing those contradictions as the unfortunate out-come of the free play of the irreducible, given character-traits of individuals. In other words, the play was informed by many of the principles of Brechtian 'epic' theatre, though this fact was only understood after the event by the members of the group.

But just as Brecht's work continues to generate profound criticism of theatrical practice, the implications of 'epic' theatre suggest to me an equally devastating attack on educational practice. It has for some time been clear (through the work of Ivan Illych, Paolo Freire and others) that the uniform organization of our institutions imposes a uniform and unexamined epistemology on all students who pass through them, and that 'schooling', extends far beyond the classroom. To offer a crude, but possibly illuminating, parallel: just as Brecht saw Aristotelian theatre as politically reactionary because, by arousing fear and pity and empathy, it purged the citizens of the drive to criticism and rebellion, so too our educational institutions, by arousing fear, pity and emulation through the catharsis of assessment, purge our students of any tendency to proceed with their understandings and use them critically.

We wanted, therefore, to include an assessed course in the body of the degree which would, by its structure, attempt to answer some of these objections. While the description quoted from the handbook is in no way misleading it is worth adding here some further characteristics of this 'epic' form of education, with comments about how and why they alter practice.

The work is seen as 'Cultural Action for Freedom', the title of a book by Paolo Freire. It makes clear that the point of education is political in the deepest sense. The point of acquiring knowledge and understanding should not be closed in on itself by the demonstration of that acquisition in assessment terms, as examinations and theses, most of which never see the light of day. In the drama course the assessment is deliberately separated off from the activities by which the students learn. In one way it is a tax we pay for being allowed to run the course as part of a grant-attracting degree course.

They write about what they've done instead, and this distancing produces some of the most interesting writing I see by degree students. The diary is given only 10 per cent because that frees it from the automatic necessity of double-marking, and that means it can be a more open, honest document. It is, on the other hand, often very good and substantial, and the contradiction between this fact and the low mark it attracts opens up several interesting contradictions.

There is no set curriculum. Students and tutor make up the course as they go along. So student choice is real and continuing. Nothing happens in the group unless the members choose that it should or assent to the choices made. The consequences of those choices have to be lived with. The students also choose what to write about for assessment.

The timetable no longer has us in thrall. We have a whole day, and if we need more time and the group so chooses we take more time. This prevents all sorts of cop-outs, which are otherwise available to tutors and students alike (e.g. 'I'd love to follow up that most interesting point if only we had the time . . .'). The course involves more than the officially signed-up students. There are members of the group who are doing the course as an optional extra to their degree. There are people who come on the course who are not 'in education' at all. One year we had a group of YOPs on the course. These 'outside elements', as they were called one year, are very valuable as a touchstone of the validity of the activities that go on. Teachers and 'real' students could otherwise collude in settling for soft options, since both groups are unhealthily interested in the course continuing smoothly.

Finally, a brief account of the kinds of work that have come out of the course. We have done a show about Frankenstein; a show about Wilhelm Reich and the sexual politics of Fascism; a show about love. We have done 'commissions': about the bomb, for a CND group; about unemployment, for a trade union meeting; about family law, for the polytechnic law department, at the request of a law lecturer, who was concerned that conventional ways of training solicitors give the students little insight into the problems they may make for their clients. One of the most interesting and 'educational' years was in 1981–82 when the ideological differences within the group became so marked and so clearly articulated that work on drama was impossible. By Easter, the group exploded with its own critical energy, but it certainly 'deepened understanding in and synthesised material from other areas of the degree' (see course aim no. 3 above); and this was demonstrated by the amount of really excellent writing that came from that year.

Most of all, the course changes. There is none of the feeling at the beginning of the year that we're in for another tour round the monuments of great

literature. Because of the reality of student choice each new group forges a
new line relevant to the concerns of their lives in that year.

Everything Changes

Everything changes. You can make
A fresh start with your final breath.
But what has happened has happened. And the water
You once poured into the wine cannot be
Drained off again.

What has happened has happened. The water
You once poured into the wine cannot be
Drained off again, but
Everything changes. You can make
A fresh start with your final breath.[2]

Bertolt Brecht.

What The Wolf Sang to Little Red Riding Hood

(Oh! Grandmother, what big ears you have!)
   The birds are crying.
   The leaves rattle, boughs crack.
   The highway is distant like the sea.
   Turn off the path; your will is strong.

(Oh! Grandmother, what big eyes you have!)
   Flowers hide. The dew climbs up the spikes of grass.
   Light sings round the shadows. Do the trees grow
   Only to warm the huntsman, like my grey skin?
   Turn off your will; the path is strong.

(Oh! Grandmother, what large hands you have!)
   And warm, my hug makes the shadows sing,
   Makes leaves turn and the blossoms flame.
   I will enter your path and melt the will.
   Listen to my hot eyes. You like my old hide?

(Oh! Grandmother, what terrible great teeth you have!)
   There is food for thought in your red hood.

Time devours and the fire too.
The moment flies, singing. Look!
The path you trod is gone!

Now he thought (his belly full of stones)
All that I made will be making its own end.
We are not here for ever.
We give thanks for the singing,
The listening and the doing.

This is the way it should be in our minds.

Notes and References

1. In *The Measures Taken and other Lehrstücke*, p. 63, London, 1977. Trans.
   Wolfgang Sauerlander. Reproduced by permission of Eyre Methuen Ltd. Trans.
   Stefan S. Brecht © 1977.
2. In *Brecht. Poems, Part Three*, p. 400, London 1976. Reproduced by permission
   of Eyre Methuen Ltd. © Eyre Methuen Ltd.

10.
English and 'The Real World'

Douglas and Dorothy Barnes

In this paper we consider some of the competing versions of the English curriculum which can be found in the final years of schooling and in the subsequent year in colleges of further education. We are particularly concerned with the different pictures of the real world which each presents. These examination-dominated years are of particular importance because they bridge the passage from school to adult life, and so look in two directions. School English (we suggest) often shows an over-restrictive concern with the pupil in a domestic context, while courses in Communications present an equally misleading picture of the world of work.

Teachers of fifth-year English classes have a clear view of their priorities. 'Last year I started off on "Childhood" and we did their memories of early days at school . . . And then we did "Violence"; we talked about football violence and that sort of thing. And then we did something on "Sex" . . .' (man in his second year's teaching). An experienced teacher, head of a secondary school English department, spoke of the contribution of English to his pupils' 'awareness of the world around them and of other people'. A woman teacher in the same department, just about to retire, spoke of the importance of pupils 'being able to . . . relate what they've read . . . to the world around them and to decide for themselves how true it is'. The head of another English department said, 'Last week I had a lesson with the fourth year about responsibilities at home, and who was doing what at home, how they felt about doing jobs at home, earning money and so on for doing their jobs . . . .'

The teachers whom we interviewed in the course of the Versions of English study[1] very frequently mentioned the importance of literature and their concern for examination results, yet two-thirds of them made references, as the teachers we have quoted did, to the relevance of English to their pupils' lives. The phrase they often use is 'their own experience'. But experience is not a simple or unproblematic idea. It seems that what English teachers count as 'experience' has its own shape and emphases; it includes some things and excludes others. In this version of 'experience' the individual is the measure of all things. Deeply felt engagement with friends and family, domestic and local experience, is valued highly. Childhood and growing up are of particular importance: the awaking self-awareness of Pip in *Great Expectations*; Jane at school in *Jane Eyre*; or Jo's relationship with her mother in *A Taste of Honey*. The experience is to be intense and self-conscious, protestant, romantic and introspective; the literature of the last 150 years provides plentiful models. It is as if our responsibility stretches only to those whom we meet face to face; wider social concerns are avoided. As one teacher who rejected 'sociological English' implied, it is first-hand experience that matters; the individual case, not the general view. English celebrates authenticity and verisimilitude, and suspects analysis and generalization. But this is, of course, an idealization; as one would expect, even those teachers who present their values in this way make adjustments and concessions in practice.

This 'personal experience' view of English can be seen to influence the lessons taught to older pupils in schools. Setting aside the teaching of litera-ture, which we will discuss separately, about two-thirds of the lessons in which the boys and girls were being taught writing showed some influence of this paradigm. Typically, such lessons would begin with the rapid read-ing of short poems or prose passages intended to suggest a topic and a mode of treatment; anecdotes were told by teachers and solicited from pupils; expressions of feeling were invited, both in the writing and in the lesson (though the latter were not often responded to); realistic detail was encour-aged, and a reverberant, quasi-poetic use of words and a tendency to moralize appeared. The implicit norm was fictional autobiography or auto-biographical fiction.

The strength of this trend must not be exaggerated, however. One way of testing it was to look at the writing actually completed by fifth-year pupils, not in terms of the topic set but of what they did with it. We grouped fiction with personal writing; as both were mainly narrative and literary, they often proved indistinguishable. Personal writing on public topics was put aside; there was little of it. It turned out that in certain classrooms the personaliz-ing trend was very powerful, but much less so in others. When we sought to find which these were, we discovered a powerful correlation with the mode of examination that the pupils were being prepared for. When they were to be examined by course work alone, 73 per cent of their writing was fictional or personal; when they were to be examined by examination paper the pro-portion dropped to 30 per cent. (For those expecting assessment by both paper and course work the corresponding figure was 55 per cent.) The choice of mode of examination did not usually reflect pupils' ability via streaming; in these schools the departments mainly chose one mode for all of their pupils. These figures indicate that alongside the 'personal experience' version of English there survived another and earlier version or versions.

When we began teaching over thirty years ago, it was not expected that writing in English should relate too closely to the real world. The norm was the 'essay', defined by a tradition of belles-lettres as elegantly entertaining writing which would enable some pupils to display their control of language without actually saying anything of importance. A revolutionary change came to the English curriculum when teachers realized that it was possible for young people to write about things that mattered to them. From class-room talk and their reading of literature, our pupils would write about the concerns of their own life-world. Did we deceive ourselves? Pupils' attitudes to English certainly changed during the Sixties: more came to enjoy writing, and we were convinced that the quality of writing rose when they were freed from demands to display their skill by meaningless word-spinning.

If writing is going to refer to the real world, then it is going to take teachers and taught into disputed areas. How should English teachers guide and shape the topics discussed? One very influential lead came in the Sixties from the English department at Walworth School, led first by Harold Rosen and then by John Dixon. Walworth School is a comprehensive secondary school in a predominantly working-class area of inner London. The English teachers there planned a course for their fourth-year pupils which began with the family and then moved outwards first to the neighbourhood and then to wider social issues. This was eventually published as the course book *Reflections*,[2] which with its imitators had a great influence upon what was to constitute English in the ensuing decades.

In the process of adopting this approach, however, a narrowing-down occurred, as if only the opening chapters of *Reflections* were being used. The pupils' concerns were increasingly interpreted as their private and domestic experience: family life, teenage rebellion, sibling rivalry, grandma (living with the family) as nuisance or confidante, and so on. Literature could furnish the models. Novels such as *Joby* or *There Is a Happy Land* provided larger-than-life eccentrics, and nostalgia for a childhood we had escaped from. 'Memories of Childhood' became what was probably the most fre-quent topic offered to sixteen-year-olds. But they are highly edited memories: if the young people retain scars they (wisely) avoid showing them. More of the fifth-form pupils whom we interviewed said they disliked writing about themselves and their families than liked doing so, and this rejection became even more marked in the lower sets. Only a minority finds it possible to couch their own intimate thoughts and feelings in a form that will allow them to be validated in the public world of school. So much has to be omitted: do we really welcome into the classroom such potential areas of experience as worries about sexual normality, police-harassment, or glue-sniffing? Some English teachers do, but most are more comfortable in the world of *Cider With Rosie* with its tamed sexuality and muted violence.

When larger public topics appear they are frequently distanced and made safe. War is dealt with through Wilfred Owen's poems; pupils are asked to write letters as if from soldiers at The Front in the 1914–18 war, now part of history. Napalm, Exocet missiles and the effects of nuclear weapons are held at a distance or omitted altogether.

We do not wish to reject the personal engagement which made for the revolution of the Sixties. At best it has led to talking, reading and writing which strengthens young people's sense that they can understand and influence the world about them, and that is no mean contribution to a secondary school curriculum that often seems to tell students that their experiences and competences are irrelevant. However, it is engagement on the teacher's terms rather than on the pupils'; when they write they quietly omit any aspects of their experience that might challenge the taken-for-granted world of liberal-minded English teachers. Much of the writing which we looked at did not seem to be exploration of experience but rather the construction of pieces to satisfy teachers. Some pupils did this skilfully; others were uncertain. One girl wrote about being snowbound:

> The snow fell heavily upon the full car as it hurried quickly to take us to Scotland. Visibility was poor and Dad had to strain his eye to keep us on the road . . . The car began to swerve gentle from side to side and I became a bit paniky. 'Ice', I thought to myself, 'Only ice . . .'

This relatively able pupil had been pulled two ways, towards colloquial phrases and towards quasi-poetic 'fine writing'. Her account reads like a fictional construction rather than self-exploration, even if it was based on a real experience. Less able pupils fell back either upon a narrative style that owed much to magazine stories or were trapped in an inexpressive style reminiscent of elementary textbooks.

> Its Monday and I get up at eight o'clock.
> I dress and have breakfast. Then I go out to
> get the morning paper. Then my Dad . . .

This no doubt corresponds to the author's experience, but the language is not being used to express its quality but merely to complete a routine task. Genuine exploration of first-hand experience seldom appeared amongst the 700 pieces we read; the most impressive pieces tended paradoxically to be expressions of opinion or highly skilled stories or entertaining journalism. When we looked at what was actually being written, much of it amounted to displays of verbal skill very like the belles-lettres paradigm we thought had been left behind in the Fifties. The reality we observed did not match the teacherly rhetoric. In spite of this, few teachers whom we interviewed explicitly rejected the 'personal experience' paradigm, though it was noticeable that teachers in some departments talked more readily about examination success, which (perhaps) represented their conception of relevance to their pupils' lives. (This is not to suggest that any of the teachers were heedless of their pupils' need for qualifications.)

It was in literature teaching that we found the sharpest irony, however. Although literature provides the model and legitimation for the personal experience paradigm of English, the way literature was taught did not match the claims made for it. Several of our teachers made the pupils' future enjoyment of fiction one yardstick of their success as English teachers: 'I think if they leave school and never open a book we stand condemned', or 'Obviously I'm interested in that bit of paper . . . all I hope at the end is they want to go and read books.' Yet much of the teaching seemed ill-designed to generate enjoyment. Pupils being prepared for O-level Literature examinations and for A-level English Literature alike frequently had to submit to a numbing plod through set texts which even at a glance contradicts the idea that each reader must recreate a text for him or herself. Yet this idea is at the centre of the 'personal experience' paradigm: the reader is to bring his or her own experience of growing up to bear on *Great Expectations* or *A Kestrel for a Knave*, his or her own experience of suspicion and jealousy to bear upon *The Crucible*. Much of the teaching we saw amounted to little more than paraphrase of text by the teacher: when teachers expect pupils to interpret what they have read this stands out sharply. The teachers who have the confidence to trust their pupils to read for themselves, who encourage them to move from *Henry V* to talk of the abuse of power, from *Jane Eyre* to the position of women, are in a minority. For the rest, books are a collection of fictional facts to be memorized and regurgitated, with little room for enjoyment or even participation.

For the first time in more than twenty years, literature-based English is faced with a serious competitor, Communications. The newcomer, like its long-established rival, makes claims which are hard to substantiate. If personal English (not belles-lettres) looks inwards for its justification, towards personal sensibility and domestic experience, Communications courses look outwards towards the world of work and of getting things done. It challenges one 'real life' with an alternative 'real life'. 'Personal' English places literature at the centre, and for its models of writing chooses the story and the essay; typically stories and essays are not written for particular audiences or occasions and may even be addressed primarily to the author in a kind of musing. Communications places action upon other people at the centre, and claims to admit a wide range of media: speech, reading and writing, diagrammatic representation and statistics. The demands of purpose, audience and occasion outweigh the claims of the author's sensibility: messages must match situation as well as purpose. It is held to be of primary importance to be able to see a colleague's point of view when discussing a disputed point, to select relevant evidence when presenting a case to a tribunal, to write appropriately when replying to a letter from a stranger, to gain necessary information pleasantly and economically when carrying out an interview, and so on. The claims of public criteria and effectiveness challenge the claims of private authenticity so long advanced by English teachers.

Are the new claims any more realistic than the old? Courses in Communications are newcomers in schools, having been developed in colleges of further education, so it is to the colleges that we look in order to test how far the reality matches the claims of the new paradigm. In practice Communications turns out to be considerably more restricted than its claims would suggest. As with English in schools there was some diversity amongst the eight Communications courses which we observed. Some of them swing to and fro between routine literacy tasks and an idealization of the world of business and industry. There might be rote-learning of spelling, or correction of lists of misused apostrophes; students must still master such 'essentials' as the Long Report, the Short Report, and the 'Memorandum'. In Communications courses, however, such exercises are now incorporated into simulated project-work: students are introduced to a world in which apprentices write reports for management and clerks prepare plans for a move to new premises. Such idealizations aside, Communications is concerned to show to students the criteria on which managers make decisions by setting them simulated managerial tasks. One lecturer suggested to us that behind Communications courses lay the hope that if more workers understood the managers' point of view it would make for a more complacent work-force, but most lecturers seemed to take what they were teaching as literal truth about the world. We were struck by the gap between the exercises in tactful letter-writing and sensitive interviewing — embodying admirable principles, valuable to employee and employer alike — and the commercial world of rivalry, competition and ruthlessness that most of us get some taste of, if only as dissatisfied customers.

The courses in Communications included remarkably little instruction in how to get one's rights, how to write to a firm selling faulty equipment, how to speak up politely and tactfully for one's own interests as well as for one's employers'. There seemed to be no reason why Communications should not help young people to manage their lives effectively, but many of the courses we saw seemed more disposed to prepare them for routine tasks within subordinate economic roles than for other aspects of their lives. This was particularly clear in the way spoken communication was dealt with, for to our surprise it was generally reduced to simulated job interviews. Finally, some comment should be made on the ubiquity of simulated messages in these courses, for from the point of view of 'personal' English this is a severe limitation. In English (the apologia would run) young people write for themselves or for a sympathetic adult about topics of urgency to themselves, and ideally this is the case. What we saw in schools was, however, very unlike this, much of the writing being as much a matter of satisfying a teacher's requirements as any Communications assignment would be.

If 'the exploration of personal experience' is little more than rhetoric, if the cultural re-creation of literature is reduced to the learning of 'ficts', if belles-lettres limits language to a meaningless display of ingenuity, and if Communications is little more than a tool of the world of business, what is left for English? Fortunately, none of these conditions entirely holds true. It *is* possible to use language to come to understand the world better, and to learn to act effectively in it. Communications courses are not by any means entirely the tools of management; English too offers much of value to pupils. There will only be space to sketch briefly how we believe English teaching should move during the coming years. We suggest four kinds of change: a widening of topics taken to be appropriate, more concern with communication that impinges upon a situation and an audience, the use of material from the world the pupils live in, and more attempt to discuss criteria explicitly with them.

There is no reason to lose the gains of the Sixties: young people do write better when they write about matters of importance to them. Some may at some times wish to explore their private experience; sometimes this may be best done through stories; but there is much to write about that goes beyond private experience. English teachers should not shy away from public issues such as war, authority, competitiveness, persecution. Sometimes this can best be approached through personal experience, but the matter should not end there. We think that continuous writing on public topics should be retained, alongside opportunities for reading and writing in a more intro-spective manner.

But not all writing is continuous, nor is it all addressed to the undefined general audience of novel and newspaper readers. Much of the writing and talking which we do as adults has a specific task to perform: in it we per-suade, present relevant information, argue a case, criticize, protest, report, or merely reorder our own thoughts. Many of the new emphases in Com-munications are admirable, so long as they complement rather than replace other forms of English. Spoken language *is* still disgracefully neglected in schools (we found); more attention *should* be given to reading, talking and writing that takes place in a context which provides criteria of effectiveness. There is no reason whatsoever why Communications courses should become solely a tool of industrial and business interests, since we all need the skills with which they claim to be concerned. If we leave young people with-out these skills, they are more at the mercy of the forces around them. It is proper that English/Communications — call it what you will — should be concerned with people's attempts to engage actively with the social world they find themselves in, rather than merely to bear it with distaste. Of course, this means a great widening of the rhetorical range of English so that at the extremes it encompasses passion, sarcasm and dispute: a balanced viewpoint is too timid a virtue.

To carry out this programme entails changes both in the content of English and in its methods. We should turn to the world about us for examples: if it is letters we are concerned with, there are plenty all about us; we have no need of the bloodless pretences of 'a letter to a friend' that betray the falsity of textbooks. Some of these letters, newspapers, forms, advertise-ments, pamphlets, reports and so on, will be taken into lessons by the teacher, but there is no reason why pupils too should not investigate how people talk and write. There is much to be said too for what might be called 'documentary' approaches, in which pupils choose a current issue of some importance, and gather interview material, collect and analyse documents, read books, as a basis first for formulating a point of view and then of pre-senting this in an appropriate public form so that it becomes a contribution to debate. Some of the best work in Communications has achieved this but it is as relevant to 'English' as to 'Communications'. Indeed, the more one con-siders what these two complementary terms refer to, the less justification there appears to be for allowing them to remain separate.

Considerable changes have already been implied in how this combined subject would be taught. The interpretation, whether of literary or non-literary material, needs to be done by the learner: using paraphrase to 'do it for them' is just bad teaching. (It did not even produce as good examination results, we found, as engaging the pupils in making sense for themselves.) Yet the pupils would continue to need their teachers' help as much as before. In discussing and categorizing 'documentary' material, in deciding the requirements of the audience they were writing or speaking for, in working out a way of performing a dramatic scene, in selecting and arranging material for a report they would need as much help as ever, but in a different mode. Much of the teaching we saw presented boys and girls with ready-made answers; not only were they answers to questions the pupils had never asked, but because they were ready-made they deprived them of any opportunity to understand the principles that informed them. The pupils would be able to satisfy an examiner, but not read or write for themselves on some other topic. This is perhaps the most profound change that we are asking for. During recent years English has become bound by intuitivist assumptions: attention is given to conventions such as spelling and punctuation but the criteria that belong to a well-ordered piece of writing, appropriateness in content and style, effectiveness for a purpose, are hardly discussed. We are urging the adoption of 'workshop' methods in which explicit discussion of criteria and methods is possible.

There were some teachers indeed who did many of these things, and it is they who give us hope that what we are recommending is happening already. There was Mr T. who had his pupils writing different versions of the same news item, Mrs B. who asked hers to come to lessons ready to present their views on *The Crucible*, and Mr A. who, by his impromptu talk about Cambodia, roused his bottom set into organizing a fund. Amongst the FE lecturers there was Mr D. who gave his students experience of practical tasks such as preparing, administering and analysing a questionnaire, Mrs F. who set up a simulated public enquiry to which various groups had to make a case, and Mrs C. who challenged and interested her Foundation course with articles from *New Society* and *The Nursing Times*. Though part of this paper refers to dead-ends and loss of purpose, these teachers allow us to end on a positive note. English/Communications can indeed help young people to develop some of the capacities which they need in order to participate fully in adult life.

Notes and References

1. The Social Science Research Council Versions of English Project, based at the University of Leeds, was a study of thirty-five courses in English or Communica-

tions, carried out in the upper forms of six schools and in four colleges of further education. The project report is published as D. Barnes and D. Barnes with S. Clarke, *Versions of English*, Heinemann, London, 1984.

2. S. Clements, J. Dixon and L. Stratta, *Reflections*, Oxford University Press, 1963.

Lucy: at school

James Berry

Leela, mi dear, all creation of man
is here, in London classrooms now.
Want to see the new body them.
Want to see faces
all shades, all shapes
list'nin' together here.

I help at school events, at Tony
an' Sharon school, as you know.
Well, on business there, I happ'n
to see the children them together
an', chile, was I amazed,
when I shouldn't be at all!

Black, brown, white — all the bodies
so smooth an' soun'! Fifteen Christmas
dinner, an' boy them pole up
slender slender in the air,
taller than you puppah. The girls,
at back an' front, they so full up
they skirt an' blouse, they could
give a strange man excuse.

White teachers have mos' black children.
But if you look good-good you see
black children a-teach white teachers,
an' you see parents lef' loaded up
with ol' time prejudice fo' theyself.

Terrors of a differen' breed, mi dear,
gett'n' lef' behin'
like spears an' bow-an'-arrows.

You see how one new year
can turn centuries upsidedown?
You see how patties
an' rottis an' roas' beef
can make feas' together?

An' all, mi dear, remind me
how I never did know
whether a Bajan or a Trinidadian
was a red man or a green man
till I come to London, an' see them,
an' get friendly with them all.

City speaky-speaky is mixed up
here, with bush talk-talk, darlin',
an' with Eastern mystery words.
Remember, Leela, chile,
how ol' people did say
'What man don't know is good to know.'

11.
No Hole in the Sky over Hackney

Alex McLeod

If you imagine a big blanket over the sky, and all the money's spread out, and you cut a hole in the blanket, where the money falls out, it wouldn't be on Hackney. It'd be falling out on richer places than that.

Kevin S., 5B Hackney Downs School, 1983

When the leaders speak of peace
The common folk know
That war is coming.

Bertolt Brecht, *A German War Primer*, 1937[1]

The General Assembly welcomes the initiative of the United Nations Educational Scientific and Cultural Organization in planning to hold a world congress on disarmament education and, in this connection, urges that organization to step up its programme aimed at the development of disarmament education as a distinct field of study through the preparation, *inter alia*, of teachers' guides, textbooks, readers and audio-visual materials. *Member states should take all possible steps to encourage the incorporation of such materials in the curricula of their educational institutions.*

United Nations Assembly Second Session on Disarmament, Final Document, 1978

The man on the wooden box told us
We would survive;
We listened to this last stranger in
Pathetic obedience.

Anthony King, *City Lines*, 1982[2]

One school has proposed a CSE course and exam on the threat of nuclear war (TES, 11 March 1983). The Education Secretary, Sir Keith Joseph, is trying to ban questions in school science exams which touch on controversies raised by such topics as nuclear weapons and nuclear power. (TES, 18 March 1983). Youth Training Scheme funds are to be withheld from colleges if teachers introduce controversial political topics; these dole sub-stitute courses, it seems, are to keep well clear of anything that might really interest their students.

Nuclear weapons seem more and more likely to destroy the world, and everything on it. Every two weeks the industrial powers spend, on arms, more than enough money to eliminate starvation and to provide adequate water, housing and education for the entire world. Should schools be con-cerned? Whereabouts on school curricula do questions about peace, nuclear weapons and nuclear war, arms expenditure and arms control properly belong? The answer is simple: everywhere, across the whole curriculum, not in some option course, nor in an occasional special programme. There's no point in making Peace Studies a separate subject, for just the same reasons as it is pointless to pretend that all teachers aren't concerned about racism, intercultural studies, sexism and gender studies, class structure and power structure. There's no justification for putting political questions into a special slot in the timetable, and pretending to keep them out of everything else.

I'd like to report some of my own experiences when discussions about nuclear weapons and nuclear war have come into my English teaching. I hope they may help to prove my point that, unless we deliberately keep them out, they are certain to arise. It's what we do with them when they do come in that we need to think about.

In October 1962, the Cuba missile crisis brought the world nearer to a nuclear strike that it has been at any time since that first use, when Hiroshima, Nagasaki and 200,000 people were destroyed as part of the A-bomb test programme. On that Friday, schoolchildren in England shook hands with tears in their eyes, not expecting to see each other again. Thousands of people panicked in the streets of Gary, Indiana, a steel town near Chicago, but that bit of news wasn't made public until months later.

I was teaching English in New Zealand. For two days, it was totally impos-sible to continue with normal teaching. As each class came into my prefab, they took up the debate. Once the questions and arguments started, there was no way of stopping. My friends in the science departments had the same experience, but with different questions. There were no problems about purposeful, motivated talking to learn.

The following year I was teaching in Walworth School in south London. *Reflections*[3] had just been published. Part III is called 'Questions of Our Time' (violence, crime, war, poverty, hunger) and the war section contains an extract from Robert Jungk's *Children of the Ashes*,[4] a report of a visit to Peckham by Winston Churchill after a bombing in World War II, a poem by Siegfried Sassoon, and photographs of devastation and war refugees.

My fourth-year class was a fairly typical one. By the third term they were a bit fed-up with using the same book so much, but it was new and I wanted to try everything in it. I was totally unprepared for their response, or for that matter, for my own. These boys and girls were fifteen, so they had been born in 1948. They had often heard their parents and grandparents talk about the war and the bombing of London.

There was absolute silence. I didn't know what to do to start up some discussion. The Churchill piece was on something they knew all about, but when we read about Hiroshima, just six months after the Cuba crisis, the message hit them hard. They knew, without my telling them, that we were no longer discussing the last war, but the next. In the discussion that followed at last, they seemed to grow about five years older, and my relationship with them had changed too; it had become, and continued to be, more adult and more trusting. That shift has, I think, always happened when I've entered into a nuclear war discussion with any class. Part of this shift arises from taking the future, and our pupils' future, seriously. English teachers have, since the beginning of education, taught about wars. The Greeks and Romans did the same. But it was always past wars, and they always ended in victory. The only break with that in my education was a heroic teacher who, in 1937, would take time off from teaching us French to discuss the coming of World War II. Our reaction then, like that of the Walworth class in 1963 and a class in Hackney in 1983, was much the same.

The United Nations declaration, quoted above, is probably the best answer to those who want to stop us including nuclear war in the agenda of English classrooms. The Bullock Report, also, makes no bones about it: 'The context (for writing) will be created from the corporate enterprises of the classroom and the individual interests and experiences of the children, cumulatively shared with the teacher and the rest of the group.'[5]

Through all the changes that have gone on in English teaching in our generation, few of us now dispute the claim that our pupils' own experience, interests and concerns provide us with the best starting points for growth. Some are still scared off by controversial issues, but I don't see how, if we accept our pupils' interests as our agenda, we can possibly avoid them. We don't need to make a decision to introduce a topic unit on nuclear war. It forces its own way in.

For four years (1979–83) I have been working and helping with a class in Hackney Downs School. John Hardcastle was their teacher, first for

Humanities, then for English. I joined them for a double period once a week from the time they were second years (12–13) until they were 16 and were taking their fifth-form examinations. It's an all-boys school.

In reporting some of the ways in which nuclear weapons and nuclear war came immediately into the work they were doing, I'm limited in many ways. I hadn't set out to document this side of their work; I was there only once a week. It's interesting, however, to look at some of the contexts in which these questions arose.

In the summer term of 1981 (third form) the Humanities programme included a substantial section on North America, including post-war history. As well as English, the programme includes drama, religious education, geography and history. John Hardcastle and Clare Widgery, the drama teacher, decided in one week to focus on a crisis point in American history, the Cuban revolution and the events that followed it. The whole class was cast as Cuban workers and peasants, revolutionary leaders, American and Russian diplomats and commercial representatives. Each group had spent some hours of class time researching and preparing their position. We video-taped the double period in which the classroom became a plenary meeting of the four groups. The arguments and counter-arguments were well-informed and fairly heated. A recurring theme, growing in importance as the meeting went on, was the general question of whether it is possible for a small poor country to be non-aligned. A short extract from the transcript gives some sense of the boys' concern; it is not a subject any teacher could ignore. At this point the plenary session had been going on for over half an hour.

Sunday (Castro)	All you two want to do is blast the hell out of each other. That's all you want to know about. (Applause) The first thing you think about is nuclear bases. War. Don't you think of how you're going to live, peacefully? Don't you think you could share everybody's thoughts? All you want is to be stronger than everyone else.
John (USA)	If we do blast hell out of each other, do you reckon you're going to survive, alone, without getting one scratch? You're going to get blasted to hell as well.
David (Cuban worker)	Yeah, but if you lot put nuclear bases on our land, then that's just going to make it worse, isn't it, because . . .
John	You're still going to get blown to hell.
David	No, but you see, all you lot want to do, as he said, is fight each other. Now why can't you lot live in peace, and accept

	each other's faults? You're just making the world war next to happen, over a little country like Cuba who's only asking for a little aid . . .
Kevin (USSR)	Rubbish, rubbish. How are we going to make a war over your country?
David	Because you want nuclear bases.
Simon Y. (Cuban leader)	Why's everybody talking about war, why do you want to start a war?
Kevin	You want to feed your people.
	(ferocious argument breaks out)
John Hardcastle	Wait, wait. Look we're getting a bit excited. I think what we want to do is try to establish why America and Russia keep threatening to blast hell out of each other.

A complete analysis of that video-tape would involve many questions about language, thought and comprehension. I've quoted it here mainly to show how this series of lessons gave these boys the chance to make full use of their intellectual abilities and language abilities, working together with their teachers on some questions about nuclear arms in the Sixties and, by implication, in the present. They reached no conclusions, but went a long way in their understanding of how the hostile confrontation of the super-powers, and especially their military spending, affects poor countries. About two-thirds of the boys are members of families who came to Britain from West Indian countries, Nigeria or Pakistan.

Once the questions had been raised, they re-appeared frequently. Most of the discussions aren't documented, but most of the writing is. At the end of the fourth-form year there were school exams. One of the questions on the English paper was: 'Write about a book that you have read recently that you enjoyed, or one that you thought was important. One boy, Sunday, chose *Nuclear War in Hackney* by Tom Brown.[6]

City Lines, the collection of poems by London school students, appeared in September 1982. There are several poems on nuclear issues. 5B at Hackney Downs were impressed by this collection. More poems were written, probably because it changed their conception of the kinds of ideas that can be expressed through poems.

Course work folders for O level and JMB were being put together. One list of suggestions for discursive writing included an invitation to 'write about something you feel really concerned or worried about.' Some wrote about unemployment, violence or racism. Simon C. put no title on his work, just a small CND sign after his name. It begins:

> Since the Sixties in Britain and all over the world there have been large
> scale demonstrations and marches by the Campaign for Nuclear Dis-
> armament. CND with the legendary 'Ban the Bomb' slogan is the largest
> pressure group in the world, ever. But the question that the masses in the
> countries whose governments control the bombs ask is, *is nuclear dis-
> armament the right way out?*
>
> There are many arguments for and against this point, but for me there's
> only one answer.
>
> Since 1945 and now governments all over the world have been
> threatening us with their atomic bombs. We must all be aware now about
> the possibility that a nuclear war could mean the end of me and you.

This is about a quarter of his essay, in which he discusses deterrence,
unilateralism, and the positions of the main British political parties. We
made some copies and most of the class read it. They talked about it and
wanted to know more. Whenever I appeared I was asked a string of
questions.

By this time I had become involved in peace and disarmament education at
the Institute of Education and through the European Nuclear Disarmament
organization. At the Institute the University Centre for Teachers ran a one-
day course on Peace Education. I had been collecting teaching resource
materials for some time. Among these was a thirty-minute video-tape, *If You
Love this Planet* made by the Canadian National Film Board. It is one of
several films they made in collaboration with Helen Caldicott, an Australian
doctor who gave up her career to work full-time to publicize the medical
effects of nuclear warfare. John Hardcastle and I decided to show it to 5B
because it discusses so many of the questions they had been raising in class.

Helen Caldicott begins with Hiroshima, takes the viewer through the proliferation in the number and destructive power of nuclear weapons since
then and shows how medical services and hospitals will be totally unable to
cope with casualties, most of whom will be left to die. The living will envy
the dead.

I took into the class on the same day two small posters, one I'd made
myself after hearing a lecture by Sir Shridath Ramphal, Secretary General of
the Commonwealth. He had said 'The money required to provide adequate
food, water, education, health and housing for everyone in the world has
been estimated at 17 billion dollars a year. It is a huge sum of money, about
as much as the world spends on arms every two weeks.' The other shows a
British family with a missile in a shopping trolley. '£18 a week on arms.

That's what the average British family spent on arms last year. And that's before Trident.'

We recorded the discussion that followed the showing of the video-tape. It lasted until the end of the morning, about half an hour, and then, with a group of boys, twenty minutes into the lunch hour. The teachers' contributions were mostly answers to factual questions. The boys talked about the possibilities and risks of unilateral renunciation of nuclear weapons, about the chances of survival ('So we're the last generation then.' . . . 'I'd kill myself.' Simon Y.), about whether the Queen and Prime Minister have comfortable furniture in their shelters, about the cost and control of the arms industries, and about what schools should do. Here is a short extract:

Ricky	If you, listen, if you think about it . . .
Simon C.	We know nothing about it.
Ricky	That's it, that's what I mean.
Simon C.	This is the first lesson we've had about it, yeah, if you think about it.
Ricky	We've had 15 . . . 16. 13 years out of our 15, 16 not knowing much about it.
Simon C.	I mean, it's probably one of the most important things we've got to learn in schools.
Ricky	It's the future, innit? Instead of learning about the past when there might not be no past.
Simon C.	I mean, once you got it.
Ricky	Hastings.
Simon Y.	You know, about what's going to happen in the future.
Simon C.	I mean we're living on . . . you know.
Robert	You can't really put the future that forward really. You can't really.
Ricky	No, but you've got to be able to understand what's going to happen, otherwise . . .
Robert	You can't really.
Simon C.	Until we can get rid of that . . . that problem, we haven't even got the basics down. It's not worth learning about bloody, you know, Shakespeare, and you know . . . all writing poems or anything until we've got the basic facts down, about what's going to happen.

Although we didn't quite agree with Simon about what was or wasn't worthwhile, we were interested in the general point he was making. We asked them to say whether they thought this particular video-tape should be shown in schools, and they were all emphatically in favour, though they were by no means unanimous in their views on disarmament. Three wanted to know about how to join CND, while others were much more concerned about military spending, poverty in Third World countries, cuts in education, housing and health in Britain. I had been told, not long before, that working-class school students, and in particular black students, were not interested in this question. It certainly wasn't true this time.

I had begun with some doubts about how my commitment to disarmament education stood in relation to my ideas about English teaching. I had none now. This doesn't mean that I think every anti-bomb film and book should be introduced but my problem now is of a different kind. The nuclear debate raises questions I can't answer — scientific, economic, geographical and historical. To carry on the discussion effectively it will be necessary to work together with friends and colleagues who teach other subjects, and this collaboration will give us courage as well as enlightenment. Thames TV's English programme in summer 1983, *Nuclear Issues*, has given us an excellent start.

As English teachers we have a particular responsibility as well as a general one. We look at how language is used, by people and also against them. While I don't agree with Simon C. that we shouldn't study Shakespeare until we know how to control our future, I want to make a connection between control of the future and control of language, and to look more closely than ever at the language of public debate, TV news and commentary, printed news, advertising, and all the quasi-advertising that passes for information. Whenever we turn our attention to the language of power and politics, we can't just study the language and ignore the issues, unless we have a very odd view of the relationship between language and thought. When 'defence policy' is used to mean preparations for attack and security is used mainly for things that greatly increase insecurity, we should be examining the policy as well as the language.

It is certain that we will be accused of bias and indoctrination, mostly by politicians. When it comes to that we are likely to be better judges of bias than they are, as was so well demonstrated by Stephen Tunnicliffe in 'English and Nuclear War'.[7] Political leaders are always convinced that it is their right to lecture teachers about balance and political impartiality in terms that are as partial and off-balance as they can possibly be. As Tunnicliffe pointed out, unless we examine the language in which the nuclear debate is carried on, we are neglecting an important part of our job.

That won't stop us being unpopular. English teachers are used to that. We only need to start discussing the way language is used against unions, women, black people, gays and peace campaigners, and they tell us that isn't what English teaching should be. But if English teaching isn't about language use, what on earth is it about?

References

1. B. Brecht, 'A German War Primer', trans. H.R. Hays, *Poems, 1913–1950*, Eyre Methuen, London, 1976.
2. ILEA English Centre, *City Lines: Poems by London school students*, 1982.
3. C. Clements, J. Dixon and L. Stratta (eds.), *Reflections; An English course for students 14–18*, Oxford University Press, 1963.
4. R. Jungk, *Children of the Ashes*, Heinemann, London, 1961 (quoted in *Reflections* op. cit.)
5. Department of Education and Science, *A Language for Life*, HMSO, London, 1975.
6. Tom Brown, *Nuclear War in Hackney*.
7. S. Tunnicliffe, 'English and Nuclear War' in *The Use of English*, vol. 32, no. 3, 1981.

12.
Home and School*

Connie Rosen

My two sons went to very formal primary schools. They had exercise books in which they wrote about the farmer-fishermen of Norway for Geography, about the way people travelled in the Middle Ages which was History, and compositions on Spring which was English. At the bottom of every essay written by my younger son was always some remark like, 'the writing could be neater', 'the writing is much tidier', 'you must try harder to keep your work clean'. They spent the rest of the time at school from seven to eleven doing intelligence tests, comprehension tests, spelling and grammar exercises, having examinations and moving places round the class as a result of the examinations. My older son, on being asked one of those friendly adult questions said he quite liked school, but he wasn't very good at Intelligence.

Outside school they played by the river, fished, quarrelled, fought, made dens. They lived in the woods and the farm and knew every inch of the area. They doggedly followed in the heels of a very good-humoured farmer on whose small Welsh hillside farm we camped, became experts on livestock, auctions, county fairs, badgers, bird-life, trout fishing and otter hunting. They knew every stick and stone of every castle and every item in Hereford Cathedral, and had climbed every hill for miles around. Not a single word of all this ever appeared in their talk or in their writing in school. No one was interested, no one ever invited them to bring any of this into the classroom.

Where were they really educated? What did they learn? What really has become part of their life and part of their personalities? My sons are now twenty-five and twenty-two years old and their primary school education is a dusty joke to them. But the questions really relevant to this article are, what

* This paper first appeared under the title 'Teachers in the Middle Years' in *Forum*, vol. 11, no. 1, Autumn 1968.

were the essentials of their real learning and could *all* the children — A and B streams alike — have learnt in that sort of way with the school working with them?

One of my postgraduate primary students is a zoologist. The science and maths graduates are very interesting in a primary situation. They have more confidence in coping with a more mathematical approach to the number work in school than other students but I don't know why they are so inhibited and so rigid in their ways of thinking. The zoology student was determined to read a story to a group of immature seven-year-olds for an hour at the end of each day in spite of the children's tiredness and restlessness. A great deal of time and effort went into persuading her to cut this down to ten or fifteen minutes and to allow some children to opt out altogether. On being asked what an eleven-year-old class from more favoured circumstances would do between twenty to four and four o'clock if given the choice, she said there would be chaos, without in fact confirming whether the hypothesis was correct. What they actually chose was to take out reading books, take out sheets of music, stand round the stickle-back tank, continue some work on fossils and rocks, painting, writing and arithmetic. She was so amazed to discover that seven-year-old children had such different personalities that she devoted her education study to examining half a dozen of them to find out how this had happened. It was the most important thing for her to have found out in the year. But when it came to discussing the importance of first-hand experience, the importance of careful observation, the need to help children record their experiences, she knew exactly what was meant and delighted the children with her rocks and crystals, insects, sticklebacks and beetles. She responded with pleasure when the children wrote about 'a stickleback flipping his tail when he wants to turn corners', or a diving beetle 'sinking his jaws into a bit of worm'. When one of the sticklebacks died she showed a couple of seven-year-olds how to dissect it and how to draw the dissection. One day one of the children put a pencil into the stickleback tank and then put it into the beetle tank, and when the beetle shot off, she reported that the children had said the beetle could smell a stickleback smell. I do not know whether beetles smell or not, but I asked her if the children could put a 'neutral' pencil into the beetle tank just to make sure it was not the pencils that had an adverse effect on beetles.

She is devoted to her science studies and enjoys the children's interest in her stick insects and beetles. Here was an interesting example of a specialist contributing a great deal, stimulating interest, helping the children to be methodical and how to record *their* discoveries, and yet unable to reach the heart of the matter until she had begun to learn that children have different personalities and learn in different ways.

It was even more difficult to persuade the student who had studied archaeology as part of her degree to take this interest to children in school. There was not a sign of this, no objects she'd dug up, no stories of finds, no slides or pictures, no mention of the Silbury excavations on television and certainly no site to visit.

I think that the best primary work is of the nature of my own two son's experience at home, exploration of their own environments, first-hand experience. Chapter 17 in the Plowden Report lists all the subjects beginning with religious education as though they were working through a grammar school curriculum, and appears to be in contradiction to the chapter before this on children learning in school. Here HMIs, 'working in a division in which some particularly good work is to be found', are quoted:

> The newer methods start with the direct impact of the environment on the child's individual response to it. The results are unpredictable but extremely worthwhile. The teacher has to be prepared to follow up the personal interests of the children who, either singly, or in groups, follow divergent paths of discovery. Books of reference, maps, enquiries of local officials, museums, archives, elderly residents in the area are all called upon to give the information needed to complete the picture that the child is seeking to construct. When this enthusiasm is unleashed in a class, the timetable may even be dispensed with, as the resulting occupations may easily cover mathematics, geology, astronomy, history, navigation, religious instruction, literature, art and craft. The teacher needs perception to appreciate the value that can be gained from this method of working, and he needs also energy to keep up with the children's demands. (Para. 544)[1]

In areas of the country where primary education is understood, there is a possibility that it may continue into the twelve or thirteen-year-old level. It is possible that the middle school may take the best features of primary work and develop them further. Whether secondary teachers who have never had experience of primary methods will be made the heads of these middle schools will again differ from one area to another. Where the children's primary school work is similar to my sons', it is unlikely that there will be anything other than Nuffield French, Nuffield science, Nuffield maths, history, geography, PE, music, art and RI as listed in Chapter 17, with so-called 'specialist' teaching beginning at nine.

I have seen team teaching going on which seemed to mean the writing of innumerable assignment cards for a group of eighty children. They moved from a card which told them to weigh something, to drawing a lady in Elizabeth costume, to burning a piece of polystyrene and painting it, to reading a chapter in a book, to writing about a dream they had had.

I have seen team teaching which started at Communications or Power or Conflict or some such generalized topic, in which many of the twelve-year-olds seemed to settle on drawing aeroplanes or film stars or making a scrap book about footballers.

Is it inconceivable to continue the environmental work of the primary school? A friend of mine is teaching Egypt to a remedial class of twelve-year-olds. They have been to the British Museum and had a lot of fun and interest, I'm sure, but why Egypt? She said it was to do with man and his environment, and the Egyptians seem, I suppose, to have been quite good at managing the environment. But perhaps the significant thing about the Egyptians was what made them unique. There were other civilizations that were pretty advanced, but what made the Egyptians outstrip their contemporaries in their level of achievement? I do not know the answer, but I suspect that I would want to know if I thought I wanted to teach twelve-year-olds about Egypt: and I rather suspect that when I discovered what was most significant to that ancient civilization, I would not think it a suitable topic after all, and would settle on an exploration of the docks.

Finally, and I do not know how long it's going to take us to do it, but I think we have got to work hard trying to think in different ways about specialisms. It may be that with more confidence and experience my archaeology student will be able to take some eleven- or twelve-year-olds on a dig. It may be that if one is taking a class of children to the docks, then the dad who was a docker and who often found lizards and beetles in the crates of bananas could come and tell the children about it all. It may be that we could invite the crane drivers and lightermen to come and talk about their work. We need different ways of looking at experience ourselves, and different kinds of people to assist children to develop. We are used to having graduates with history degrees, maths, science, English and the rest. It is possible that a history graduate will be interested in local history and first-hand documents and manuscripts but it is not inevitable. We need people who have studied architecture and building materials, industrial archaeology and technology, ornithologists, town planners, poets, musicians, and artists, and it only works if they are interested in what they are doing and in the children they teach.

References

1. Plowden Report, *Children and Their Primary Schools*, HMSO, London, 1967.

13.
Doing Teaching English

Peter Medway

This is an interim sharing of thoughts which arise, sometimes tangentially, from research which is incomplete. I am studying English curricula as they are taught to eleven- and twelve-year-olds (mainly twelve) in secondary schools and middle schools in an area of the north of England.[1]

The study of Douglas and Dorothy Barnes with Stephen Clarke of English curricula at ages 15 to 17, reported in another paper in this collection and in the book *Versions of English*,[2] was my starting point. My thinking owes much to that team, though responsibility for misconceived ideas in this paper is mine.

From their data on school fifth-year curricula Barnes, Barnes and Clarke were able to distinguish several 'versions' or paradigms of English towards which the various observed curricula could be seen as tending. One of the dimensions in terms of which they defined their versions was 'detached — engaged'. Early on in my search for versions at the twelve-year-old level I thought I had hit on a clear case of each polarity: in one school a teacher who taught writing as a craft, set assignments (fairy stories, funny stories) which did not require the pupils to display feelings or inner selves, and read with the class a book which was entertaining, non-realistic (about a witch) and remote from personal issues; in another a teacher who set writing about personal experience, prepared for the writing by inviting pupils to discuss feelings and states of mind, and read a book which dealt in a serious manner with the existential situation of a realistically portrayed child. But not much later it became clear that for the second teacher the psychological exploration was ritualistic, that he was really giving a set of recipes for doing 'personal writing' and that the criteria by which he evaluated the writing were ones of simple competence in the written language and not of achieved self-expression or psychological insight. Despite appearances, this 'version' was hardly less 'detached' than the first, though the assignments and the themes of the attendant instruction seemed to derive from a pedagogy in which the engagement of pupils' feelings and identities was paramount. Contradictions like this were what I continued to find. Elements of practice which appeared to be realizations of a particular coherent view of English would occur as free-floating optional items in a repertoire, often in association with ones seeming to derive from quite incompatible approaches. There were no strong organizing rationales, and no 'versions'. Rather there appeared to be a vast à la carte menu in which anything could go with anything else: writing escape stories with reading poems about rain with grammar exercises with personal accounts of fear featuring in a display on *The Boy Who Was Afraid* with watching Middle English.

The search for clear alternative paradigms proving fruitless, another sort of pattern suggested itself which, for the time being at any rate, looks a more promising way of representing the complexity of the scene. I was struck by the difference between teachers who offered specific arguments that their approach would achieve this or that end or was necessary because of this or that circumstance, and those who simply said what they did. I realized that my examination of the different curricula had unconsciously been conducted in the light of an implicit question: what is this teacher trying to achieve by this practice? — to which the possible answers that I had in mind, and which I hoped would differentiate between teachers, were ones like 'self-understanding', 'tolerance', 'cope with demands of everyday life' or 'master a range of written discourse'. The fact that some teachers offered no such accounts made me see that the question was not always appropriate. There was in fact no reason to assume that teachers were doing whatever they did in English in order to achieve some aim beyond it. Quite conceivably they might be setting themselves simply to 'do teaching English'. A comment by Martyn Hammersley, quoted by Barnes et al.[3], lent support to this view: a teacher

> does not begin with a set of goals and develop means to achieve them: he is socialised into a culture which simultaneously provides a collection of routine concerns and practices which themselves define teaching (until further notice) and a set of accounts spelling out its purposes.

The interesting question then was, what for the different teachers constitutes 'doing teaching English'? Beyond which, further questions suggested themselves: where do the definitions come from?, what sustains them and changes them?, what is implied in them for pupils' chances of learning? Here I can do no more than offer a tentative answer to the first and some observations and speculation relevant to parts of the others.

It does indeed appear that among these teachers there is a set of practices which counts as 'doing teaching English'. Variations are possible but they are variations from a basic 'unmarked case', the standard minimum curriculum for which it is unnecessary to offer justifications. Deviate from this, by omitting or adding a major component or by modifying one in a major way, and you will feel under some obligation to give explanations or to specify ulterior aims, whether in terms of pupils' needs, or *these* pupils' needs, the nature of language learning, the demands of society or whatever.

The 'unmarked case' as it seems to operate in the schools to which I have had access is a threefold curriculum — a *trivium*. Three major categories appear to be prescribed and within each category a general pattern of activity, with options at certain points. *Literature, writing* (or composition) and *'language work'* are obligatory — the last item referring to 'comprehension' plus instruction and exercises, outside the contexts of literature and writing, in (one or more of) punctuation, spelling, syntax, grammar, vocabulary and usage. The treatment throughout is 'detached': craft and skills, performance, mastering conventions, cleverness, study, enjoyment, as against feeling and insight, expression, unlocking resources, truthfulness, experience, learning. Literature means reading a 'class reader' together, about one a term, basically for enjoyment rather than as an induction into the specialism of literary studies, but with the occasional character study/plot summary/review, *plus* a few poems *plus* introduction of the terms 'metaphor,' 'simile' and 'alliteration' *plus* some provision for individual reading. Writing I shall deal with below, and 'language work' I shall leave out of account in this paper.

Conformity to such a standard minimum curriculum is not necessarily blind or unconscious. Teachers may enact the whole package in a spirit of commitment to some elements and doubt about others. They may then offer justifications for engaging in practices they don't believe in: 'I'm not a great believer in comprehension but they do a lot of it in the high school so you'd better have some experience of it.' The standard curriculum does not derive its solidity merely from the rigidity of mental categories; behind them are some real external constraints.

To consider the literature component in more detail. The novels read were nearly all written post-1960. Generally there is no indication that teachers are using the books to achieve anything beyond whatever it is that reading books is assumed automatically to result in. No *particular* understanding of self or society, for example, seems to be sought. The books are simply run, and that is 'doing literature'. Pupils' 'involvement' in the text is what counts as success and justification — though there is apparently nothing against cashing in on this motivation to get imaginative writing. There is however some tension between this pleasure-oriented principle of procedure and a widely felt need to set exercises which nod in the direction of academic literary study (character studies and so on), and one is reminded that it is the latter which has traditionally been at the centre of the English specialist's professional identity and that it is the prevailing version in the high status, university-oriented areas of the English department's work, i.e. with older and selected pupils (see *Versions of English*). The pull of this centre can sometimes be discerned in 'marked' cases where teachers with top sets begin to induct children into literature as an autonomous discipline with systematic attention to language, style and structure. Sometimes there is a clear intention that the values and insights of the book be deeply internalized (i.e. an 'engaged' approach); sometimes the emphasis is on a (still 'detached') appreciation of how the book 'works'. In such classes I have had the unmistakeable sense that the teachers feel at home — that they are doing what comes most naturally and are practising what they feel to be their real craft.

The *Versions* study found that at 15 the size of the literature component declined sharply with the ability label of the set. My data suggests a quite different picture at 12: literature (essentially in the form of the class reader) is a consistently large component. I cannot claim to be able to explain this but certain considerations suggest themselves as relevant. An arguable account of one strand in the history of English teaching in the Fifties and Sixties runs like this[4]: deep commitment to literature as a source of values (certain literature, read in certain ways) reached down from Leavis's Cambridge via its graduates into the grammar schools; many of these grammar school teachers took their commitment into head of department posts in the new comprehensive schools; here however the sort of literature-based curriculum designed for the selected minority could not be straightforwardly replicated with the unselected majority; that particular stream of values and cultural concerns had to find another channel through which to flow. The solution which emerged 'worked' in classroom terms and accorded well with the 'whole person' ideology of comprehensive education, thus ensuring the survival of English as a well-resourced core subject: an alternative realization for the same deep purposes was found through writing instead of literature — 'engaged' personal or creative writing as against the traditional 'detached' essay and composition.

I can attest from my own experience to the urgency of the need for such a resolution. When I started teaching at Walworth School, London, in 1964, in a department where literature was valued and there was a good knowledge of available material, the second-year book stock was such that the titles I selected as *most* likely to appeal to the middle streams were *Shane, Children on the Oregon Trail* and *Call of the Wild.* Teaching them was an uphill struggle. With restless classes the temptation to cut literature to a minimum was a strong one. In that school writing had indeed filled out to occupy the major space, and in it were invested our best energies and expectations.

But literature has not in the event withered away — far from it. What has happened is new books — books which work. The result is that the English teacher now has little difficulty in finding for every year, at any rate up to third year secondary, three, or even six, books which can be expected to go well. From being the problem, literature has become the solution. Relevant to an explanation of this enthusiastic espousal of children's literature may be some characteristics of English teachers' working situation. To point out that there are other pressures on teachers besides the need to bring about learning is to be not cynical but realistic. (A more revealing question than the one which I had in mind at the start of my study may sometimes be the one posed by Sharp and Green: 'To what problems are these [practices] viable solutions for the teacher?'[5]) Unlike any other teachers except those of mathematics, English teachers have to keep the entire population of under-16 pupils occupied for two to three hours a week in full class-sized groups. Small wonder that an activity which has the power to engage classes in quiet absorption, and which has the legitimation of 'literature' behind it, is readily adopted, nor that there is little urgent probing of what *besides* experience of books gets learned in the process.

There are after all many worse things that children could be doing than enjoying books (some forms of 'language work', for instance). In some schools where an English curriculum based on fiction has replaced a much drier diet writing now also flourishes, there are displays around the school and morale is high — English is for the first time really felt to work. Yet one teacher's remark that now the literature provides the pupils with the experience to write about, which previously they lacked, activates a latent unease in me. Is some sort of enclosed culture developing which is losing touch with the real world?

The writing curriculum turns out to raise similar issues. The 'unmarked case' looks like this: *fiction* is the major element ('detached' fiction, that is: conventional genres, remote or unfamiliar situations, emphasis on effects of suspense, excitement, amusement) with some (minimal) *instruction* in 'writing a story' *plus* (once or twice) *essays* in the role of 'participating citizen' (fox-hunting/hanging/caning/school uniform) *plus* (once or twice) *utilitarian-bureaucratic communications* (letter of complaint, accident report) *plus* optional other items in small quantities, such as '*description*' and *auto-biographical narratives*. About this curriculum two things can be said: that it is heavily literary in emphasis, and that what is represented is largely unreal. By 'literary' I mean to indicate writing which presupposes 'aesthetic' rather than 'efferent' reading, in Rosenblatt's terms[6], reading of which the point is in the experience induced by the transaction with the text rather than in what might be abstracted and taken away from the text for use or application in other contexts. Not only does the fictional writing fall into this category but also most of the non-fictional description and narrative, and also the 'pseudo-documents' produced in some classes: these invented diaries, letters, posters and so on are functionally quite distinct from real documents. In one class a pupil-produced newspaper simulated the layout, language and other features of a newspaper but contained no news. The contents were invented. It could only be read 'aesthetically', for enjoyment of the skill of the imitation or the verisimilitude of the stories. That writing in English should predominantly mean literary sorts of writing is simply taken for granted. It is almost never argued for. Yet the rhetoric of aims and principles in English is almost always about the development of language, effectiveness in language, competence in language, ability to communicate or express oneself, or the acquisition of language resources — all in *general* terms: there are no clauses limiting the responsibility mainly to the literary modes.

The point about the non-real nature of the referents is a related one, as the case of the pseudo-newspaper showed: the imaginary nature of the contents and the assumption of an 'aesthetic' reading were aspects of the same phenomenon. A sort of unreality extends, too, to many of the 'descriptions' and poems ('A snowy day', 'Fear') which, while not overtly fictional, are characterized by a generalizing remoteness from concrete reality. Then, of the non-literary texts, even those which look like a real communications to specific audiences for specific purposes (letters, reports and so on) turn out also to be unreal in each of those respects.

Thus between writing which is about non-existent realities, literature which is exclusively fiction and 'language work' on bits of language which have been made up for the occasion and in which the appearance of empirical reference is illusory, it is possible for pupils to spend almost their whole time in English in some insubstantial limbo. The language may almost never engage with the facticity of an actual state of affairs. Indeed, the possibility of a language used heuristically as a means of interpreting and understanding, of making the world available to thought, does not seem to be allowed for in the prevailing implicit model of language. Functions which are not literary (or 'creative' or 'imaginative') are indiscriminately consigned to the category of 'practical' (read, 'merely practical'). The bi-polar view suggested by Whitehead's 1966 account — the ability . . . to use one's native tongue effectively in all its modes, '. . . in its everyday utilitarian functions as well as for the more subtle imaginative and emotional purposes which make up the province of literature.'[7] — still apparently informs contemporary writing about English: 'That's why, then, literature, and especially story, take up such a central focus in the book. Other practical uses of language are important. . . .' (David Jackson[8]) ('other' = 'practical'?) and is detectable in the rationales of teachers I have spoken to who oppose the interesting 'creative' work to the boring but occasionally necessary form-filling, report-writing, etc.

Infrequently in the curricula which I have sampled (and I suspect more commonly in some schools which did not fall within my study), the topic addressed is indeed some aspect of the real world or of experience, and what looks like a language to probe and explore, to get at the reality, is being employed. Yet even here the appearance of reality-orientation may be misleading. Robert Hull[9] characterizes such situations in an illuminating way. He finds English (and not only English) to be full of propositions which appear to be empirical but are actually 'grammatical', in a sense which he adapts from Wittgenstein's[10]. In other words, these are statements the successful 'carrying-off' of which is a matter less of getting it right about the world than of getting it right about how words are used. 'Discussing', and then writing, about a photograph of a solitary person on a promenade, the pupils were not so much examining the realities and realistic possibilities of such a situation as getting taught the elements of what counts in English as an account of one: 'constructing the grammar of a lonely person on a promenade', as he puts it.[11]

The implication of the 'unmarked case', if I have roughly got it right, seems to be that the criteria for 'doing English' may simply be that language of certain kinds be made to flow. The pupils must be generating and receiving messages about which the important thing is not whether they tell you anything but that they are the right sort of messages, composed of prescribed categories of elements articulated to interact in preferred ways. Thus for a teacher to direct the language outwards with the intention of penetrating the world is to deviate from the unmarked case and to work against the grain. Attempts to make language the means to knowledge are difficult to sustain, so firmly is it built into the institution of English that language, not knowledge, is the end. (English teachers, after all, don't *have* to have their pupils achieving insights into reality; they *do* have to have them writing.)

My final point is about teachers whose particular commitments and per-spectives have led them well away from that minimal unmarked case (and here I draw on my wider experience and other sources beyond the present research). There *are* English teachers who get a genuinely heuristic language going. The area of reality examined is usually limited to some aspect of the private sphere — the immediate physical and social environment and the responses of the self — but there is no mistaking the genuineness of the pupils' involvement in the learning and discovering. David Jackson, on the evidence of the work reported in his book (and despite the quotation above) is clearly such a teacher: one could hardly ask for more convincing evidence of children pursuing meaning for themselves. Yet, as a careful reading shows, the end to which all these processes are being led is an under-standing not of life but of literature. While adopting not only the rhetoric but the essential practice of a pedagogy aimed at making language a means of apprehending reality, Jackson is in fact helping his pupils to find the meanings through which books and poems will 'speak to them'. In other classrooms that process of excited exploration, searching and discovery, skil-fully initiated, coaxed along and built to a powerful momentum, achieves its eventual culmination in . . . a piece of writing. So what was going on was just *inventio*, a stage in the production of a discourse when the ideas for the writing are found. Such writing is conceived not as part of a process — a pro-visional stocktaking, say, before continuing — but as its end and final dis-charge.

Thus the disabling limitation, language for language's sake, inherent in the standard minimum version of the subject can also afflict the most con-scious and critical practitioners. When the pupils become committed participants in a self-directed learning process which promises to lead them to successions of new understandings, English seem unable to rid itself of the last minute compulsion to throw the switch and sidetrack the enterprise into some specialist enclosure — of writing or literature. The writing and the literature are fine and valuable but the crucial achievement of English, which has empowered pupils (if only here and there) not only to find their voices but thereby to pursue for themselves the understandings they feel most in need of, is too central to the educational enfranchisement of the majority to remain subordinated to the requirements of a culture which puts language first. Is it possible for English teachers to break out of the received definitions of English and let their pupils learn, trusting that the language will be well enough attended to in the process?

Notes and References

1. The data consists of detailed observations of the lessons of six teachers over a period of a month, responses of 67 teachers to a questionnaire sent to a random sample of schools, interviews with half of the latter and, in most cases, some examination of pupils' work. I should stress that the response rate (41 per cent) to the questionnaire does not warrant confident extrapolation to the whole sample nor, *a fortiori*, to English teachers as a whole in the area. Nevertheless 67 teachers is not an insignificant number (over 10 per cent of the estimated total of teachers teaching English to twelve-year-old classes in three LEA areas) so that the patterns emerging are of some interest. The findings I report here should be regarded as tentative and provisional.

   The research is being carried out at the University of Leeds with the support of a Social Science Research Council studentship.
2. D. Barnes and D. Barnes with S. Clarke, *Versions of English*, Heinemann, London, 1984.
3. Ibid., chapter 1.
4. I owe these ideas to discussions with Douglas Barnes.
5. R. Sharp and A. Green, *Education and Social Control: A study in progressive primary education*, Routledge and Kegan Paul, London, 1975, p. 13.
6. L. Rosenblatt, *The Reader, The Text, The Poem*, Southern Illinois Press, 1978.
7. F. Whitehead, *The Disappearing Dais*, Chatto and Windus, London, 1966, p. 12. Quoted by Steven ten Brinke in *The Complete Mother-Tongue Curriculum*, Walters-Woordhoff Longman, Groningen, Netherlands, 1976, p. 11.
8. D. Jackson, *Continuity in Secondary English*, Methuen, London, 1982, p. 7.
9. R. Hull, 'Aspects of the Relation Between Language and Learning in a Comprehensive School', unpublished D Phil thesis, University of Sussex, 1982.
10. Ibid., chapter 4.
11. Ibid., p. 254.

14.
The Politics of Drama Teaching

Garth Boomer

Students require an education in curriculum as in sentiments in order to discover what they assumed — with the complicity of their teachers — was nature, was in fact culture; that what was given is no more than a way of taking.

Adapted from Richard Howard in the preface to Roland Barthes, *S/Z: An essay*, Hill and Wang, New York, 1974.

But schools declare themselves as surely as people do. And children learn to read the implicit meanings more quickly and thoroughly than they learn many prescribed tasks. 'What does the place say to me?', they ask and look for the answer in every intonation of the institution. In finding the answer they also discover what it is possible for them to say.

Connie and Harold Rosen, *The Language of Primary School Children*, Penguin, Harmondsworth, 1973, p. 21.

In drama classrooms throughout this country children are being taught the politics of their teachers. By politics I mean the teachers' beliefs about desired power relationships between people and about how power can be used in a community of people. By politics I also mean *enacted* politics not *espoused* politics, the living example of the teacher *in situ* as the curriculum unfolds in the school.

The micro-community of the drama class is also subject, of course, to the politics taught by the school which through every artefact on display, every word written in reports, every rule made, every person praised, every textbook chosen, speaks profoundly to the students about what is valued here, how one is expected to live here, what one is allowed to say here, and who makes what decisions *here*. Because such political messages come to the students through the very pores of the school body, they are profoundly militant. They make war and peace selectively and rarely operate 'in uniform'. Congruent values are subtly stroked; incongruent values may be attacked with a battery of weapons ranging from corporal assault through to the less visible withholding of affection or the persistent generation of uncomfortableness.

Where the drama teacher's politics, as defined, are largely incongruent with the politics of the school, it is likely that students will experience various kinds of confusion about political messages. The drama teacher subject to the same militant school politics as the students, will, if not continually vigilant, carry school political contamination (from his or her own point of view) into the classroom, for example, simply by reluctantly complying with a school requirement that homework be regularly set. The teacher will be tacitly demonstrating compliance with a misguided authority if the issue is not explicitly discussed with students, or openly confronting the fact of strategic compromise for survival if the issue is explicitly raised. In the latter case the teacher will also be demonstrating, in the eyes of many teachers, some form of professional disloyalty.

This brings us quickly to questions of personal integrity, authenticity and honesty. It also leads one to reflect on what I have termed elsewhere, the 'complicity of tact' in schools[1], the phenomenon of keeping secrets for the so-called good of others. 'They are not yet ready to handle it' or 'It would cause more trouble than it's worth' or 'The parents wouldn't like it' or 'One day (as with Father Christmas) they will understand'. In all cases of secrecy 'not saying' is a political act, confirming the people who do not have this information in the belief that what they already know is sufficient, maybe even true. If information is the fuel of power it is an act of subjugation. It secures the power of those who have the secret.

What I have to say applies to any teaching at any level but I am convinced that drama because of its potent 'life' connections illustrates the politics of teaching more dramatically than any other subject. It should be clear from my preamble that I am about to address questions of *knowing, controlling, telling* and *acting* in drama teaching. It will be my contention that many drama teachers are unwitting agents of oppression, perpetrating each day acts of covert terrorism out of habit.

I wish to question some habits of drama teaching in order to unmask the politics of habit and to diagnose the likely toxic effect of strategies which power at students rather than empower them. This will lead me also to look closely at the politics of surprise which goes to the very heart of drama teaching.

Habits and contexts

I shall assume that the easy targets of criticism are well known to you and that you share, without explication, an understanding of the sapping narcosis which attends persistent tambourine bearing ('Circus, Circus'); teacher direction of class plays ('Help *me* realize *my* fantasies'); a staple diet of student-generated improvisations ('Trap them where they are'); a regime of mime last week, puppets this week and voice production next week ('Who skilled Cock Robin?'); or 'doing' periods and the plays of the 'greats' for examination purposes ('Distancing, dissection and dessication'). Habitually employed, such routines leave students feeling that knowledge and power reside elsewhere. These have been part of the drama teachers' contributions to containment of the citizenry and progressive socialization into acquiescence.

I shall assume also that the school makes many potentially harmful things non-negotiable for the teacher but I will not treat the politics and ideology of such contexts as forty-minute lessons, classes of thirty, assessment by grading, using drama as a 'sink' (or drain) subject or giving drama to a specialist at the primary level (a particularly effective way of painting it into a corner).

I take it for granted that every teacher of drama is to varying degrees at war with such contexts and that students are also implicated in the struggle. My focus will be on the curriculum *text* which is jointly made by teachers and students within the context of school and society. What happens when the door closes on the drama room or space and the action begins? How is the script written? What in the fullest sense does drama in school *mean*. What lessons are learned?

As a test case I shall present an hypothetical drama teacher who is as rhetorically committed to empowerment of students as Dorothy Heathcote and who has gone well beyond the cruder forms of *training* through drama.

The script

Let us eavesdrop on a unit of work with a year 10 drama class of twenty-year-olds.

The teacher brings into the class a video recording of a television programme exploring the bone-marrow disease commonly known as Gargoylism which eventually proves fatal for children but not until they have become horribly grotesque, malformed and brain damaged. The programme explores the traumas of two sets of parents as they battle with doctors to save their children through a process of bone-marrow transplants from relatives. Eventually one child dies and one survives with a reasonable chance of a normal life. At the end of the programme we see doctors at the overloaded hospital having to decide which of two new patients with terminal illnesses will be admitted to undergo the possibly life-saving operation. The one omitted is likely to die while waiting.

The class discussion following this programme is intense. Issues such as euthanasia, the cost to the community, the right to abortion (the disease can be detected in the embryo), and the ethical and emotional strain on parents and doctors are canvassed. At a certain point, the teacher says she would like them as a class to work up their own dramatic exploration of some of these issues over the next few weeks with a view to showing it to another year 10 class.

Before the lesson ends they decide fairly amicably to develop an improvisation around the basic situation delineated at the end of the programme. A choice must be made between two patients. The stakes are life and death. The teacher undertakes to come up with a suggested plan of action for the next lesson.

In the next lesson, the class agrees to the teacher's plan that one group form to improvise being the relatives of one patient, while another is to become the relatives of the other patient. There is also to be a group of doctors and medical staff and a group of 'concerned' citizens (a minister, a politician, a reporter, etc.). The teacher takes on the role of chief surgeon and the task is for participants in each group to develop a character, to begin discussion and to prepare for preliminary discussion with the chief surgeon.

In the next lesson, each group in turn has an improvised session where it confronts the chief surgeon who, in each case, manages to throw in unforeseen complications and counter-arguments. In a debriefing session the whole class reflects on the emerging plot, comments on ways of proceeding and suggests improvements on the improvisation to date.

From here, on the next day the teacher organizes the students to re-group to marshall further arguments. However, instead of them meeting the surgeon again, they find that they are to meet another group, though unprepared for it. The teacher has thrown this in as a means of further stretching them and to widen their appreciation of other perspectives on the dilemma.

This proves to be a lively session. In the de-briefing for the day they discuss good points and points of potential growth as well as considering where to go from here. They decide they need some time to write some embryonic scripts in terms of issues, stances and unfolding action rather than specific lines.

After the script writing, they go back over two scenes (with the chief surgeon and with another group). They then face the difficulty of how to round off their presentation to make it cohere for the spectator class. With some teacher prompting, it is resolved that they will all attend a formal meeting of interested parties at which the chief surgeon will hear the pro's and con's and make a decision. The improvisation will end with the chief surgeon's summing-up and decision.

Because none of the groups has really grappled with the wider political/economic restrictions on the hospital, the teacher decides privately that the chief surgeon will refuse to operate on either patient, as a public protest, until the government makes more funds and resources available. This, she knows, will create a rich base for further class discussion of forms of protest, leading nicely into the next experience she has arranged — a class viewing of the film *Gandhi*.

The improvisation is eventually polished for performance. It is very well received by the spectator class and there is excellent spontaneous discussion (theatre-in-education style) after the presentation.

The teacher is well satisfied that students have come to grips with issues of power, control, decision-making and vested interest. She feels that this experience has raised political awareness and complicated simplistic views about how decisions are made. She herself, as a female chief surgeon, has modelled assertiveness against constraining authorities.

This teacher is highly regarded by students and fellow staff members, though considered to be a bit radical and 'bolshy' in the themes she has students consider. Many other drama teachers covet her ability to take risks and to trust in the power of students to work up their own scripts. The principal values her because she allows him to demonstrate publicly, through her students, that his is a school where students can stand up and put on a show. Drama is not some kind of mystical dark-room ritual in this school.

Having admitted that such teaching goes well beyond present 'par-for-the-course' teaching in our secondary schools, in terms of allowing student initiative, I wish to look at the politics of her enactment of the curriculum; at the texture and intentions of the text.

Analysis of the script

Two crucial questions in any analysis of a political 'text' are 'Who wrote the script?' and 'Whose interests are being served?'. Within the hospital script, it is true that the students develop much of the script in collaboration with each other, but the parameters of the plot and the territory to be explored have been pre-empted by the teacher who has made a crucial shaping deci-

148   *Garth Boomer*

sion in introducing the video-tape. The teacher administers their labours and, with their consent, organizes the mechanics both of the classroom meta-script (managing the time allocation, the movement and the activity sequences) and the emerging class 'hospital' script (controlling group focus, patterns of interaction and key aspects of plot resolution). Student decisions are made largely about issues to be raised and attitudes to be presented within the offering they have agreed to prepare with (or for?) the teacher.

Indeed much of the meta-script is submerged because we do not have direct access to the teacher's intentions. Why did she choose the Gargoyle video? What skills, knowledge and attitudes, precisely, was she hoping to promote? How much of the script seen in retrospect had she already imagined? Did she have some form of evaluation in mind? What criteria did she have for any evaluation? What degree of deviance from her imagination of the script was she willing to tolerate? There are clues within the unfolding classroom drama which suggest that she did indeed have a powerfully conceived script in mind. She may have been surprised by some of the inventions of the students within the play, but by and large one gets the feeling that things happened as planned. The teacher wrote the script and the students agreeably fleshed it out.

The question 'In whose interests?' is harder to answer. The teacher would no doubt answer along these lines 'In the interests of the students' articulateness, awareness and capacity to plan and of fostering their growing ability to work together tenaciously towards a goal.' Furthermore they were obviously interested. Co-operation was high. There was little resistance.

But what teacher interests are also being served? In the first place the teacher has professional interests, connected with being a good drama teacher, with professional kudos. Then there are her interests in control, public approval and the excitement of seeing what the students will make of it all. She seems to have had quite a good time, taking on the starring role, throwing in plot complications and appropriating the last words. Maybe it was in her interests as a lover of acting to be in the limelight. Another way to ask the question is 'Who wanted to do it in the first place?' Clearly, the students came to accept what the teacher wanted. They are gently manipulated into the act — the contract to pretend. 'You pretend to be other than students and I'll pretend to be other than teacher.' And yet within the pretence, teacher continues to be in charge, in role. The pretence is not in the direction of playing at being powerful. It is playing at being trapped. The simulation mirrors the entrapment of the classroom outside the pretence. By seemingly divesting herself of the teacher role, the teacher intensifies her power.

Surprise

Another litmus test for power is to ask 'Who knows what is going to happen?' The ones being most surprised, are the ones with least control over their own destiny. The more one is subject to surprise, the more vulnerable one is.

The drama teacher would conceivably produce the following evidence. The students knew the following:

- they were to explore a shared theme known to them
- they were to perform the outcomes to another class
- the teacher would help to organize them
- they were responsible for developing their own parts.

At the curriculum planning level, then, they knew what was required and in the play within the plan knew what they had to explore. They agreed to do this.

But what did the drama teacher know which was unknown to the students? She knew:

- why she was doing this work
- why she chose this particular set of teaching strategies
- how she would organize each lesson (in advance of the students)
- how she would evaluate its success.
- how she would intervene to push the students' thinking
- what she hoped the students would learn about.

She had information and clear intentions which enabled her to teach *deliberately*, *systematically*, *productively* and *reflectively*. The daily consequence of her plan in action empowered her to adjust and move forward to the resolution.

By contrast, the students could not be deliberate learners because they did not know what they were supposed to learn about. They knew what they were supposed to do and how but they did not know, in the fullest sense, why. They knew only part of what the teacher had in mind. They were therefore 'surprised' each day by the teacher's revelation of what they were to do and within that they were further surprised by the unpredictable turns of the teacher — in and out of role.

It should be noted that such surprise is so much part of school that students do not perceive it as surprise. Whereas with their peers they shared the vulnerability of unpredictability, with their teacher in and out of role they were relatively vulnerable to pre-meditated teacher shifts. It is interesting to contemplate what would have happened if the teacher had suddenly been taken ill and had handed over to another supervising teacher. Without the teacher's devices, left to their own devices, would they have resolved the plot in ways which would have surprised their teacher?

Certainly the students had intentions within the pretence — to explore and resolve a conflict with a view to performance. Outside the pretence they had no clear learning intentions other than to act in collusion with the teacher to see if the task could be done. They pretended to be students. After the act they could see and talk about what they had 'surprisingly' learned from the experience. Experience thus acted upon them rather than vice versa. Because the students did not know what they were intending to learn, the consequence of their in-role drama could not be potent for them (as the teacher's were for her). They could reflect upon the consequences of the mechanics of their plotting and acting, because the intention to perform was explicit, but they could not reflect in a *focused* way on the *content* of what they were exploring. The teacher, secure in the knowledge that they were, perhaps *despite* themselves, exploring gutsy political and ethical issues, was content with the content. The students, because this was not explicitly on their agenda, were, ironically, contentedly 'dis-contented'.

The teacher might contend that she could not predict how the students would handle their improvisations and how they would develop the issues. She was thus put in a position of having to react, as pedagogue, to student 'surprises'. While she knew the broad plot, the details could not be predicted. But this is little more than the surprise teachers of any subject anywhere have to cope with as students make variable responses in variable ways to the set curriculum. Teachers *expect* to be 'surprised' in this sense so that it is not really very surprising, merely temporarily annoying, diverting, stimulating or challenging. Habitually the teacher's job is to take what comes and shape it, with varying degrees of latitude, towards pre-figured ends. These moments are mere hiccups in the balance of power.

The balance of surprise would have changed had the students negotiated the teacher into the role of giver of information and demonstration as commissioned by them. You cannot learn your lines for such a classroom. You must improvise from a position of some vulnerability and certain fallibility.

Secrets

This drama teacher, allegedly committed to the empowerment of her students, critical of existing power relationships in society and in the school and powerful in her own teaching, is out of habit and some delusion, I would say, teaching dependence and powerlessness because she has not confronted the fact that, in addition to experience and status, she holds secrets which constitute power and could constitute increased power for others, if shared, particularly with those who live in schools. Or if she has reached the point of knowing the power of her secrets, she has decided that there is as yet no point in, or no good to be derived from, telling them to her students. Perhaps it is because she feels that they would not comprehend. Or it may be that she operates on the false analogy that you do not need to know about car engines to drive a car.

It is habitual for teachers to write curriculum scripts. It is not habitual for teachers to question the politics of habit. Here is a partial list of information which the teacher could have decided to give her students.

- Why she chose to introduce the 'Gargoyle' video.
- What she had in mind as a way of exploring it further.
- What she hoped students would be learning about and doing in this unit. (Not *what* they would learn, which can only be foreseen by rat psychologists and animal trainers.)
- Why she considered this important.
- What role she was going to play and the kinds of things she intended to do.
- The relevant parts of her learning or teaching theory upon which she based these plans.
- Her predictions, with reasons, as to why this unit of work would succeed as a learning experience.
- The political and educational reasons for performing to another class.
- The criteria by which she would evaluate the curriculum unit itself and the individual performance of students (how they would be tested).
- The degree of negotiability she would allow in framing the script and the performances (what decisions could be made by students).

She must know all this to write the curriculum scripts. Perhaps she had not admitted some of these secrets even to herself but, when she has, she can then make them available to the students in terms that they can understand.

If the students remain in the dark about all this, the curriculum will seem to them to be somehow *given*, *impermeable*, maybe even *magic* if the teacher is as charismatic as this one. It will not be considered by students to be pertinent matter for them. It is the teacher's 'show business', not theirs.

Teachers who do not take students behind their curriculum set to show how it is done, have:
either not thought about it,

or consider curriculum production and management issues are of no real
concern to the workers,

or are unwilling to spend the time and energy which would then need to be
expended each time a new 'script' was to be introduced,

or think that the students would reject such intimacy as a tactless breaking
of the established rules and roles of teaching and learning,

or do not want to be an alienating Brecht with respect to their own theatre,

or would find it threatening.

The list could go on, for the fact is that few teachers *do* take this step. My
own informal research has yielded a full crop of 'Yes, buts . . .' whenever
coming clean about the curriculum and the school is suggested. These 'Yes,
buts' are not to be sneered at. They are significant, real and perceived
aspects of the teacher's contestation for room and power in the school.

It seems, however, that *theoretically* most can see that students who are
illiterate with respect to the school and the curriculum (who cannot 'read'
the place in which they operate as students) are gravely at risk and likely to
be 'done in' by schooling. And yet, it is considered a radical and dangerous
step to break the complicity (or is it conspiracy?) of tact where the successful
pick up the passwords according to privilege and chance. It is almost taboo
to *tell* students how the place works, how the curriculum is constructed and
how to negotiate for reward. In whose interests is this information withheld?

By choosing not to tell, not to make their own teaching explicitly problem-
atic for students or being naïvely unaware of the possibility of telling,
teachers are teaching a politics which condones information capital and
privilege, cultural discrimination against the young and the division of
mental labour.

Trust

Returning to our hypothetical drama teacher, we need to correct some tendencies to score easy points. In a mediated exchange a few years ago, I got the
impression from Dorothy Heathcote that the key to good drama teaching is
the *trust* which students have in their teacher.

This teacher has the trust of her students. If over time the students learn
through experience and consequences that the teacher cares about them and
is working in their interests then there is no need, says Dorothy Heathcote,[2]
to get into convolutions of negotiation and explanation. Our hypothetical
drama teacher would argue that she should not be judged on the basis of one
unit; that because of her genuine *intention* to empower this will permeate the
curriculum in subtle ways and eventually take hold without the need for self-

conscious dwelling on it. She might also argue that one must always move the students gradually from their learned helplessness in most classrooms to new regimes where they can progressively take up more power and responsibility. Rebellion and rejection too often accompany sudden shifts in the teaching roles. My present stance is to reject these counter-arguments.

I have said elsewhere that *trust*[3] is a worrisome concept. I am continually on my guard against those in power over me, no matter how 'good' they are, and I require continual demonstration and negotiation to confirm that I am not being manipulated against my own interest. Indeed the more trustworthy the authority, the more I need to be alert. 'Trustworthy' people are often warm hosts to the invisible bad habits of society. In my own teaching these days, I deliberately seek to alienate my students from my teaching performance by showing them what I am about. I wish to rouse their suspicions about what I say and do so that I will be tested before swallowing. I always try to teach the meta-text along with the text. This is my contribution to the breaking of the reproduction of dependence that the schooling industry usually achieves.

In these resolves I continually fall short, catching myself out in compromise, contradiction and insidious bad habits. While striving to set up a collaboration of equals. I accept that as teacher I have 'unequal' power. For this reason, the contradictions of my classroom are more pleasing than the harmonies. They indicate that my authority is questionable.

Struggling and penetrating

Returning to the drama teacher *constructed* in this paper, I need to draw attention to the fact that this is *my construct* cited for my own purposes. Real teachers would tell a far more complex story of subtle changes in power and influence as students exercise their capacities to resist and to charm teachers in their own interests. They would also, no doubt, set their script writing in a context which includes far more complex industrial, ethical and physical constraints than I have sketched out in my convenient hypothesis.

Nevertheless, I have tried to suggest how it is that all of us, no matter how finely tuned our consciousness, will teach with variable integrity, authenticity and consistency.

> . . . ideologies are not abstract ideas merely 'held in the heads of people'. As recent European social theorists remind us, they are constituted by our whole array of commonsense practices and meanings that are lived out as we go about our daily lives. Furthermore, they may be internally inconsistent. These commonsense practices and meanings are often 'deeply contradictory, shot

through with [both] ideological elements (and) elements of good sense'. Thus side by side with beliefs and actions that maintain the dominance of powerful classes and groups, there will be elements of serious (though perhaps incomplete) understanding, elements that see the differential benefits and penetrate close to the core of an unequal reality.[4]

We are at once opponents and agents of the hegemony of schools. Our students also vacillate from subversion of some parts of our regime to reinforcement of some of our comfortable habits. Just as we as teachers are engaged in a continuing struggle to penetrate social reality, so should our students be encouraged to struggle and penetrate.

In drama classrooms throughout the country children are being taught the politics of their teachers, the politics of the school and the politics of the nation. Drama teaching can be a powerful vehicle for helping students to penetrate and interpret what is happening to them.

Notes and References

1. In 'Reading the Whole Curriculum', unpublished address to the National Reading Conference, Darwin, Australia, August, 1982.
2. See *NADIE Journal*, 1981.
3. 'The Politics of Pretending and Intending', unpublished discussion paper.
4. Michael V. Apple, 'Analyzing Determinations: Understanding and evaluating the production of social outcomes in schools', *Curriculum Inquiry*, Vol. 10, No. 1, 1980, p. 61.

15.
Language and the Learning of Practical Skills

Michael Hamerston

The purpose of this paper is to identify some features of language in the processes of teaching and learning practical skills. Polanyi's work on skill provides a convenient theoretical foundation for examining the learning of practical skills by first-year apprentice plumbers. The transcript material and examples quoted in the paper were collected from workshop practice sessions in a London college of further education.

Anyone who teaches physical skills knows how difficult it is 'to put into words' exactly what we want our learners to do. Or, more importantly, how we want them to do it. Similarly, skilled performers find it extremely difficult to describe their skills to someone else. The problem is that a practical skill consists of more than language is able to convey. The limitations of verbal language have been identified intuitively by a first-rate automotive engineer who was asked to talk about his skills as he fitted a camshaft to the renowned Cosworth racing engine:

> What I'm doing now is feel. You can't really describe that. You don't know what experience you've got until you think about it. Well, I don't anyway.

Re-building racing engines and tuning them to high performance draws, then, on skills which are neither dependent upon language nor amenable to logical specification in language. An inability to give explicit expression to the rules which guide skilled performers is a phenomenon common to fields as diverse as automotive engineering, plumbing, painting and music. But Polanyi[1] demonstrates that this is not simply a failure of articulation, an inadequacy of language. Rather, it represents a fundamental distinction in knowing, a boundary between what may be known explicitly and what may be known implicitly.

Polanyi provides a detailed exploration of skill in general which can illuminate our particular interest in the skills of plumbing. The exercise of plumbing skill is equivalent, in Polanyi's terms, to the practice of an art, the explicit rules of which are in themselves not adequate to create skilful performance. 'Rules of art . . . can serve as a guide to an art only if they can be integrated into the practical knowledge of the art.' Plumbing, like all arts, has its maxims which seek to guide the hands of craftsmen but Polanyi is concerned to probe the nature of the 'practical knowledge' into which such maxims may be integrated. He argues 'that the aim of a skilful performance is achieved by the observance of a set of rules which are not known as such to the person following them'. In this sense, then, the essential rules for plumbing remain inexplicit or 'logically unspecifiable', and continue embedded in a tradition which allows them to be passed by example from master to apprentice. A learner is required to trust his master's technique even when its effectiveness cannot be analysed in detail. 'By watching the master and emulating his efforts in the presence of his example, the apprentice unconsciously picks up the rules of the art, including those which are not explicitly known to the master himself.' This is to suggest neither the existence of a static repertoire of skills in any craft nor that the creation and integration of new skills at the level of the unconscious occurs in the absence of guiding frameworks. On the contrary, Polanyi argues for two kinds of awareness, focal and subsidiary, which participate in the discovery, performance and maintenance of skills.

We use our focal awareness, in line with our intentions to produce meaningful changes in the materials at our disposal, to guide, and to monitor the results of, our activity. Simultaneously, our subsidiary awareness of muscle-control, tools and working procedures allows us to make unconsciously those adjustments which lead, by accreditation at the level of focal awareness, to adequate skilful performance. It is in the merging of focal and subsidiary awareness that the unconscious, unspecifiable rules of action exist. If a plumber, for example, attends focally to what is essentially subsidiary, his performance will be paralysed. If he attends to his gripping of a mallet rather than to the effects of his beating at lead, the lead will not submit itself to his intentions within the meaningful schema of the craft. If the actions of gripping the mallet, manipulating the lead, positioning the feet and so on are experienced subsidiarily in terms of their contributions to intended outcomes, the learner may select out those features which facilitate his performance,

> without ever knowing these as they would appear to him when considered in themselves. This is the usual process of unconscious trial and error by which we feel our way to success and may continue to improve on our success without

specifiably knowing how we do it — for we never meet the causes of our success as identifiable things which can be described in terms of classes of which such things are members.

Thus the skill of beating a cylinder from sheet-lead, for example, remains logically unspecifiable for a plumber because the 'specification of the particulars would logically contradict what is implied in the performance.'

The operational field of particulars encompassed by subsidiary awareness includes not only the neuro-muscular elements of the craftsman's body but also the tools which function as purposive extensions of his body. Polanyi emphasizes that the learner must place his reliance in certain objects, tools or limbs, as capable of achieving or signifying something in line with his intentions. 'Thus reliance is a personal commitment which is involved in all acts of intelligence by which we integrate some things subsidiarily to the centre of our local attention.' Tools function as extensions of our bodies, assimilated 'as parts of our existence. We accept them existentially by dwelling in them.' This assimilation requires an intelligent effort to construe a coherent perception of one's activity. The learner's awareness has to be populated with those otherwise irrelevant elements which now become salient to the situation by virtue of the operational results achieved through their application. Tools disappear as objects in their own right, subsumed by unconscious interpretation of the interaction between them and the objects of their attention. Polanyi argues that this loss of consciousness on the part of skilled performers is accompanied by new awareness of activity 'on the operational plane'. Such awareness is not, therefore, brought about merely by repetition of physical acts. 'It is a structural change achieved by a repeated mental effort aimed at the instrumentalization of certain things and actions in the service of some purpose.'

Polanyi regards the accumulation and exercise of skill as proceeding from certain intentional changes of being whereby a craftsman pours himself into 'the subsidiary awareness of particulars, which in the performance of skills are instrumental to a skilful achievement'. Alan Garner[2] has captured this quality of indwelling in his description of a blacksmith at work:

> Grandad put the hot end into a hole in the swage block, and pulled down until the strip began to bend. He drew it out a short way, and bent it again. The metal was losing its colour. 'Now', said Grandad. 'Give her a good un! Come on! Queen Elizabeth, Chapel and all!'
> The lever went up and down, and William with it. The forge roared. Grandad held the strip with long pincers and paddled it in the fire. He kept looking at the bellows handle, as if he was measuring it, but most of the time he was watching the heated iron.

'You'll often wonder why a smith works in the dark', he said, 'and here's why. It's nothing dubious. You can't judge colour if the sun's putting your fire out. It's pale straw we're after; pale straw, and not a touch lighter. See!' He pulled out the strip. Where he had bent it in the swage block was yellow but not white. He moved quickly now and turned the rough end in the hollow cup, pressing but not forcing the softened iron to the perfect curve, so that the cup in the block gave its shape to his hand. Then he laid the strip aside. It changed from straw to cherry.

In the exercise of his skill, Grandad attends to his swage block and his pincers; he measures the action of the bellows against the intensity of the forge communicated to his strip of iron; he judges the receptivity of the metal by its colour; he manages conversation, and he works quickly with hands and arms when he feels the moment is right. That is not guesswork. All of these particulars and others have been integrated subsidiarily to the centre of his focal awareness of what is finally given as shape to his hand, to his intentional conception of a sled runner. Grandad holds his knowledge implicitly and does not attempt to specify logically, in detail, the rules by which he performs skilfully. He does, however, alert his grandson to the critical nature of heat in blacksmithing, first by regulating William's activity at the bellows, and second by offering the approximative characterization, 'pale straw'. These explicit uses of language to establish joint attention by master and beginner to salient features in a particular context are suggestive of how language might contribute to the construction of coherent perceptions of activity for teachers and learners of practical skills in workshops and on-the-job. I would like to explore the proposition that language is useful in shaping and controlling a learner's awareness of activity in line with his intentions to develop and perform appropriate practical skills. Here is a story about a plumber which begins to show how language can contribute to learning the logically unspecifiable:

> The plumber and his apprentice were called to fix some pipes in an old house. In the course of the work, the plumber noticed that his apprentice was having difficulty with a particular joint. So the master said to the lad: 'Spit on it, Richard, spit on it!' The apprentice, not understanding what the advice meant, returned a puzzled glance. And the master said: 'Look, my son, a plumber's sweat is worth nothing, but a plumber's spit — now that's gold.'

The story describes a brief instructional act consisting of an attempt by the master to encourage his apprentice to spit. Importantly, however, the spitting has to be done within a particular set of actions and for a particular plumbing purpose. The master uses his language to draw attention to the relevance of spitting in certain circumstances, and to reinforce that relevance by distinguishing the value of spit from that of sweat. The master's admonition invites the apprentice to perceive spit as advantageous in plumbing. Spit is identified as one more tool at the plumber's disposal, waiting to be integrated into the complex of skills which stand between the craftsman and the materials which he manipulates. And once a plumber has learned to make spit work for him, he has no difficulty in making perfect sense of the story because it reverberates within his 'practical knowledge of the art' of plumbing. A plumbing teacher explained the story to me like this:

> There's a lot in there. I'll explain that to you. Well, basically, the idea of spit relates back to the old tradition of joint-wiping. Right? Now, if you wipe a joint with a blow-lamp, the tendency of the tin in that was to drop to the bottom. Right? Now, when you wipe a joint, to prevent the tears of tin collecting and preventin' you gettin' a clean line on your joint, you spit on it. And the fact that the spit is cooler, it stops the tin droppin' and it holds it. And this is where obviously this is originated from. From what I can make out there what you said. Because if he's, if you're talkin' in terms of sweat, 'cos it's sweat, he burns his bloody self. Whereas if he spits it, he's at the distance where he achieves the object and no harm is done.

It is important to see the difference between the story and the plumbing teacher's explanation. In the story, the master is not concerned to explain anything to the apprentice. Rather, he directs the learner's attention to an appropriate technique, leaving him to test it out for himself. The master says, in effect, 'If you spit in the correct manner, the job will go more easily.' The apprentice is urged to test out the advice by systematically modifying his spitting until it becomes part of the skill of joint-wiping. As the 'tears of tin' are palpably prevented from dropping to the bottom, the learner integrates his spitting into a network of skills which constitutes the wiping of joints: he is not learning to spit but to wipe a joint. In the plumbing teacher's explanation there is similarly nothing concrete which could teach an apprentice to spit more effectively. The explanation tells us why spit makes for better joint-wiping by spelling out a low-level theory of thermodynamics. But, like the master's instruction, the explanation has the potential to draw the learner's attention to what is critical in the skills required for joint-wiping. The plumbing teacher says, in effect, 'If you direct your spit in a manner which cools the material, the job will go more easily.' Successful joint-wiping can neither be taught nor learned to a recipe. It has to be learned through experience. When the skill has been mastered, when the apprentice becomes master of the skill, knowledge of the skill remains largely unconscious. In practice, a plumber gives little conscious attention to spitting on his work except for that first occasion when he is instructed to do so by someone-who-knows, and on those few subsequent occasions when he is deliberately testing out the instruction to see if it 'achieves the object'. If you ask a plumber how he learned to wipe a joint, he is likely to answer, 'Through practice. Practice makes perfect, you know.' There can be no precise instructions about how to spit for more successful joint-wiping. It's something that plumbers 'get a feel for' in the same way that automotive engineers get a feel for fitting camshafts to Cosworth racing engines. Systematic trial and error guided by intentional projection and awareness of outcomes gradually refines the performance until it is skilled.

The master of a skill is someone who knows how to control his awareness when the skill is being performed. He knows from a sense of feel what refinements are necessary in the integration of movements which produce skilled performance. A teacher of skills is someone who, while recognizing the essential implicit character of 'rules of art', has the capacity to identify and to articulate the critical features of skilled performance so that learners know where to direct their awareness for the refinement of technique. The potentially important role played by language in this process of channelling awareness is illustrated clearly in the story of the master and his apprentice. Language is an extremely efficient system for attracting and directing the attention of others. It is possible, of course, to achieve similar results by physical intervention or by demonstration. For example, the master plumber in the story might have made his point simply by taking over the wiping of his apprentice's joint. But language is structured precisely in the way that is needed to identify the relevant, and to exclude the irrelevant, features of human action in circumstances where learning might occur. We might speculate, then, that good teachers are those who effectively alert their students to the critical features of the skills needed for mastery of a particular craft. My observations in workshops have identified at least four ways in which language is used to direct students' awareness to the critical features of the skills they are trying to learn. The four language strategies range from the very brief and directive to the very extensive and tentative. What is common to them all, however, is the functioning of language as part of a larger meaning-making system which includes objects and non-verbal processes. The four strategies demonstrate the value of language in facilitating effective co-ordination of teachers' and learners' attention with relevant features of the physical world upon which they have an intention to act. The categories overlap in important respects and should, therefore, be regarded as nothing more than a convenient way of distinguishing the major differences between various uses of language.

1. Incidental instruction in correct practice

This is a good place to start because it marks the boundary between non-verbal and verbal intervention by teachers. As such, the category can help us to understand the increase in power which language provides for instruction. Sometimes, a teacher will observe that a student is having difficulty because he is using the wrong tool for the job. In these circumstances, the teacher might put his student on the right track by handing him a tool more appropriate to the job. In other words, the teacher's intended meaning is carried in the simple action of producing the tool which itself draws attention to a critical feature of correct technique. In practice, of course, interventions like this are frequently accompanied by language such as, 'Here, you'll find that this makes it easier', or, 'You'll never get it right with that. Use this.' When the problem has to do with a process rather than with a tool, language is extremely efficient for instruction. A teacher can move around the workshop offering brief directions or rules of the craft as he observes the problems encountered by individuals: 'Don't bend it too far', 'Be careful with that torch — you don't want it too hot', or, 'Never put lead pipe in the vice!' The effect of instructions like these is twofold. First, the student's attention is directed to a feature ignored by his current behaviour. Second, a thinking process is initiated inviting the student to consider and test out in action a new hypothesis appropriate to the skill he is trying to master.

2. Demonstration

Teachers give demonstrations before students attempt new skills and when those attempts break down. In my experience, the most effective demonstrations are those given when a student has attempted a skill but is unable to carry the process to a successful conclusion. Here are two examples.

An apprentice was attempting to make a branch-joint in copper pipe. The work was not going well because of faulty technique which threatened to damage the pipe. When the teacher observed the danger, he stepped in, took up the tools, and proceeded to demonstrate correct technique. He achieved this first by completing the job, and then by going back over the process in slow motion with a commentary: 'Start off with the tool vertical. Then do your leverin'. Work towards the heat.' The language is brief, but it functions as a check mechanism. The language holds the apprentice's attention and focuses it on the features which must be controlled if the job is to be carried out successfully.

Language functions in exactly the same way in this second example of demonstration by a teacher when two apprentices called for assistance after reaching the point of breakdown in a difficult job. The apprentices were

162 *Michael Hamerston*

attempting to make lead slates which require the beating of a cylinder from, but in the centre of, a flat piece of lead sheet. They beat the material too hard, for too long and in the wrong way, resulting in fractures which brought work to a halt. When called and shown the failed materials, the teacher responded by working with a new sheet of lead. He showed how the job should be done, mostly by beating loudly. The teacher paused occasionally to make brief comments intended to keep the apprentices' attention fixed on the critical features: 'Make use of this hump by moving it into the centre', 'Now you can slip your block in underneath', 'Don't be afraid to hit it', and so on. Again, the language is brief, but it functions to control the process of observation through which the apprentices are able to relate what they see of the teacher's successful technique to their own experience of beating at lead. But, essentially, the students learn by observation. They observe the process and manner of beating, they see the changes in the material, they relate these to the feel of their own experience and create the correct techniques retrospectively. By chaining acts and consequences in reverse order, they identify what is subsidiary in order to integrate it in their own next attempts. Language occupies a relatively small percentage of the demonstration time, but it is central to identifying the properties of lead and the features of its response to beating which must be managed by a skilful slate-beater.

3. Clarification of task

Because language allows us to talk meaningfully about things which are both present and not present, we are able to use it to plan our future actions in advance. We can get our ideas straight before we attempt to carry them out. Apprentices in workshops rely on their teachers to define appropriate procedures, to specify relevant materials, and to provide a global plan for activity as one model gives way to the next. The transcript which follows is a typical exchange initiated by a plumbing apprentice as he moves into a new activity based on a network of pipe connections and fittings for a simulated bathroom system. The conversation occurs as teacher and apprentice stand together at a bench loaded with some components and an empty board to which the pipework will be attached.

> Peter   I want one of them there, don't I?
> Teacher Yes.
> Peter   Does it matter whereabouts I put this hexagon nut?
> Teacher Now, this one's a plastic one, isn't it?
> 5 Peter   That one's a plastic one.

Teacher	That one's a plastic one . . .
Peter	So I put one of them big . . .
Steven	[Indecipherable]
Peter	I've got one here.
10 Teacher	Where's the other one?
Steven	I've got it here.
Peter	He's got the other one.
Steven	Here y'are. I don't muck about.
Peter	I don't need it at the moment anyway, do I?
15 Teacher	Um, no. As I say, the best thing to do is to put the two in there, right?
Peter	Yeah.
Teacher	Get the bottoms . . .
Peter	Righto.
20 Teacher	You can get your copper runs in there, can't you?
Peter	Yeah.
Teacher	That should keep you reasonably happy.
Peter	That one and that one?
Teacher	On an elbow. Right?
25	That one, in fact, you run in here.
Peter	In there?
Teacher	That goes on there. Right?
	That one's a lead one.
Peter	What's that one there then?
30 Teacher	Well what you want is a short of iron . . .
Peter	Yeah.
Teacher	and then an elbow . . .
Peter	Yeah.
Teacher	Right . . . See what Alf's got . . .
35 Peter	Yeah.
Teacher	Now, that one will be a lead one. So you'll have a plumber's union in that elbow . . .
Peter	Yeah.
Teacher	and then you'll have a cap and lining behind there for your tap
40	connector. You'll see the fittin's that you use in there.
Peter	Right.
Teacher	OK?
Peter	Yeah.

Clarification of task depends on negotiation. Indeed, Peter's needs can be properly served only when his understandings and misunderstandings are transparent to the teacher. Verbal language embedded in its context of reference is an effective medium for creating that transparency as the participants responsively negotiate their way forward. Peter initiates the exchange with two straightforward questions in lines 1-4. The teacher answers Peter's first question, but ignores the second as he begins to think his way into the problem before defining 'the best thing to do' (lines 15-20). At line 22, 'That should keep you reasonably happy', the teacher is satisfied that Peter's problem is solved.

However, Peter shows by his questions that he, in fact, misunderstands. The questions at 23, 26, and 29 expose Peter's failure to grasp all that he is required to do. The question, 'What's that one there then?' (line 29), in particular, is pivotal in provoking a detailed and systematic account of the task which the apprentice succeeds in absorbing. Notice the way 'Yes', 'Yeah', 'Right' and 'OK' function to signal understanding, and to demonstrate that both participants are attending simultaneously to the same things. Peter negotiates an understanding of what he is required to do through conversation supported by the materials with which he must work. The teacher responds to Peter's need for clarification with increasingly detailed explanations until a satisfactory global plan for the apprentice's activity has been established.

4. Problem-solving

The role of language in solving problems of a practical nature is similar to that discussed in the previous category. Most importantly, language again functions to help teacher and student 'think through' a problem. Problem-solving is also similar to demonstration because it occurs in response to difficulties encountered somewhere along the pathway to completion of a job. But problem-solving is different from demonstration in that the teacher does not take over the job himself. Rather, teacher and student explore the difficulty together, gradually working towards a new understanding which forms the basis for further activity. In this example, Robert has called for assistance after an unsuccessful attempt to secure a cap and lining in a length of lead pipe.

> Teacher   See, a lot of people get hold of the cap and lining, just smash it in the end of the pipe, don't give it a thought. Really you should give it a couple of taps, see how far it's gone in. If it's insufficient, then give it a little bit more. But you must have 75
> 5   mil. You see . . .

Robert	Well, I've got 75 mil . . .
Teacher	Well, yeah, but you've got to be careful you don't get your [Indecipherable] . . . I mean, if you withdraw this slightly and dress that down, if you get yourself a bent bolt, just start
10		dressin' it back with the bent bolt there, right, that will enclose it. And that will then make the taper shorter. You see, at the moment . . . at the moment, you're nosin' into there.
Robert	Yeah.
Teacher	Well, that's too much. Really, you want to reduce that by
15		about, oh, you want to try and cut it down to about 10 mil.
Robert	That's too long anyway, so if I do it in that end . . .
Teacher	Alright, same difference. If you want to re-do it, that's up to you. You'll have to turn that off and start again if you wish. But try not to get it entering by much more than 10 mil.
20 Robert		10 mil.
Teacher	You see, you want that about. Give it a little bit, then check it. [Robert hammers] Do it bit by bit. Be careful with that because the pipe will split.

The teacher solves Robert's problem with a complex instructional act. Robert needs to know, first, what an ideal cap and lining insertion is like, and, second, where his work has fallen short of this ideal. The teacher begins by referring to a common mistake (lines 1–2) before directing Robert's attention to the errors exhibited in his particular job. Then, features of an ideal job are detailed (lines 4–5, and 19) while providing instruction in the process required to achieve a satisfactory job (lines 2–5 and 8–11) as a prelude to guiding Robert immediately through the appropriate procedure (lines 21–23). Having drawn careful attention to the critical features, and having won Robert's agreement in lines 13 and 20, the teacher is able virtually to control the apprentice's hands as they move towards a goal which is now more clearly perceived and understood.

Before leaving the four categories, it is worth considering a further general point. The reader will have been aware of many occurrences of words such as 'it', 'this' and 'that' in the transcript material. Frequently, it is a mystery as to what these words refer to. And yet it is obvious that the participants in the conversations are totally clear about their meanings. Take, for example, the teacher's directions to Robert in lines 8–11. When the teacher says, 'just start dressin' it back with the bent bolt there, right, that will enclose it', the word 'it' refers to two quite different things. In the first instance, the teacher is referring to the lead pipe; in the second, to the cap and lining which is to be enclosed by the lead pipe. Similarly, in lines 14–16, the teacher's 'that' refers to the enclosure while Robert's refers first to the overall length of the pipe in which the cap and lining is to be enclosed, and then to one end of that pipe. This kind of language works for Robert and his teacher because it is embedded in a situation which they both share and understand. They allow their attention to shift flexibly from one thing to another, and, because they have a tacit agreement to attend to the same things simultaneously, they experience no difficulty in understanding the changing patterns of reference contained within their language.

In situations where learning is being done through experience, much of the meaning represented in verbal language is implicit. Workshops and laboratories are stocked with meaningful objects. They are places where productive learning occurs without the need for explicit language. Tools, materials and actions support the meaning of language: language, in turn, supports the meaning of tools, materials and actions. Language is not required to say everything because physical and non-verbal features of context fill in the gaps. Language should, therefore, be seen as one of the tools available to teachers and learners as they experience directly the feel of certain skills. So that any importance we want to attach to language will arise because of its efficiency in directing learners' attention to the critical features which must be managed in the performance of a skill. In the four categories of use discussed above, language was an efficient component of instruction, performing an alerting function and a planning function to direct attention to critical features in a shared context of purposive activity. These functions are characterized by the highly implicit nature of language. But the plumbing teacher's explanation of the spitting story demonstrates that language may also be useful to learners of practical skills when it becomes explicit and performs a summarizing function which Olson and Bruner[3] have termed 'deuteropraxis'. By this process, it is argued, we are constantly trying to reorganize

> what we know so that it may be translated into symbolic systems . . . both for the purpose of facilitating the communication that is required for the survival of the culture and for the purpose of rendering one's own personal experience comprehensible.

Deuteropraxis leads to economic framings of experience in the form of rules, suggestions or aphorisms. The master plumber's aphorism dealing with the value of plumbers' spit is an example of information organized into a form appropriate to cultural transmission within the plumbing trade. So, too, is the plumbing teacher's more elaborated explanation. Olson and Bruner believe that such accounts are useful in instruction because learners often find it difficult to link actions with the consequences that follow. Deuteropraxis accounts, 'whether in the form of an abstract equation, a principle, a noiseless exemplar, or an appropriate model, have the effect of "time-binding" or virtually simultanizing temporal events and thereby surpassing ordinary experience.' The process of 'time-binding' is clearly evident in this transcript of a conversation which followed the lead-slate-beating session discussed under the heading, Demonstration. After the apprentices had gone on to produce their own lead slates successfully, I asked the teacher to comment on why his demonstration had been effective:

	Michael	So, what do you reckon you did to put them straight this morning?
	Teacher	Well, they were obviously stretching the material too far. But you don't need to stretch it that far. All you really want is the
5		height, the initial height, and then you've got to draw the bottom in, but what's got to be appreciated is, that when you're dealing with a sheet, you're talking about stress with that particular operation. Now what you've got to do is counteract for the stresses that are involved. You know, if you're stretching
10		it, then you've got to reinforce it. And this is what they were doing. They were bouncing the metal up into a bloody great mound and, the fact of the matter was, they stretched it to such an extent that it just couldn't be reinforced any more.
	Michael	Right. Now you've just given me an explanation which is
15		fairly technical.
	Teacher	Yeah.
	Michael	And it's not one that you gave them. You know that my interest is in language. So that I was interested, this morning, in what was non-verbal in what you did and what was verbal . . .
20	Teacher	No, the difference is, the difference is I had the piece of material in front of me this morning . . .
	Michael	Absolutely!
	Teacher	So I could put my words into actions and physically demonstrate what I was trying to say.
25	Michael	Yep.
	Teacher	But when you're trying to explain it technically, you've obviously got to have a little bit of an assumed knowledge. Well, you've *seen* what I done this morning, so I am assuming that you appreciate what I'm saying when I'm using technical sort
30		of jargon.

The teacher makes a clear distinction between describing and demonstrating the process of making lead slates. The deuteropraxic account is subordinated to what has already been seen of the doing. In other words, the account makes sense because it can be held referentially against a set of shared experiences. There is an important difference between talking about the process in the absence of the material and being able to put 'words into actions and physically demonstrate' what language is inadequate to show by itself. The inadequacy of language by itself to teach lead slate-making is revealed by the teacher's description. Although the description is very detailed, I doubt if we could use it to master the skills of slate-making. Remember that when the teacher was demonstrating he said, 'Make use of this hump by moving it into the centre.' That brief statement means at least as much as, if not more than, the seven 'time-binding' lines (3–10).

In the context of beating, the hump represented the boundary between stretching and reinforcing. Itself the product of stretching, the hump becomes the means of counteracting 'for the stresses that are involved' in having stretched the material elsewhere. Such complicated formulations are unnecessary in context, however, where the progress of the hump and the effect of its movement in preventing fracture may be observed directly. And yet the deuteropraxic account is portrayed as useful to someone who has already seen the skill performed or attempted to perform it. Olson and Bruner assert that such accounts are 'indeed powerful . . . as a summary of experience' by serving as 'pointers from which experience is progressively assimilated'. Thus the teacher's detailed description may be helpful to learners who have tried to beat lead slates because it elaborates their understanding of what is occurring in the piece of lead sheet. It may help them to relate their intellectual grasp of what they are doing to the feel of the thing. The detailed description may heighten awareness of the critical features by drawing attention to them in an increasingly elaborated and abstracted fashion which is precisely what the teacher did earlier when he explained the effect of spit in joint-wiping.

The learning of practical skills in workshops is achieved through a marriage of direct contingent experience, observation and instruction. Instructional acts aim to create awareness of critical alternatives in the processes and of critical features in materials. Language functions as one element in these complex acts. Its principal role is to initiate and maintain joint attention to salient features in the broader context of action. Often, however, this function is as well performed by deliberate gesture or simply by doing. Language is, therefore, powerful by virtue of its economy in workshop teaching but learning does not stand or fall by the quality of language exclusively. In this sense, the model of learning processes in the workshop, *vis-à-vis* language, is very similar to that proposed for early language development by Bruner[4] (1979), which emphasizes the communicative intent of participants realised through joint action and joint reference in a meaningful context. The alerting, planning and summarizing functions of language contribute an important dimension to instructional strategies in the broader meaning-making system represented by the workshop. Through an efficient process of identifying relevant alternatives, language participates in the structuring of a complex invitation to learners to perceive and to accept the relevance of certain skills, and to pour themselves intentionally into the subsidiary awareness of particulars instrumental to the performance of those skills. Perhaps the importance of language will diminish as learners approach their objective of skilful performance, as they move unconsciously to pick up 'the rules of the art'. But language will continue to function as a useful element in the conscious shaping of experiences from which learners may create for themselves a powerful shape for the unconscious knowledge of appropriate practical skills.

Notes and References

1. M. Polanyi, *Personal Knowledge*, Routledge and Kegan Paul, London, 1962.
2. A. Garner, *Tom Fobble's Day*, Fontana Lions, London, 1979.
3. D.R. Olson, and J. Bruner, 'Learning Through Experience and Learning Through Media', in *Media and Symbols*, edited by D.R. Olson, National Society for the Study of Education, Chicago, 1974.
4. J. Bruner: 'From Communication to Language — A psychological perspective' in *Language Development*, edited by Victor Lee, Croom Helm, Open University, London, 1979.

16.
Contemporary Developments in the Public Assessment of English

Keith Kimberley

In the classroom, assessment is primarily related to the learning of individuals or groups. It is the means by which the teacher decides what to do next, by which the student is able to check how things are going, and by which parents get some information on their children's progress[1]. This is not to deny that teachers also use assessment for purposes of social control nor that use is made of school assessment procedures to grade and select students for differential treatment. My main point, however, is that the central role of assessment in school is to provide shared understandings between teacher and student and these understandings are mediated through a considerable variety of situations, formal and informal.

By contrast, public assessment of English has a very different centre. It has functions which go far beyond describing, for the benefit of the student, what he or she can do, functions which are deeply embedded in the structure of society. It requires for its operation the labour of teachers and a professional caste of examiners and administrators. The considerable logistical and financial arrangements involved are subject to market forces. The content and structures are subject to control by government.

It should perhaps first be acknowledged that there is a great variety of mechanisms for dividing up the population in relation to their future prospects which operate *outside* the public assessment systems. It is clear, for example, that employers and those who guard entry into post-compulsory education often by-pass, or disregard, the handful of assorted certificates that applicants carry in their bags and pockets, and do this on the basis of criteria not available to public scrutiny[2]. Nor is there a straight-forward relationship between what certification gives evidence of and the way in which 'users'[3] of certificates regard them. It is common for a grade boundary (GCE O level Grade C/D for example) to be used as a 'qualification' cut-off point despite the known inaccuracies of such grading[4] and irrespective of the range of differentiated attainments and abilities that such a crude grading may represent.

Public assessment of students at 16-plus is not seen primarily as of benefit to the student. Both systems like GCE O Level and CSE, which are fully established, and those like TVEI and CPVE, which are in the process of evolution, have as their central function the differentiation of the students who have taken courses based on their syllabuses and thus of sorting and grading people for their various career destinations — including unemployment. Students are continually exhorted to strive to get the best for themselves but the grading and sorting is done primarily in the interests òf the economy rather than their immediate personal benefit. The assessment systems provide *justification* for subsequent divisions, established for the vast majority of the population by their having taken (or even by not having taken) some form of examination at 16.

This function of differentiating the population one from another at 16 is performed with varying degrees of arbitrariness and approximation; some systems accumulate evidence across long stretches of time while others confine judgement to an end-of-course timed test; some have a highly competitive base involving the grading of students relative to each other and aim for a high degree of comparability between subjects and others assess according to publicly agreed external standards or criteria. Existing systems consist of a mixture of several of these elements.

In addition to this function, public assessment systems effectively define the school curriculum[5]. This is usually seen as a desirable feature of examinations in that they offer a means of keeping a check on both what is being taught and the efficiency with which it is being taught. Additionally, new examinations offer the opportunity to change the curriculum from outside schools.[6]

The policy of the present government is expressed in terms of changing the traditional balance of central and local influence over the curriculum and, logically, sees the examination system as a crucial site for extending central control. In its editorial on the speech given in January 1984 to the North of England Educational Conference in Sheffield by Sir Keith Joseph, *The Times Educational Supplement* commented that,

> the whole of the examination exercise is about redefining — and curbing — the curriculum. Sir Keith and his advisers hold that the key to higher standards is a narrower, more clearly defined, curriculum controlled by the agreements which are reflected in the criteria.[7]

Such moves are in keeping with the traditional relationship between examinations and the secondary school curriculum. What is new in the proposal is that the assessment objectives *implicit* within examination boards' procedures, and made muddy by the additional complication of the grade boundary defining negotiations which they engage in each year to decide how many candidates their statistical data will allow them to push up or down, should be made *explicit*, defined more tightly and thus provide the criteria against which individual students can be judged, thereby avoiding the need for the whole business of judging one student against another.[8] None of this appears to change the situation greatly for students and their teachers. The essential elements remain unaltered: the curriculum will be determined outside the school with the likely consequence that it will constitute the fourth- and fifth-year course which the students and teachers will follow.

These twin functions performed by public assessment of *differentiating students* one from another and *controlling the curriculum* are central to the issues which this paper seeks to address in relation to the assessment of English. Central questions appear to be:

1. What resolution can there be of the student's need to present information about him or herself without being differentiated, despite the complexity of the evidence, in terms of crudely simplistic grades?
2. What degree of centralized agreement over the curriculum acts beneficially for the student, teacher and society alike? Or, to put it another way, what degree of interference and specification operates as a straitjacket which, by its rigidity, precludes the engagement of students and teachers in the very processes which generate high levels of achievement?

Two related strands will be pursued: the future of examinations at 16-plus and current LEA enthusiasm for 'graded tests'.

Examinations at 16-plus

It seems, with hindsight, a remarkable feature of the Certificate of Secondary Education (CSE) system that there was achieved, within its framework, a flexible means of:

*   exploring and debating in whose interests a student was being assessed;[9]
*   investigating and extending the nature of the evidence gathered and the means used to assess students in relation to their language performance;
*   rethinking the curriculum of the last years of compulsory schooling.

Work on the Certificate of Extended Education (CEE) in the early Seventies developed these possibilities further but the test bed for new ideas was, from the outset, to be found in the school-based Mode 3s, where the course could be constructed with a view to the school's particular situation and *before* deciding on examination procedures.

As the principle which seems to be implied in the present Secretary of State's policy with relation to examination at 16 is that the curriculum defined centrally should lead to assessment, it may be worth considering CSE experience as offering an alternative view from that of tightly maintained central control, though not from the idea of curriculum-led assessment. Certainly the shifting of the centre of gravity away from narrowness of curriculum and approach owes a very great deal to the framework of teacher participation set up for the CSE and in particular to the work done by practising teachers in syllabus construction on advisory panels and in the context of their own schools. Coincidental with this shift was a raising of expectation of what students of all abilities can become interested in and can achieve in terms of understanding and expression.

Despite both the, then, prevailing behaviourist psychology and the preoccupation of English teachers of the period with O and A level, CSE English was established on the basis that language performance should be assessed across a *wide range* of *interdependent* skills with full respect given to the *contexts* and *purposes* in and for which language is used. The alternative model of assessment, then rejected, was one which takes as its basic assumption that skills in language can be separately and precisely defined and then tested by arbitrary and limited sampling taken under conditions from which motive and context for their use have been eliminated.

By contrast, CSE English syllabuses, broadly speaking, can be seen to stand for a shift in English assessment priorities from a narrow range of test items (essay, comprehension, précis, standing for wider competencies in 'English Language', for example) to attempts to sample performance across a wide range of language use — a similar approach later being adopted by the Assessment of Performance Unit for its own distinct purposes. Development work in CSE since then has, however many fits and starts it may have suffered, rightly become the source of guidelines for examination reform at 16-plus. In the proposals of the Joint Boards[10], for example, there is a major role for the use of course work as a means of assessment both in relation to written performance and response to literature[11]. Further, whatever Black Paperites have urged to the contrary, CSE Mode 3s, though fully involving teachers in an initiating role, have not given teachers unbridled freedom any more than the use of Joint Matriculation Board's O level Syllabus D (100 per cent course work) has meant that standards have been lowered at O level. In practice, both exercises have been subject to a high degree of inspection with justifications for content and method of assessment having to be made clearly explicit. Both have involved the development of criteria against which performance could be assessed in the form of descriptions of what is expected at each grade level. Both have involved both the teachers and examination boards in developing a high level of professionalism.

At this point, it may be helpful to look more closely at present government policy as outlined in Sir Keith Joseph's Sheffield speech[12]. This, as suggested above, appears to shift some of the ground that has hitherto been taken for granted by government and the examination boards (if not by teachers), that it is essential for students to be differentiated *relative to each other* (that is by the norm-referencing procedures currently used by the 16-plus examination boards) and also that it is the government's intention to bring

> 80–90 per cent of all pupils *at least* to the level now associated with CSE Grade 4, i.e. *at least* to the level now expected and achieved by pupils of average ability in individual subjects.[13]

The Secretary of State hopes this will be brought about through the partnership between teachers, parents, governing bodies, LEAs and the government, 'each performing their proper role in response to the needs of the pupils and of the country as a whole'.[14] What he is concerned to assert is the 'proper concern' of each of these parties and he is careful not to privilege teachers. Those of us with a more optimistic view of teachers' professionalism, and of local government, may feel that his approach conversely privileges central government. We might ask whether there may be greater advantages to be gained by trusting teachers, governors, parents and LEAs to the extent proposed in the Second Report of the Select Committee on Science, Education and the Arts, where it is suggested that an explicit statement of a school's curricular aims made public in the community has a greater chance of meeting the needs of a changing plural society than central directives on the curriculum[15].

But does this mean, I hear you saying, that students will be assessed on what they, individually, can do and that the tyranny of the GCE boards is at last to be broken? The answers appear to be 'yes' and 'no' respectively. On the first, the Secretary of State is quite definite:

> Much excellent and committed work goes into the preparation and teaching of our examination system. Unfortunately the system does not enable us to measure what candidates can do.[16]

There is, as always, a sting in the tail. The passage continues with,

> because it does not set absolute standards of competence, skill and understanding which pupils of different abilities are expected to attain.[17]

Thus we have recognition of the need to remove the ludicrous competitive element but the price to be paid is in centrally agreed 'grade-related criteria' which are perceived as '*absolute standards*'.

On the second point, the speech throws up the following elucidation of the Secretary of State's intention:

> For example, it entails the objective that in any subject far more pupils than at present should reach the level of knowledge and skill now associated generally with an O level Grade C, *on the basis that this level will be fully maintained*.[18]

The last phrase is glossed elsewhere in more general terms:

> By comparison with 20 years ago, our schools are offering more pupils a broader education, and a larger proportion of pupils are successful in examinations at 16-plus. In all this, the level of attainment associated with an O level pass has been maintained. It needs to be maintained in future. We have a good base for scaling greater heights.[19]

So should we put out flags of welcome for the Secretary of State's initiative? I suspect not too many and not too soon. The proposals, while seeking to raise the achievements of the majority and showing a remarkable realism about the difficulties which teachers face in the classroom, do not seem likely in practice to reduce the élitist nature of the system, while A level stays unaltered and the domination of the GCE O level boards is maintained.

A brief look at some of the elements in the relationship between central government and the examination system may be helpful here in providing the wider context within which to view the evolution that is taking place at 16-plus. At the time of writing, the long-standing question of whether to bring together the CSE and GCE examinations into a single system is still not resolved and, interestingly, the Secretary of State sees his initiative as required regardless of whether it is decided to 'merge' or to 'harmonize' O levels and CSE.

This muted approach to 16-plus reorganization is in keeping with the decision of Mark Carlisle, when he was Secretary of State, to give responsibility for the top grades to the GCE examination boards in any common system of examining, thereby re-stating in a slightly different form the relationship in which CSE was from the outset tied to its GCE overlord. This sought to prevent CSE boards developing too radical alternatives to traditional modes of examining and was based on two false assumptions: that the 'narrow' experience of CSE boards prevented them from understanding what is involved in assessing the work of the most able and that the shifts in curricular priorities and examining techniques which were pioneered within the CSE framework had less to offer a new system than the largely unchanging methods of the GCE boards. In spite of the achievements discussed above, some of this thinking evidently persists since otherwise the experience of the CSE boards in gathering positive evidence of what students can do across a wide range of language activities would immediately recommend a merger and rule out even the possibility of the GCE boards continuing to go their own way.

Another government intervention which may give some reason for caution is to be seen in the development of subject-specific criteria by which the syllabuses of all 16-plus examinations are to be judged. This, at first glance, appears an eminently healthy and rational development and, despite earlier fears of a narrowing of English to a narrow set of behaviours, the criteria which have been developed by the Joint Council of GCE and CSE boards are written at a level of generality and common sense with which it is difficult to take much exception. They describe a subject which can include a wide variety of practice and possibilities. On the other hand, there may be significant consequences which will follow from the Joint Board's recommendation that the oral component, while compulsory, should only feature on the certificate as an endorsement. 'Users' are likely to read this as a devaluing of the oral component and a reinforcement of the written elements. There is also enshrined in the criteria the continued separation of language and literature which seems likely to maintain the separation of two kinds of students in schools. Additionally, the use of differentiated papers has been strongly recommended by the Secretary of State for 'English Literature' and is to be investigated with respect to 'English'. I suspect few English teachers will relish the implications for their practice of differentiated papers or sections of papers, though they may welcome the Secretary of State's obvious distaste for short answer and multiple-choice questions, and his important commitment to course work being part of all modes of examining.

Now that *grade-related criteria* are to be formulated for the 16-plus examinations, it looks as if teachers can expect even more close attention from central government to the details of what constitutes English. The Secondary Examinations Council[20], which has been set up by the DES to vet and monitor those examinations which fall within its terms of reference, appears to be subject to specific instruction by the Secretary of State and ultimately to have to refer its recommendations back for the Secretary of

State's approval or rejection. Thus, one way of interpreting these consecutive exercises concerning criteria is as a means of signalling DES authority over the examination system; an authority which the Secretaries of State seem to be applying to detail as well as to the broad outlines of policy.

Graded tests

The DES is, by contrast, with its close interest in the future of 16-plus assessment, lukewarm in its response to the general enthusiasm which has been generated around the 'graded test' concept. In the DES consultation document *Records of Achievement for School Leavers: a draft statement of policy*, graded tests are seen as likely to have value in some key subjects and mathematics is cited as an example (following the Cockcroft Report recommendation), but it seems that the concept is seen as limited in application to the less able. No mention was made of 'graded tests' in the Sheffield speech though the proposal for pilot projects on records of achievement is cited as an important policy objective. It may be that Sir Keith Joseph has some reluctance to get into a technical debate about the differences, theoretical and practical, between varieties of 'graded test' and assessment based on 'grade-related criteria'. The DES is clearly aware of the limitations of the application to English of the concept of a sequence of learning objectives through which students progress at their own speed:

> Pupils learning their own language do not progress through a sequence of language objectives but constantly expand and adapt familiar components of the skills of speaking, listening, writing and reading. There are in existence no graded tests in English which match up to educational need and there must be doubt about the feasibility of developing such tests. Other approaches to recording and assessing individual progress in this subject will therefore need to be investigated.[21]

For the University of Oxford Delegacy of Local Examinations and the London University Examination Board 'graded tests', however, would seem to have the attraction of enabling them to extend their interests into new areas and acquire new areas of expertise. Of the LEAs, who have initiated the developmental work, the Inner London Education Authority has expressed a determination to find answers to under-achievement, truancy and disaffection; their policy paper *2524*, describing the present examination system as incapable of giving 'a fair picture of the achievement of many pupils', and proposing that 'graded tests' should be viewed as a 'promising approach' which might become the basis for developing 'alternative and additional methods' to the present 16-plus examination system with hoped-for outcomes of better motivation, a freeing of assessment from specific age linking, and giving students a record of positive achievement[22]. On learning of Sir Keith Joseph's speech in Sheffield, Frances Morrell, leader of the ILEA, suggested he had been engaged in a systematic theft of the ILEA's idea.[23]

Tim Brighouse, the Chief Education Officer for Oxfordshire has similarly expressed hopes for the demise of even a reformed 16-plus system and favours certificated 'in the round' descriptions of what students can do, which combine 'the rigour of external validation with the assessment that comes from the flair and fizz of the outstanding teacher and the lively school'.[24]

Breathing the same heady air, Bob Moon, member of an Oxford Certificate of Educational Achievement Steering Group, summoned up a vision of the last year of compulsory education for four fictional students:

> The school no longer takes subject O levels in English Language or the arts. Each of the four has covered a programme leading to graded tests assessing a basic level of written and spoken communication. Paul has already acquired the top level, Jenny level 1 and Stephen and Louise are debating whether to attempt the one from the top.
> Paul has begun a Mode III O level-type literature course which takes him away from the group. He joins older students who have opted for this, one afternoon a week.[25]

Even in a flight of fancy 'graded tests' do not appear to have brought about the demise of the 16-plus system and the functions it at present performs. Here, following Brighouse, Bob Moon appears to see the instrumental uses to which 'users' put English Language O level being supplanted by a 'graded test' in a 'basic level of spoken and written communication'. Literature has become something you do with consenting adults in an alternative system of 'O level type examinations'! By comparison the DES proposal, may appear to the English teacher to adopt a more constructive stance:

> A list of objectives (for English teaching) which commands general support might enable teachers to appraise their pupils' progress in different modes of language, using course work rather than timed examinations as their source of evidence, on a basis which users of the record could accept as reliable.[26]

Such a procedure does not, however, retain much of either *grading* or *test* about it.

The theoretical difficulties associated with 'grading' fall into three main categories: those which concern the idea of progression in a series, with each of the stages acting as a prerequisite for the succeeding stages; those which concern the ways in which content is distributed; and those which imply a developmental theory. Goldstein and Nuttall raise some of these in a review of the technical issues for the Further Education Unit:

> Whilst almost all students are taught on a broad principle of progress, this progress is not tied to the linear development of an unvarying set of objectives and there are many different ways of progressing through the same syllabus. Mastery of the objectives at one level may therefore not be essential to the study of objectives at the next level, and graded tests could easily become simply modular tests, that is, tests on self-contained content that can be taken in any order and whose material can be forgotten without apparent penalty after the test has been taken.[27]

Studies such as David Jackson's examination of continuity and linked development in English from eleven to eighteen[28] give detailed evidence to support the view — if such support should be thought needed — that progress in English is not a simple linear development. Typically, some of the stages are marked by achievement in a specific context while others, especially those concerned with process, are realized in a more diffuse manner.

It remains to be seen what is to be proposed for English under the heading, 'test'; whether, for instance, the term may be used to cover a wide range of procedures which could include the sampling of a student's work or whether the interpretation will be narrowed down by means of narrowly defined objectives. In a recent foray into this territory, Keohane proposed *proficiency* tests in English and maths in addition to the CSE subjects taken[29]. Though now shelved, it is difficult to see how this proposal would have resulted in much more than tests of grammar, spelling, punctuation and layout.

Tests of this narrow kind find some favour with students because of the limited demands made and, similarly, there are teachers who find security in narrowly defined objectives. On the other hand, such arrangements would be likely to encourage teaching for the test and discourage the raising of levels of expectation of what all students can achieve. Much of the success with students in their last year of compulsory education which has been achieved by English teachers[30] can be seen to derive from their opening up of the whole field of language and the experience of literature to students from across the whole ability range and a reluctance to separate out students in terms of their 'basic level of spoken and written communication'. In the words of a submission to the ILEA Working Party on Graded Testing by Kidbrooke School English Department,

> Our O level English results are proof that students benefit from working in a

situation where expectations are maintained at the highest level for all children as long as possible; children who are written off by failure in tests give up.[31]

Theoretically, tests which can be taken at the right moment for the individual student should be attractive to teachers committed to individualized learning. In practice, they know the devastating effect on the expectations of Bob Moon's Jenny once she realizes that she is confined to stage 1. It is also worth noting that the HMI report on graded objectives in modern languages in Oxfordshire showed up the difficulty of organizing testing to suit individuals:

> On the whole, however, it tends to be confined to the less able pupils who all take the test at the same time. Even where groups have this measure of homogeneity it is clear that some pupils are being faced with too easy a test which for others is still too difficult.[32]

The English teacher's concern with negotiating a series of routes for individual students through the full range of uses of language is made in the knowledge that the students come bringing considerable linguistic resources. The teacher's job is seen to be to stretch, extend, and introduce new possibilities. In this context, students need regular, positive feedback but are also aware that the ultimate objectives are long-term ones of autonomy in relation to their reading, writing and talking. It is perhaps crucially in terms of expectation that the contrast between assessment of attainment in a first language and assessment of a language learned during secondary education is at its greatest. As seems to have been recognized at the DES, a test of communicative competence in a modern language after a number of terms of classroom study[33] is a very different matter from the assessment of all-round attainment in a language which has been spoken with virtually full communicative competence from around the age of five and written and read with increasing proficiency thereafter. Graded tests in English might, if the same model were followed, be very limited and limiting. In the English classroom, genuine communicative situations can be established at the drop of a hat. It remains to be seen how any 'graded test' in English could be used to assess, in its richness, what students can do with the language they encounter and have at their disposal.

On the other hand, some elements which are to be found in contemporary 'graded test' discussions are already part of good assessment practices and might well be extended. Chief amongst these is the recognition of the central importance of giving positive feedback in the day-to-day transactions that take place in the classroom, reflecting back positive achievements being made, both short- and long-term. In the best English classrooms there is a core of informal student-teacher negotiation which involves making expectations and criteria for success explicit. There is also development work being undertaken by English teachers in schools and Communications teachers in FE with respect to 'negotiated assessment' in which the student has a say in setting the goals to be reached. Some of these arrangements have been given a quasi-contractual basis — though this may be a more realistic proposition in colleges of further education than in schools. 'Negotiated assessment', by making explicit both the intentions of the student and the expectations of the teacher, gives the student an increasing control over his/her learning.

There can be similar student involvement in the selection of a portfolio of work at the level of selection and in jointly evolving criteria for selection. The gathering together of written work and, if feasible, its oral equivalent, provides a focus for student self-assessment as well as enabling a student to show development over time for external moderation. As indicated above, the use of a selection of specific items of evidence, suitably moderated, has substantial development work behind it in the CSE and JMB Syllabus D traditions where the practical difficulties of administering course work moderation in the 16-plus system have been largely overcome. A positive alternative to the 16-plus would necessarily draw on this work, combining it perhaps with a full descriptive statement of a student's language performance. The immediate priority seems to lie in suggesting ways of describing or presenting what students can do which are both flexible and precise, which reflect positive achievements over a wide range of interdependent skills and in which assessment remains close to students' intentions and in the contexts in which language is put to use.

Conclusion

History is ever with us. The debates on public assessment of the early Sixties centred on how assessment could be made available to a wider cross-section of the ability range and new life breathed into an inadequate curriculum. Then, too, there was much discussion of the means required to enable teachers to take on the job of teaching with enthusiasm and enable the students to have a sense of their achievements.

The ferment within the DES, the examination boards, and the LEAs which we are witnessing now has a similar focus but, if history has any lessons for us, we should not be too optimistic that a new dawn is beginning when assessment will be seen to follow rather than determine the curriculum and when assessment will function first and foremost in the interests of the student. In 1965 the consequence of failing to reform GCE O level was that the CSE certificate, despite the curriculum development it spearheaded, was limited in value, particularly in the lower grades. 'Graded tests' may also become irretrievably linked with those of lower ability. Similarly, the future 16-plus examination system, whether 'merged' or 'harmonized' will still remain interwoven with the traditional, narrowly academic A level system; though the 16-plus of 1985 and thereafter will be operating alongside a new set of separately controlled forms of assessment and certification for pre-vocational courses (TVEI/CPVE).

I hope we will have learned some lessons from history. It would be a great pity if we were to lose the ground won by the Mode 3 pioneers and allowed the formulation of national criteria for English to cause us to forget that teachers in their schools or groups of schools were able to make their criteria explicit responsibly at a local level. Provided explicit statements about the curriculum are made by the school to the LEA, the parents and the community, there seems little reason for having other than the very broadest of national guidelines. In a different climate of political priorities, a nation-wide extension of the Mode 3 principle might, with appropriate safeguards, look both desirable and feasible.

Similarly, the hard-won knowledge of how children's language develops over time must not be displaced by the behaviourist model rejected once before. Somewhere behind the moves for 'graded tests' and 'criterion-referencing' lies a desire to achieve certainty about complex processes by pre-specifying precise objectives and by not specifying at all in areas which are not easily reduced to simple formulae. The complexities of the competencies involved in the use of language must be kept in the public mind.

At an abstract level, the '16-plus' and 'graded tests' have a tendency to coalesce. 'What constitutes the subject English at the end of compulsory schooling?' can be rewritten as 'What can an able student do with language?'. Both are in a sense public questions and the answers are in large measure defined by the need for students to meet society's demands. The second also has a developmental history: for 'less able' we also read 'less mature', 'less experienced'. I think the implications of this are twofold:

1.   There is as yet no public agreement on what constitutes English beyond the Joint Board's criteria. The government intends that there shall be. At a level of specification less general than the existing criteria, there will be disagreement and a battle for definitions.

2.   The 'graded test' exercise has revealed, what most teachers knew already, that we have no 'simple' developmental theory which can support syllabus design and assessment. We do have, however, a great

deal of complex knowledge of the processes involved which needs to be shared more widely.

Public examinations are maintained by an ideology which defines its functioning as concerned with 'standards' while playing down its role in the maintenance of social divisions. The operation of examining boards is portrayed as unproblematic, consisting of the use of supposedly objective measures in whose rigour and fairness the public can have confidence, the myths of objectivity, reliability and comparability being the stock-in-trade of both examination professionals and central government[34]. Thus, at a time of great competition for employment and places in further education, it is convenient to be able to assert that decisions of exclusion are based on judgements external to the schools tied to rigorously defined, even *absolute* standards, and that the whole business of examining is being kept strictly under review by the Secretary of State.

Notes and References

1. For an analysis of school-based assessment of English see A. Stibbs, *Assessing Children's Language*, Ward Lock, London, 1979.
2. An instructive example of this use of hidden criteria, in this case at A level, was reported in *The Times Educational Supplement* of 15 September 1983. Gail Marshall, hoping to read English at Keble College, Oxford, applied by the entrance exam and interview route only to find herself rejected despite A grades at A level in English, French, RE and General Studies, and a B grade in History. The Warden of Keble commented, 'We believe our entrance examinations are a better indication of suitability than A levels. Gail was a very able candidate but not as able as her competitors', backing this up with the comment that the interview enables the college to see behind the layer of 'special coaching'. Gail's parents saw her lack of 'special coaching' and her comprehensive school's lack of hidden links with Oxford as easier explanations of the unfairness. The implication of the Warden's pronouncement is that those with high grades in English and related subjects at A level have been force-fed with academic skills and knowledge behind which Keble must look for further indications of ability! They operate, that is to say, on criteria other than ability in English as defined by what gets grade A at A level.

   An example of by-passing evidence of students' general educational achievements at 16-plus increasingly can be seen in the use by employers of YTS schemes as a means of selecting likely employees.
3. There is some irony in the term 'user' as employed within examination circles. The interests of the 'user' of examinations are often cited as of critical importance and myths created about their wishes for particular kinds of evidence, assessment procedures and reporting on results. Students, teachers and parents

are *not* 'users' of exams.

4. Schools Council, *Standards in Public Examinations: Problems and possibilities*, 1980.

5. HMI, *Aspects of Secondary Education in England and Wales*, HMSO, 1979. The HMI revealed that many schools in their survey had no syllabuses other than examination syllabuses in years 4 and 5. The HMI did not call for a major reappraisal of the structure of the present system.

6. The 'backwash' effect of the CSE exams in 1965 was to throw into relief the inadequacies of the existing curricula of secondary schools and to suggest new content and emphasis. For English teachers it legitimized the use of a wider range of literary texts and kinds of written expression.

7. *The Times Educational Supplement*, 13 January 1984.

8. DES Press Notice 1/84, 6 January 1984.

9. This has been particularly noticeable in debates within advisory panels and in discussion with examination committees about Mode 3 and new or revised syllabuses. That these could on occasions raise issues of principle, rather than technical issues concerning examining techniques, was demonstrated by the resignation of the Metropolitan Regional Examination Board's Chief Examiner for English on the occasion of the rejection by the Examination Committee of the English Advisory Panel's proposal for a Syllabus B which it was thought would, because of its increased course work component, be a more positive way of enabling candidates.

10. Joint Boards representing GCE and CSE interests have produced proposals for English in a common system of exams and, in some parts of the country, pilot schemes under existing regulations are well established.

11. For a full account of these principles and developments see M. Raleigh, *English Exams at 16*, London Association for the Teaching of English, 1980.

12. DES Press Notice 1/84, 6 January 1984.

13. Ibid.

14. Ibid.

15. Select Committee on Science, Education and the Arts, *Second Report: The Secondary School Curriculum and Examinations*, HMSO, London, 1982. 'The public statement would be the basis for a regular process of self-assessment by the school which we believe would generate a dynamic rather than a static curriculum.' (p. xxxii)

16. DES Press Notice 1/84, 6 January 1984.

17. Ibid.

18. Ibid.

19. Ibid.

20. The Secondary Examinations Council, a DES-nominated body, was set up in 1983 as a consequence of the separation of the Schools Council's curriculum and examinations functions.

21. DES, *Records of Achievement for School Leavers: A draft statement of policy*. DES consultative document, 1983.

22. ILEA, *2524*, October 1982, p. 7.
23. *The Times Educational Supplement*, 13 January 1984.
24. *Education*, 24/31 December 1982.
25. *The Times Educational Supplement*, 17 June 1983.
26. DES op. cit., 21.
27. H. Goldstein and D. Nuttall, *Profiles and Graded Tests: The Technical Issues*, Further Education Curriculum Review and Development Unit, Department of Education and Science, 1983.
28. D. Jackson, *Continuity in Secondary English*, Methuen, London, 1982.
29. DES, *Proposal for a Certificate of Extended Education*, HMSO, London, 1979.
30. The interim report of the ILEA working party set up by the Chief Inspector (Schools) 'to evaluate the nature and forms of assessment in English investigating the feasibility of using graded tests as part of the process of developing pupil profiles', notes that '16-year-olds in the ILEA, through their own and their teachers' efforts, are doing a great deal better out of the present system than they were intended to when it was set up'.
31. Kidbrooke School English Department submission to the ILEA English Working Party on Graded Tests.
32. DES, *Survey of Modern Languages Graded Tests, Oxfordshire*, HMSO, London, 1983.
33. DES, op. cit., n. 21; also A. Harrison, *Graded Objectives and Tests for Modern Languages: An evaluation*, Schools Council, London, 1982.
34. For a discussion of the issues of comparability, reliability, objectivity and validity see Raleigh, op. cit., n. 11.

17
Talking About Television

Bob Ferguson, Phillip Drummond and Manuel Alvarado

TV is strong on talk. It is the medium of 'chat-shows' where we are spectators of its talk, it is the medium of news-programmes where it talks directly to us. It is the medium of 'talking-heads'. The dominance of sound, and in particular dialogue, on television may be reinforced by the nature of the televisual image, less sophisticated than its cinematic counterpart; the 'flow' of television ensures that this vocality remains unbroken. Television's powers of social speech are open to a number of interpretations. One reading follows metaphorical interpretations of the status of the medium by regarding television, with McLuhan, as an extension of the central nervous system in its various appetites and drives. A politically determinist interpretation would on the other hand prefer to follow Althusser in defining television as a major agency for achieving social consensus and hegemony through the specific powers of discursive practice, television as the eminently acceptable voice of State.

Whichever of these lines is chosen, a number of underlying features of the medium are at once apparent. First, television is a 'language system' not only in terms of verbal 'speech' but in terms of the broader linguistic features — for instance visual and narrative structures — which shape its output. Second, the 'language system' of television, like any other, does not merely 'reflect' a given world transparently or 'realistically', but contributes to the construction or expression of that world through processes of mediation. Third, it would appear that, on the whole, television prefers to see itself as a one-way system of communication, speaking *to*, but rarely speaking *with*, its addressees. Fourth, television rarely speaks about itself, does not in a developed sense reflect upon the very fact of its own pre-eminence in the arena of social speaking, the closure of its own monologic form, or the mediating tendencies of its preferred stylistic and structural protocols.

How then can we develop a response to the talk of television, and to the positionality from which it speaks? Specifically, how can we develop an educational rationale and strategy for such a form of dialogue, within the framework of a broad curriculum commitment to what we might call Television or Media Studies in the widest sense? Our answer here is offered through specific reference to a recent case of popular attention to television, the June 1983 DES Report *Popular TV and Schoolchildren*. This Report, though small-scale, nonetheless provided current views on the social role of television for young people in the schooling age range, and hence on the potential relationships between the discourses of television and of education. It also generated considerable cross-talk between the various media themselves, offering extremely valuable evidence of the way the press in particular would wish to speak about TV and about education. It is this triangular set of discourses — TV, the press, education — that we speak to here.

Commissioned by the Secretary of State for Education and Science, HM Inspectorate convened a group of fifteen teachers to study 'the values and images of adult life' presented in a series of popular television programmes over a five-week period March-April 1982. The group concentrated on four categories of programme: drama (*Crossroads, Dallas, The Dukes of Hazzard, Hill Street Blues, McClain's Law, Minder, We'll Meet Again*); light entertainment (*Emery, Family Fortunes, The Gaffer, The Glamour Girls, The Kenny Everett Show, Mind Your Language, Shelley, Top of the Pops, Whoops Apocalypse*); news and current affairs (BBC and ITN news broadcasts, *Nationwide, Panorama, World in Action*) and science/features (*Tomorrow's World, Police*). Three main issues arise. First, the Report comments upon popular preoccupations with the representation of sexuality, and of violent behaviour, on TV. No conclusions are drawn about the latter, but it is wondered whether the repeated representations of violence lose their capacity to shock, or even develop an appetite for more, whilst with regard to sexuality the group was less worried with the notion of over-explicitness than with general exploitativeness in the attempt to attract large audiences, or to secure an easy laugh (particularly in the case of *The Kenny Everett Show*).

Second, the Report is concerned with notions of 'identification' between young people and screen-characters and personalities, particularly where attitudes towards authority and the status quo are concerned. Anxiety is expressed about a disparate range of tendencies: anarchic definitions of heroism; restricted definitions of 'success'; confusing representations of

Law and Disorder; 'antagonistic' rather then 'diagonal' representations
of debate within news and current affairs, and somewhat cynical representations of politics and politicians. The Report's third area of concern covers
representations of social groups. Here a number of social groupings are seen
to be under-represented, or represented more fully but unfairly — old
people, the handicapped, the unemployed, ethnic minorities and foreigners
to this country. The changing position of women, the positive aspects of
marriage, and the interests of the regions were, in a mixed bag, equally seen
to be undervalued by the medium.

There is much that should be welcomed in the Report, particularly in
terms of its openness to debate, the ideological acuity of many of its insights,
and its strong institutional understanding of the need for specialist training
in co-operation between the broadcasters and the educators. We whole-
heartedly agree that

> There is an undoubted need for arrangements at appropriate levels to enable pro-
> gramme makers, teachers and parents to explore together their different but
> related responsibilities in understanding better the impact of television upon the
> young and seeking to ensure that it is a positive constructive influence

and that, going further still,

> specialist courses in media studies are not enough; all teachers should be
> involved in examining and discussing television programmes with young people.

On the whole, we take the Report as a progressive contribution of a formal
kind to educational discourse about TV.

We would also wish to register certain reservations. The programme-
sample, while intriguingly eclectic, is highly selective, and the period of the
research restricted. The method of analysis, too, is not clearly explicated, in
terms of the nature of the questionnaire applied and the relative assessment
of teachers'/pupils' views. There is correspondingly a discrepancy between
direct evaluation in the area of TV fiction, often based upon the conjectural
framework of psychological realism and consensual moralism, and the treatment of TV news and current affairs, where a more complex consciousness
of both television protocol and audience-participation in the decoding
process is apparent. Underlying this unevenness, and perhaps traceable in
the Report's somewhat jumbled structuring, is a revealing tension between
conservative and more radical tendencies — the former fuelling anxieties
over the representations of authority and status quo, the latter energizing the
Report's concern with the inadequate depiction of minority and oppressed
social fractions in the institution of TV.[1]

The complexity of the Report described above might have left it a minority document had it not been for the overarching discourses of the other organs of the media, in particular the press, which caught up the Report in a front-page furore that on the one hand obscured the range of issues under debate and, on the other, redefined the debate in ways which pose fresh problems for studies of the media and for attempts to transform the terms in which we talk of television. Here, the press emerges as the essential public translator of a specialist Report for an audience who will almost certainly never see the original. The voice of that translator, we shall be suggesting, was itself confused, alternately accommodating and aggressive, as it sought both to take its distance from, yet profit from proximity to, the world of television; or rather, aspects of the world of television selected and reduced from the broader perspectives of the Report.

Scandal is the keynote of reports on the Report, scandal focusing on the attempted corruption of the young, a corruption with two nuclei: sex and violence. In certain cases — for example, the *Daily Mirror* (22 June 1983) — it is possible to link the two with a word calculated to attract both the prudish and the potentially corruptible, 'smut': thus the front-page headline: 'SEX, SMUT AND VIOLENCE. CHILDREN ARE BEING CORRUPTED BY TV SHOWS'. Here the reader is offered both potential indignation, and potential titillation, an ambiguity narrowed down by the nature of the more detailed story following on a later page. Here a photograph of the comedian Kenny Everett is spread across three columns, accompanied by the caption in letters over an inch high: 'KENNY'S NAUGHTY BITS "ARE JUST CHEAP SMUT" '. The quotation-marks within the captions are significant indicators of the *Mirror's* eventual distance from the findings of the Report; the photograph, as we shall see, is calculated to outrage or delight, depending upon the position of the reader. There is no unitary discourse at work here. Instead, we would want to argue, a range of optional meanings is offered, which is designed to draw together and unite readers of the *Mirror* as, precisely, readers of the *Mirror*.

The photographic image shows Everett with a semi-clad girl seated on either side of him in a large cane chair which places their breasts on his eyeline. He has his nose and eyes buried in the brassiered left breast of the girl on his right; the girl on his left wears no brassiere, but her black fishnet stockings and suspender belt are prominent. The *Mirror's* caption reads: 'EYES DOWN: Kenny enjoying the fun with a pair of shapely helpers'. Seen in isolation, such a caption suggests that the *Mirror* is a paper which values the readership of sexists and lovers of the bawdy over that of anti-sexists or moralists, but seen in the context of the paper's moral outrage, it also presents its message with a confidence in the retention of ideological equilibrium and consensus.

The brief article which accompanies the image provides several examples of sketches from Everett's shows plus information illustrating the criticisms offered by the writers of the Report. We are told that the Report says: 'The obsession with women's bodies and the reliance on sexual innuendo to get quick laughs reflected overall a degrading and offensive attitude to women.' The *Mirror* adds:

> This sketch could qualify for that description. A starlet called Cupid Stunt is interviewed by a cut-out picture of Michael Parkinson. She says she is making a sequel to E.T. It's called T.I.T.

The puzzle for the reader of the paper could be one of identifying just what is being implied about the Report and television in general. There are clear contradictions between the scandal reported in the headline and what can only be described as journalistic cynicism in the presentation of the Report. The emphasis throughout is on sex viewed in terms of a traditional chauvinistic sexism, rather than on violence. There is no overt praise or condemnation of the Report but there is more than a tacit acceptance of Everett as good bawdy fun for discriminating adults, even if it might be unsuitable for younger viewers.

Other newspaper responses to the Report were more outspoken and some carried editorial comment. There was not, as one might have expected, support for the concern of the teachers over the declining standards which television viewing may be causing. The TV Editor of the *Daily Express*, James Murray, said (23 June 1983) that the authors had confused education and entertainment. He then redirected the arguments about media influence towards the schools themselves:

> There is a striking absence in this latest teachers' report of any analysis of school influences on children's behaviour.

For Murray, programmes like *Dallas* are 'hokum', and 'Everybody — even youngsters — enjoys a rich slice of hokum.' Phrases such as 'this latest teachers' report' and 'a rich slice of hokum' position Mr Murray's discourse somewhere between disparagement of prudery and amazement at the *naïveté* of teachers faced with the everyday enjoyments of everybody, including youngsters. What he does emphasize as an important factor in relation to media influence is the 'copycat effect', which he claims, without evidence, was alarmingly demonstrated by the 'riots' of 1981. He is concerned about a programme which showed the swallowing and regurgitation of a live fish, but the different 'effects' of Kenny Everett do not bother him.

He points out that children love inventing jokes about 'chamber pots and tinkles', and would presumably see little difference between this and the 'fun' of representing a woman with the aggressive Spoonerism of 'Cupid Stunt'. The discourse of the *Daily Express* is very similar to that of the *Mirror*. It is a defence of the complex but utterly tolerable status quo in the face of moralizing, self-righteous educators who do not inhabit the real world and are less and less capable of looking after 'unruly schoolchildren' who are, after all, potential rioters.

The final example we wish to consider is the editorial of the *Daily Telegraph* (22 June 1983), which offers a dazzling display of fundamental contradictions insidiously overlaid by reason. It begins, in a familiar stratagem, by appealing to all thinkers to identify themselves by agreeing with the case on offer. The first brief paragraph dismisses the possibility that television is likely to turn children into sex maniacs and gangsters in favour of television as producer of deadened minds. The criteria which establish the relationship between sex, violence, television and deadened minds are not enumerated. The Report is, however, allowed a modicum of unexceptionability by its occasional attainment of the level of 'common sense'. Its authors are, nonetheless, identified as authoritarian prigs who are 'not a lot less dangerous than the sex and violence we all deplore.' They think, says the editorial, that women should not be 'flawless ornaments, beautifully attired and always decorative'. They are further described as conservative and yet subversive, anti-materialists, who hold 'anti-capitalist' notions.

About Kenny Everett the editorial has the following to say:

> The sexual innuendo of the hapless Mr. Kenny Everett makes them flush like maiden aunts, as would, one suspects, the jokes of Mr. George Robey.

It has to be said that the signifiers with which Everett operates, including the wearing of a wig and an enormous false front with breasts which rear above the plunging neckline, could not be construed as constituting mere 'innuendo'. Nor, by any etymological standards, could Everett be called 'hapless'. The *Telegraph's* language serves the purpose of glossing over the weakness of the arguments put forward. The reference to 'maiden aunts' is not so much imprecise as doubly sexist. The invocation of George Robey is ambiguous. One is not clear whether it would be good for the authors of the Report to hear a few of George Robey's jokes or whether the *Telegraph* is saying: 'if you think Kenny Everett is bad, you should hear George Robey!' But the likelihood remains that, in effect, George Robey is regarded by the *Telegraph* as an established and reputable sexist and racist comedian who could teach both authors and Everett a thing or two.

We have dwelt at length upon the way the dailies addressed the Report because the case illustrates the skewing of important if tentative educational initiatives by another powerful medium. That medium, we are suggesting, serves its own interests in creating, through its chosen speech-acts, another kind of audience to witness its discussion of the world of television. It is this 'greater power' — fuelled by half-grasped alarm over, on the one hand, assumptions about the rise of social permissiveness, and, on the other, by the increasing multiplication of media delivery-systems such as video and cable — that must additionally be addressed, we are then arguing, since it would have been these very misreportings which made up the mass readership's grasp of the Report, not only in relation to television, but to education too. (The 'educational' press itself, it might be noted, gave the Report scant attention, leaving the field open to the popular travesties.)

A number of conclusions occur to us. Media Studies, we have been implying, is both the study of a number of concrete institutions — for example, television, cinema, the press — and the study of the languages or discourses that flow between them and which they use to place and redefine each other. In the case in question, the tentative beginnings of a discourse from another kind of institution, that of education, was in effect obliterated, or at least travestied, by the superior force of the larger journalistic commentary. What challenges us as media educationists, therefore, is the need to strengthen and consolidate not only our analytic interests in the languages and discourses of media, but to strengthen the institutional voice with which we speak. It is to the 'working future' of the Report that educationists should now turn their attention, and to the forging of those institutional collaborations — between media practitioners and media educationists — that commitment must be made.

Reference

1. For a fuller discussion of the Report see D. Lusted, 'Feeding the Panic and Breaking the Cycle', *Screen*, vol. 24, no. 6, November-December 1983, pp. 81–93; and D. Lusted (ed.), *Popular TV and Schooling*, BFI/University of London Institute of Education, forthcoming.

18
Riddle Me Real

Some thoughts on English and gender

Margaret Sandra

> 'This here is a riddle', George said.
> 'I'm listening.'
> 'Two Indians was walking on a trail. The one in front was the son of the one behind but the one behind was not his father. What kin was they?'
> 'Less see. His stepfather.'
> George grinned at Portia with his square blue teeth.
> 'His Uncle then.'
> 'You can't guess. It was his mother. The trick is that you don't think about an Indian being a lady.'
> Carson McCullers, *The Heart is a Lonely Hunter*, 1943[1]

George's riddle is one of several of its kind which depend on the invisibility of women. The answer to the riddle remains a problem for many adults but there is a generation growing up now who can see the answer immediately. Unlike Portia, their eyes have been opened to the obvious by a combination of factors. The main influence for a change in perception of the role of women has come from the Women's Movement and the support and opposition it has generated in the media. And since the majority of teachers are women, it is not surprising that feminists have made an impact on the curriculum so that it is possible for my friend Pat's daughter Pam to pronounce the riddle as 'about sexism', clearly revealing an awareness, adequate or not, of the way gender is a socializing process to which we are all subjected, whatever our race, class or creed:

> If a test of civilization be sought, none can be so sure as the condition of that half of society over which the other half has power — from the exercise of the right of the strongest.
> Harriet Martineau, 1837

The process of putting gender in all its aspects into the education agenda is relatively new but women have been speaking out against discrimination and oppression for centuries. However, as Dale Spender has pointed out in *Invisible Women*,[2] our resistance and struggle regularly disappear from the history books and generations of women have to rediscover their strength in a common cause. What I hope to do in this chapter is map how some English teachers, influenced by their own beliefs as feminists and feminist sympathisers, have worked over the last twenty years to put gender on the agenda for English teachers. In divining how that process has been a part of a larger progress in understanding our personal constructs, we have been helped by institutions like the Institute of Education and departments within it like the English Department, led by thoughtful, permeable people under whose tutelage, students and teachers have raised the difficult questions of class and culture, race and gender in relation to the teaching of English.

> I was taught that the way of progress is neither swift nor easy.
> Marie Curie, 1923

Gender has been the most recent of the difficult questions to be asked. There are some who would maintain that it is not worth attempting an answer until the question of class has first been solved. My position, implicit in this chapter I hope, is that there is no *one* 'real' answer and that progress depends on pursuing each thread, individually and collectively, for the common good. Given that rather pious hope, I want also to emphasize that although all questioning of the filters through which we view education lead back to the question of power, this most recent question of gender produces particular discomfort because it is about sexuality. Since the mere mention of sex education regularly produces cries of anguish about the preservation of innocence, it is not surprising that the wider implications of gender conditioning have produced resistance in the form of trivialization, silence or blunt opposition. In addition, fear of open expression of sexuality is underpinned by a mostly subconscious understanding that men have a great deal to lose if the power relations between the sexes are breached.

So it is not surprising that throughout the Sixties and Seventies there has been conscious opposition to those who wished to question sexism and oppression in education since it inevitably implied a challenge to the power of the *status quo* in the West, i.e. white males. On the other hand, there have been powerful pressures, both economic and philosophical, on society as a whole which make the waste of talent and imagination caused by sexual oppression very debilitating for nations, whether capitalist or socialist.

It is through the tongue, the pen, and the press that truth is principally propagated.
Angelina Grimke, 1836

American feminists, emerging out of the equal rights movement of the Sixties, have helped to create the climate and conditions needed in this country to open up the question of sexism. Ellen Moers's book, *Literary Women*, written between 1963 and 1976, became available in this country in 1978[3] and helped to fuel the Women's Studies lobby. Similarly, Elaine Showalter's *A Literature of Their Own*, published in the same year by Virago,[4] fuelled the debate about literary representation and criticism started by Germaine Greer,[5] and Kate Millet.[6] I was particularly influenced by Andrea Dworkin's *Woman Hating*[7] and Jill Johnston's courageous *Lesbian Nation*.[8] Adrienne Rich[9] and Mary Daly[10] mounted a fierce attack on heterosexuality and Judeo-Christianity, and a major assault on linguistic research was established in Thorne and Henley's *Language and Sex, Difference and Dominance*.[11]

Thanks to publishing collectives and to the buying policies of an increasing number of radical bookshops in the Seventies, these books and many more came onto the market in Britain, under imprints such as Virago, The Women's Press and Sheba. These publishers, and others established by women for women, have rescued from oblivion the work of many women which had been received, applauded and forgotten by patriarchal literary criticism.

In politics, social studies and psychology, the work of women like Juliet Mitchell,[12] Ann Oakley[13] and Jean Baker Miller[14] contributed to the raising of consciousness which enabled publications like the Virago series, *The Gender Trap* by Carol Adams and Rae Laurikietis,[15] to come into schools as the first generation of teaching materials officially aimed at providing teachers with resources for the classroom. In this highly personal view of those who contributed to change, I have not the space to identify every author or contributor who deserves to be included, but I do want to set the scene for what follows — a history, through my personal perspective, of how gender became a 'real' issue in English teaching for me.

A change of heart is the essence of all other change and it is brought about by a re-education of the mind.
Emmeline Pethick-Lawrence, 1938

There can be few teachers of English in London and the South East, as well as places further away, who have not experienced the influence of the English Department at the Institute of Education, either through the work of individual members of that department or through what many regard as the extended department in the form of the London Association for the Teaching of English (LATE). As a probationary teacher in 1964, I was quickly adopted onto the LATE committee from whence I did not emerge until many years later — a valuable process from which many have benefited, largely because the Association's close links with the university mean that a classroom teacher can retain contact with the newest theories and the best classroom practice as and when they become available.

In 1971 I was seconded to the Institute, for the Role of Language in Education course. That diploma has been a source of much richness to those fortunate enough to take it, and it laid the foundations, in its exploration of language, of an awareness of both the oppressive role of language and its capacity for change. The questioning I learned on that course, much of it still unexpressed except within my head, led to a friendship based on similar questioning of the system, particularly in terms of how sex and sexuality were ignored in the theories we struggled with. Our concern led us to propose, in 1975, to organize a commission at a conference of NATE, the

Source: Casey Miller and Kate Swift, *Words and Women; New Language in New Times.*[16]

national extension of the London Association for the Teaching of English (a quip for all of us who are regionalists). Our commission offered teachers a chance to consider sex, culture and class. At the planning stage we were asked to remove references to sex in the brochure as some local authorities might refuse grants to teachers who wished to attend on the basis that sex, sexuality, sexism might not be considered appropriate areas of discussion for English teachers! Despite this set-back the commission attracted large numbers who wanted to debate the impact of sexual socialization and education, and we produced a small booklet. However, our debates hinged largely on the debilitating effects of sex stereotyping on girls and boys, particularly in books and the media, a reasonable response given the period.

Despite the success of the commission and the publication earlier in 1974 of the National Council for the Teaching of English (NCTE) guidelines on language and sexism, the initiative for raising gender as an issue remained with the grass roots as far as NATE was concerned. The flag was taken up again in 1977 by a group of women studying at the Institute of Education in a variety of disciplines. They began to meet regularly with the aim of bringing a feminist perspective to their studies and their genesis owed much to Dale Spender, then a research student and teacher at the Institute. A number of papers under the group title *Feminist Research Group* were published, and several of these later formed the basis of the Women Against Sexism in Teaching and Education (WASTE) papers which were presented at the 1978 York NATE conference. We met there as a working party, having been refused full commission status by NATE executive, and our presence at York was marked by opposition which expressed itself in our posters being removed or defaced, our papers left unprinted, and general condescension. Such behaviour served, as one would expect, to sharpen resolve and the National Working Party on Sexism and English Teaching gained members and began to meet regularly, drawing support from all corners of England.

The working party concentrated its attention on examining language and its role in the socializing process. We were much helped in this work by Visiting Professor Cheris Kramerae and Dale Spender whose PhD at the Institute of Education on language and gender was being supervized by Harold Rosen. Her book, *Man-made Language*, an earlier version of her thesis, made a major impact on educationists of all kinds when it was published in 1980.[17] It helped to open up a whole aspect of classroom performance which had not been explored before. She challenged the invisibility of women and girls' experience in the classroom and by doing so changed fundamentally the debate on language and social class by adding, indelibly, gender to the dimension.

The 1979 NATE conference was held at the London Institute of Education and the working party, invited this time, was able to widen its support in London so that the first LATE day-conference was organized on gender in 1980. It was remarkably successful and revealed, I believe, the way in which the Women's Movement and the debate generated by the working party were coming together to promote an understanding amongst English teachers that talking about gender and English teaching could not be divorced from the personal aspects of both these things. The argument is that each person is a sexual being and that gender is a socializing process over which we can exercise control.

The growth of interest in LATE is due to some extent to the pressure from many of the probationary teachers who joined the ILEA from the Institute English Department. Although not given a high profile, the question of gender has been raised on each PGCE course for several years, accompanied at the postgraduate level by encouragement to explore the relationship between gender and English teaching. This gave me an opportunity to study the effect of the introduction of boys into an all-girls secondary school and the consequences for their English work.

> Where young boys plan for what they will achieve and attain, young girls plan for whom they will achieve and attain.
> Charlotte Perkins Gilman, 1898

My interest had been generated by Dale Spender's work on language and her own observations in my school of the way in which boys took up teacher time, both physically and verbally. My own observations confirmed this and I was struck particularly by the reduced amount of time boys appeared to spend on reading and writing in school. Did this account for boys' lower pass rate in examinations at sixteen? If so, how does one account for the remarkable success of girls in English by comparison, given that most of their textbooks, both language and literature, are by men, about men, and embody masculine values?

The question of relative performance of girls and boys has been a matter for concern to the Department of Education and Science (DES) and to the Inner London Education Authority (ILEA) for a considerable time. The DES first published a paper in 1974 but their surveys have concentrated on highlighting a deficit model of girls as under-performers in science and maths and very little endorsement has been given to girls for their success in English and modern languages. The latter would seem to be particularly important in a country within the European Economic Community but there is no sign of female linguists or eloquent English speakers taking over the EEC Parliament or international business. Instead, we see girls continuing to service those who *do* run those areas, as their personal assistants and secretaries. As Dale Spender has said elsewhere, women's success is continually redefined by a patriarchal society to serve the needs of those who hold power. The question we have to ask is, whose interests does it serve to have significant numbers of boys regarding reading and writing as a bore, and significant numbers of girls discounting their highly effective literacy? Both questions enter the debate on class and race at a point which I find more meaningful than the position taken by some that the only real issue is class, as if one dimension is more real than the other. Gender, like race and class, is a process of socialization. Change is possible if we are prepared to open our minds to it, and that depends on questioning not just the conditions of oppression, but also how they are articulated.

Up to now most published theoretical writing about education has come from men. Their words and structures shape meanings into paragraphs and chapters and books which set fact apart from fiction, the poetic at the other end of the spectrum from the transactional. They purport to reveal objective truths which actually alienate and mystify. By bringing a feminist perspective to the study of education we can see that much of it in the past has been a study of boys' education, where girls' different behaviour has often been interpreted as 'deviant' or 'not statistically viable'. By putting girls' education back into the picture we can focus on performance through a gender filter, an act which is bound, in my opinion, to be fruitful.

> And if education is always to be conceived along the same antiquated lines of mere transmission of knowledge, there is little to be hoped from it in the bettering of man's future. For what is the use of transmitting knowledge if the individual's total development lags behind?
> Maria Montessori, 1956

The Seventies produced a wealth of grass roots education publications, one of which owed its emergence to LATE. The magazine *Teaching London Kids* (TLK) grew out a series of three one-day conferences organized by LATE to look at English and social class. Harold Rosen created the title for the conferences and it provoked just the right amount of interest, and disgust at the use of the word 'kid'. We attracted large numbers of London teachers who later became the audience for the magazine. Aimed at English teachers initially, it still publishes a wide range of articles covering issues of social class, culture and race. I owe much to those friends in the collective and it was under their influence that I began to see the parallels between what was then the emerging debate on multicultural approaches and my developing awareness of sexism.

There was the question of 'tokenism', the inclusion in groups of a representative female or black to assuage liberal consciences, an act still perpetrated regularly in media discussion programmes. There was the growing awareness of a dearth of positive images of women for girls in school which paralleled the lack of positive and appropriate multicultural material. The demand for more black teachers raised the consciousness of many teachers, that whilst the majority of the profession were female, education at every level of responsibility is dominated by men. The identification of good non-sexist literature and the encouragement of new writing to fill the cultural and ethnic gaps in the curriculum have been valuable pursuits, producing books like Gene Kemp's *The Turbulent Term of Tyke Tyler* and Robert Leeson's *It's My Life* for use in schools. As the search goes on for material which reflects current issues and offers positive images, the American influence on school literature has been very apparent.

> Our school education ignores, in a thousand ways, the rules of healthy development.
> Elizabeth Blackwell, 1860

However, the 'out with the old, on with the new' approach has its critics, rightly so, since schools clearly cannot afford to throw out all their current book stocks. We simply cannot afford to replace them, even if we could be sure that the books we would like now would still be appropriate in ten years' time. Fortunately for teachers in London, the English Centre, the ILEA-funded central resource centre, has a fine record of taking the initiative in problems like these. Thanks to the ILEA English Inspectorate and advisory service, considerable progress has been made on producing materials for teachers on English and gender. A list of them is available in booklet form, and the emerging discourse on why gender is a serious influence on the teaching of English has been disseminated in *The English Magazine* produced by the Centre. Most significantly, the new materials are not merely an attempt to offer a different approach. Implicit in their production is the assumption that positive images on current issues are not sufficient in themselves. The gender and cultural assumptions in a novel, play or poem need to be made explicit in a number of ways, not all of them overt. Pupils need to be led to examine their own assumptions about sex roles and stereotypes through approaches which are not didactic or pedantic. Pupils should be able to develop a healthy awareness that challenging traditional assumptions about the roles of women and men is in their own interest.

It is probably true to say that the largest scope for change still lies in men's attitude to women, and in women's attitude to themselves.
Vera Brittain, 1953

As we move into the new technology and the shrinking supply of work, as we expand our service industries and as physical production declines, changes in how men and women live will be forced upon us at even greater speed than they are now. The debate for English teachers must continue to be about how the study of language and literature can prepare girls and boys equally for a society in which class and cross-cultural influences combine with an attack on gender assumptions to produce new ways of working in the classroom. The main impetus of such work must come from classroom teachers, supported by their local authorities and by provision of time to develop resources. Changing attitudes depends on giving people time and space to *experience* change, which is a lesson developed by the feminist movement in their use of consciousness raising.

As teachers struggle with questions about gender conditioning they will also need to face up to questions about their own sexuality. Homophobia will need to be exposed if men are to deal with their masculine strait-jackets. Homophobia, or fear of homosexuality, permeates our society, petrifying gay teachers and pupils and stunting the natural expression of emotion in men and boys. It acts as one of the most powerful controls on male behaviour in schools and for that reason arouses strong feelings. It is actually probably true to say that the largest scope for change lies in men's attitude to men so that men can work to free themselves from the debilitating effects of macho-capitalism.

Open and honest sex education which places emphasis on feelings and mutuality must be given to boys as well as girls. At present many English teachers find that they are the informal transmitters of such learning through discussions arising out of novels and poems. We cannot expect to achieve equality in the school curriculum whilst boys are kept wilfully ignorant of female sexuality. And their own sexuality is distorted by all but the most basic facts of sex of which the most important is the myth of the uncontrollable sex urge. A further problem as we move towards a multicultural literature in the English classroom, will be the problem of cross-cultural conflict over the roles of women. Probably some of the most valuable insights in further work will be gained when politically black* women bring their perceptions to bear on this work.

* A term created by the Lewisham Black Women's Forum to include all ethnic minority women.

English teachers have been in the front line of change on so many changes in the curriculum that I am sure they will tackle gender as an issue with equal courage. They need to be prepared by their training to deal with the problems I have outlined and they will need support for their school initiatives from local education authorities committed to anti-sexist policies. It is going to be a tough learning experience but we are changing the world, aren't we?

References

1. Carson McCullers, *The Heart is a Lonely Hunter*, King Penguin, Harmondsworth, 1981 (first published 1943).
2. D. Spender, *Invisible Women. The schooling scandal*, Readers and Writers Co-operative, London, 1982.
3. E. Moers, *Literary Women*, The Women's Press, London, 1978.
4. E. Showalter, *A Literature of Their Own: British women novelists from Brontë to Lessing*, Virago, London, 1978.
5. G. Greer, *The Female Eunuch*, MacGibbon and Kee, London, 1970.
6. K. Millet, *Sexual Politics*, Avon Books, New York, 1972.
7. A. Dworkin, *Woman Hating*, E.P. Dutton, New York, 1974.
8. J. Johnston, *Lesbian Nation: The feminist solution*, Touchstone Books, Simon and Shuster, New York, 1974
9. A. Rich, *Of Woman Born*, Virago, London, 1977.
10. M. Daly, *Gyn-ecology: The metaethics of radical feminism*, Beacon Press, Boston, Mass., 1978.
11. B. Thorne and N. Henley, *Language and Sex, Difference and Dominance*, Newbury House, Rowley, Mass., 1969.
12. J. Mitchell, *Woman's Estate*, Penguin, Harmondsworth, 1971.
13. A. Oakley, *Housewife*, Penguin, Harmondsworth, 1976.
14. J.B. Miller, *Towards a New Psychology of Women*, Penguin, Harmondsworth, 1978.
15. C. Adams and R. Laurikietis, *The Gender Trap: A closer look at sex roles*, Virago, London, 1976.
16. C. Miller and K. Swift, *Words and Women: New language in new times*, Gollancz, London, 1976.
17. D. Spender, *Man-made Language*, Routledge and Kegan Paul, London, 1980.

Changing English; English Changing

Heather Kay

CHANGING ENGLISH

C linging Angels
H aggling
A ches
N agging
G angling
 I nane
N eighing
G ag!

ENGLISH CHANGING

E asing
N ice
G iggles
L ines
 I ncline
S ail
H ail!

19
Speaking of Shifters

Margaret Meek

When I can, I read with pre-school children and those around six years old a picture book by Pat Hutchins called *Clocks and More Clocks*. In it, Mr Higgins, a gentleman of Victorian cast, eccentrically clad, finds a clock in his attic and wonders it it tells the right time. To make sure, he buys another clock for his bedroom, one for the kitchen and a fourth for the hall. But when he rushes up and down the stairs to see if they all tell the right time, (the pictures show the reader that they do), he finds they are different by about two minutes. Mr Higgin's friend the Clockmaker inspects the clocks. When he compares them with his watch he finds each is reliable. So Mr Higgins buys a watch and then, 'all his clocks are right'. Children of five can re-tell the story exactly but are not sure at first why Mr Higgins never found all his clocks telling the same time. As readers, they attend to the clocks but rarely to the time it takes to climb the stairs.

Piaget didn't know about Mr Higgin's human problem but it lurks in his investigations of children's developing understanding of logical time: duration, simultaneity, movement and velocity, which leads their steps towards the intellectual constructs of physics. Besides drawing some comfort from the fact that this growth in understanding *takes* time, my heart warms to the child who told Piaget that bigger things are older than smaller things, and things which have stopped growing have stopped getting older.[1] I have often wondered what Piaget made of children playing at 'What's the time, Mr Wolf' and moving through space one step at a time, and why he didn't watch and listen to early music lessons where a minim is matched in duration with a crotchet so that the tune will be right. Would his continental logic let him accept

> Time present and time past
> Are both perhaps present in time future
> And time future contained in time past . . .?

I doubt if he knew that Isaac Watts believed children to be capable of understanding:

A thousand ages in thy sight
Are like an evening gone.

The plain fact is, children's notions of time are intimately bound up with their language development before the objective and subjective meanings of time are within their grasp of consciousness. Not a day passes without alerting them to the preoccupation adults have with time in all its aspects. 'I've told you time and time again . . . there isn't time . . . we're wasting time . . .' No other topic illustrates so well the capacity of ordinary language to be 'a treasure house of expressions appropriate to what is specifically human in experience'.[2]

When children investigate clocks and watches they know that the verb is to *tell* when you say what the time is. Their initial experience of 'to mention in order' is the same as 'to make known, to narrate'. OED supports this, for these are the synonyms it gives for *tell*. Or, as we might say, to tell is to count and to recount, for what we and children essentially tell in order is stories. Narrations and the annotation of time are inseparable. Their bonding is linked with whatever counts as memory, whether in reciting multiplication tables, or in the actual remembrance of things past, or the 'virtual memory' that Susanne Langer says is the imaginative force that transforms language into literature. What follows is a speculation about the part played by stories written for children in the development of their understanding of time.

Jakobson, writing about the grammatical phenomena that Jesperson called *shifters*, says:

> The concept of the shifter has seemed to me for some time to be one of the cornerstones of linguistics, although it has not been sufficiently appreciated in the past and therefore demands more attentive elaboration. The general meaning of the grammatical form called a shifter is characterized by a reference back to the given speech act that uses this form. Thus the past tense is a shifter because it literally designates one event that precedes the given act of speech . . . The desirability of including grammatical tense in linguistic usage occurs in a fairly early stage in the child's acquisition of language, at the moment when the beginner ceases to be satisfied with a direct verbal reaction to what happens before him at a given moment.[3]

Clearly one of the major organizing devices in which shifters play what Jakobson calls 'a tremendous role' is narrative, spoken or written. In remarking that English is a particularly rich language for the study of tense and its literary uses, Susanne Langer suggests that 'in the use of verb forms one finds devices that disclose the real nature of the literary dimension in which the image of life is created'.[4] My argument is very simple: children come to understand very complicated notions of time both by telling stories and by reading those specially written for them where time is the author's chosen theme. Stories are patterns of shifters.

Children's oral narratives

Long before they can sort out the verb as a time system children have developed cultural understandings of before and after, yesterday and tomorrow, early and late, day and night, days and weeks, how to recollect and anticipate birthdays, seasons, holidays, festivals, for all that adults sometimes treat these awarenesses as crude approximations to the reality acknowledged by those who live by diaries and timetables, or who measure the fractions of a second. Children are denied 'historical sense' until quite late in their school career but that might be because adults make such a business of the naming of historical parts. There was no insult when my seven-year-old nephew asked if I was born in the Middle Ages. He was simply discovering the difference between *medieval* and *middle-aged* and he framed his question as best he could. The simplest nativity play in a primary school makes the time paradox very clear: here is the *presentation*, now, of an event that is a narration of what happened a long time ago, yet the drama occurs every year at the same time.

Most research claims that, after the first explorations of the pre-sleep monologue, the earliest conventions of story-telling practised by middle-class children in Western-type cultures are 'formal beginning, formal end and consistent past tense.[5] The narratologists quote E.M. Forşter's 'The King died, the queen died of grief' as 'minimal connexity'. Those who, like Sachs, study children's narratives quote: 'The baby cried. The mommy picked it up.'[6] The work of Shirley Brice Heath and others makes plain, however, that although narration is a universal human competence, we may have to revise our understandings of *how* stories are universally told as well as inquiring further into what they are told *about*, and how they regulate time.[7]

Propp's famous analysis is of quest tales. They tell other stories now, not only in Trackton, but in Brixton, Birmingham and Glasgow. When we have done with structural analysis we may have to look more closely at stories which seem to conform to our cultural expectations in the delineation of time, and at those which challenge them, especially in our new multicultural societies where we all look at the same clocks but not always in the same way. Harold Rosen showed us that besides being grateful to narratologists we have to look at what they neglect: 'It is best not to plunge straight into the most sophisticated forms of written narrative or even into written narrative at all, but rather to consider narratives that are as universal as language itself'.[8] He looked at natural narratives, the stories people tell, to explore their relationship to culture and cognition.

A significant extension of his ideas is in the work of Carol Fox who is studying the natural narratives of children.[9] She collected 86 story monologues in thirteen months from her five-year-old son Josh. Her analysis of these is as detailed as anything in Genette's *Narrative Discourse*.[10] They make it quite clear that we are only at the beginning of a new stage in our understanding of children's narrative composition and competences in situations that are not confined to classrooms. Here is Josh at five years nine months, with half of his story:

> Once upon a time, there — there — there's just a — just a very clean bin. Once David and Joshua got in the bin, and they flew right away. And as they flew away, they flew — right past space, and higher 'n space, and they went higher and higher, until they — reached God's palace, and when they came to God's palace, they told him to h — help, because a wicked witch was just — was just down on earth. So — he gave him — them — some — some — mag-ic powder, that could melt witches — so he got the magic powder, and once — the wicked witch was behind him, but he's just walking along the street, until he came back, and then he sprayed it on — then she melted, and then he walked back to the dustbin, and David and Joshua got in — then they flew right away — until — they — they came back to God's palace — the roof — they were — on the roof of God's palace — and then they said — said — 'Let's go down — I don't like it — like it' said Joshua — so they got down — and then — he — the — he gave them a balloo' — balloon — because — because — erm — because that dustbin was getting dirty. So — they got in the ballon and flew away — and then — they went — to — to — to the Emerald City — when David and Joshua were th — there — he — they went — they went — to see — to see Mumby, but she wasn't there — then he went to the Land of the Munchikins, but she wasn't there — but she was somewhere hiding in the Emeral City. Then they saw her, and then . . . he told her to *get* — the guard of God's palace, and then she did, and then she made a special power instead of doing — doing it to Tip she put — put on — the guard of God's palace — a — and vinegar and things, and then *he* was dead.

When I hear tapes of Josh telling his stories and read the transcripts I know that every narrative theorist on Culler's bead-roll[11] who makes the distinction between *story*, the sequence of actions and events, and *discourse*, the narration of these, should attend to children's narrative monologues. From their earliest attempts, especially when tolerant adults let them tell on, they incorporate a wide range of elements from the stories they have heard as well as from the events they have experienced. These elements are linguistic and *literary* as well as recollections or psychological intentions that move them to narrate. The work of the Cragos supports this.[12] They traced their child's interaction with book stories from the first days of her being read to and although their analysis is different from that of Carol Fox they also show the pervasiveness of time in the intertextuality of her story-telling. Stories are embedded in storying. So clear is this, that I assume it into part of the argument of what follows. Children build the author's or teller's story time into their stories, and thereby gain an extended 'virtual past' from fictive as well as factual narration.[13] (Harold Rosen's narrative of narrative has, as its prime instance of how stories are told in families, his mother's repeated reference to 'the king and his diamond scarf pin!')

As Josh narrates, he incorporates not only his cultural view of what a story is, but also his recollection of the tales he is weaving together and the almost submerged memory of his first hearing of them. His remembering organizes his consciousness; his re-telling makes two pasts present: the past of the tale itself and of the telling. As he goes on, he refocuses the combined pasts and the present.

Children's memories are necessarily short over actual time but (and here we do need Joyce, Proust, Dorothy Richardson and Virginia Woolf), the poetic structure of Josh's making allows him to combine the intricacies of genuine, and necessarily recent, memory with 'the artistic devices that achieve its semblance'. In response to the invitation, 'tell me a story', Josh is learning the play of the text, the play of shifters. He demonstrates Ricoeur's assertion that 'a story is made out of events to the extent that *plot* makes events into a story'.[14] Josh is discovering how to make plots. He places himself and his listener at Ricoeur's 'crossing-point of temporality and narrativity', where he is exploring various aspects of time. For all that he lacks a mature historical sense which would impose on him a strict linear chronology, he is free to explore Genette's *anachronies*, 'the discordance between the two orderings of story and narration', in his own way.

Josh is also using his narration as *action*. He knows that stories in books do not change, so he makes his own story give him a narrative identity; he is both the teller and the told, a shifter. 'Along with shifts of temporal and spatial points of reference', says Jakobson, 'he acquires the idea of the shifting roles of the participants.' As he does so, Josh is focused on the present, on creating an illusion of simultaneity.

Suffice it that, when they go to school, children who have had stories told or read to them are strikingly competent in their use of shifters. In their organization of extended narrative monologues they make Pitcher and Prelinger's 'continuous past tense' seem too simple a description of how they tell and recount. They know that stories, that is, language, can transport them across space and time. What joins Josh to James Joyce is his creative ability to signal time. Joyce is breaking free from the time concepts that Piaget is concerned with; Josh has still to learn them. He will do so in school when he engages with measuring and mathematics. At the same time he will write to please his teacher stories that begin with getting up and finish with going to bed as he struggles to put the linear time sequence together. He actually does better than that. Here is Josh at eight and three months. He is now *writing* a story called *The Last Chime of the Bells*. He borrowed the title from *A Christmas Carol*.

One winter night in Wales three children were at home. Just then the bells started to ring. The bells of the church, that is. That was the first time in three years that the bells had rung. So then the boys ran out of the house that they lived in and went to the church.

Utterly secure in narrative time, Josh's story not only locates its characters and its readers but also demonstrates his competence in creating the illusions of simultaneity and duration in a linear narration. He has learned from his storying and from reading and listening to compose as complicated a pattern of shifters as any he will need before he comes to understand the synchronic and anachronic features of time itself.

Josh's narratives help him to say how time shifts. He also acquires the stock of common phrases that let him declare his inchoate feeling-plus-knowing that 'time and the hour runs through the roughest day'. Keeping pace with him, writers for children link his growing understanding of the succession of events, of duration and simultaneity, with their presentation of time, narrative time, the out-of-time-ness of dreams, and the within-time-ness that is the act of reading itself.

Time in stories for children

So far we have allied the development of children's notions of time to the development of their language as they interact with people around them, as they listen to stories being told or read, and as they themselves tell stories. We know from their re-tellings that the simplest narrative time they recognize is that of the fairy tale: 'once upon a time when wishes came true', 'once there was', 'one summer's day.' This narrative time is firmly in the past, a universal unspecified past of the deep structure of our common humanity, a time that joins listeners and readers to a folk memory that stirs and shifts as in our daily living we remember the everyday tales of our grandparents and parents.

Fairy stories became children's literature in the eighteenth century when they were written down, when childhood was invented and when more children began to learn to read. Since then we have had other kinds of children's literature to diversify and instruct the young according to the convictions of the author and the persuasions of the period. When they read what has been written for them (or for adults, for that matter) children engage with a whole new range of time schemes, including the linear extension of plots over time and the ways of signalling time passing ('three months later . . .'). They come to understand that narrative time is much more complicated than a single succession of incidents. Picture books with apparently straight-forward narration, like *Mr Gumpy's Outing*, *Tim All Alone*, and even those without words, like Raymond Briggs's *The Snowman*, engage their readers in a present preoccupation with narrative events that determines, as Ricoeur suggests, 'the existential now'.

Skilled authors and artists give even the youngest reader in this 'now' a virtual past which serves as memory, and a future which they anticipate as the end of the tale. Narrative time lasts as long as the book is being read and in memory thereafter. To re-enter the time-shift of the text the reader has only to read it again. Here is Maurice Sendak suggesting a long time to pre-schoolers, time long enough, that is, to separate Max from the unpleasant supperless retribution imposed on him for his 'mischief of one kind and another':

> . . . an ocean tumbled by with a private boat for Max and he sailed off through night and day and in and out of weeks and almost over a year to where the wild things are.[15]

When Max goes back home, the order of the words is reversed. I want to suggest that the apparently simple poised rhythm of that sustained sentence without commas, and the artist's calculation of where the pages turn offer something to the study of a phenomenology of children's understanding of time.

Later, children read for themselves stories which continue in longer episodic strings this narrative pattern of characters in action over time. Young readers are best pleased, it seems, by a rapid movement of organized events, a plot, on the time basis of 'what happens next'. Willingly and unbidden they read a whole series of tales by the same author, usually one considered by teachers, librarians and critics as lacking in literary merit. Yet, despised as texts and deplored as ideology, these are often storehouses of reading experience, not least in the presentation of the conventions of narrative time and in the deployment of shifters. In a significant exposition of *Shock for the Secret Seven* by Enid Blyton and Roald Dahl's *The Twits*, Charles Sarland shows how the authors of children's popular fiction are no less skilled than more approved writers.[16] 'Virtually every technique that is available to adult authors may be found in embryo here.'

Sarland's analysis makes it plain we are wrong to imagine that because the narratives of Blyton and Dahl appear unambiguous on the surface, children can handle only simple stories straightforwardly told. His further point is that, within undesirable ideological frameworks (Blyton is racist and sexist, Dahl morally dubious), both writers develop stories that specifically challenge those very frameworks, even though they are not finally overthrown. 'My contention is', says Sarland, 'that it is the challenge to the cultural order that children find absorbing rather than the re-establishment of it at the end of the stories.' Here again is Jacobson's idea of 'the shifting roles of the paticipants'. For quite young and inexperienced readers, the reading of Blyton increases their confidence in handling predictable narrative conventions that include a wide range of anachronies.

I have quoted Sarland at length for two reasons: to endorse his belief that subtlety in the deployment of narrative time is not exclusive to writers whose work attracts critical attention as 'literature', and also to suggest that children's authors who make time the focal preoccupation of their narrative are doing something significant for children who are encouraged, helped, able and willing to read their work.

The challenges of time

There are many arguments why demonstrably skilled authors take the amount of trouble that they undoubtedly do with texts for inexperienced readers. These authors say that writing for children presents difficulties that can be a challenge. One challenge is that children's books are their *first* literature, however defined. Free as they are from ideas about what a book *has* to be like, children give adults leave to divert and instruct them, a tolerance which ingenious story-tellers are quick to exploit, especially nowadays with the help of new publishing techniques and transworld readership and distribution. Another challenge is for the writer to create new kinds of story-telling, to explore ways of making a text for those for whom imaginative play is a natural way of extending both language and learning. Story-books are essentially 'zones of proximal development'[17] for both the authors and the readers.

The openness of young readers to the experience of reading means that authors can create alternative worlds and alternative time. The author writes a story, the oldest, most universal form of told time, and makes narrative time new for new readers. The author's concern is with inventing narrative time *and* with the challenge of making plain for the young 'the backward and dark abysm of time' as an idea. In a book for children, time is a scheme of shifters that the reader takes on in interaction with the text and thus with the author. The most obvious way for an author to exploit this interaction is to count on childhood as the privileged time for dreams, day-dreams, fantasies and imaginative play because these are all, in one sense, out of time. And here lies the next challenge: to make time seem *now*, while being never, yet moving *through* time to the end of the story.

Lewis Carroll tried it. Amongst many of the games he played in *Alice*, he used the dream-like framework to unsettle time. In the topsy-turvy Wonderland Alice knows how time works but the adults don't. She says:

'You see the earth takes twenty-four hours to turn on its axis . . .'
'Talking of axes,' said the Duchess, 'off with her head.'

The discussion of time at the Mad Hatter's tea-party is the most elaborate play of shifters. Carroll's way of playing with episodic time sometimes makes younger readers uneasy; there are too many shifts for the inexperienced; they are not sure how to predict 'what happens next' nor to reason that all will be well in the end. Alice escapes situations rather than engaging with them. What Carroll does well is to shake loose a reader's notion that stories have to be based on conventions of sequences of realistic time. Narrative time is its own kind, and reading time, time-withinness, turns, as Ricoeur suggests, 'a plot into a thought'. This is what happens in the kind of children's books that publishing cataloguers call 'fantasy'. The time scheme of everyday life is abandoned for another. When C.S. Lewis's children enter Narnia through the wardrobe the days are plainly different.

The most skilful writer in this thronged field which includes science fiction writers as well as Tolkien, Mary Norton, Joan Aiken, William Mayne, and Aidan Chambers, is Alan Garner. He rejects the wardrobe-type device for re-ordering time as dreams and star-treks. He concentrates on time as place, especially the place where his family has lived over centuries. He loops his narrative time to include layers of mythology, traditional tales, legends and stories, thus calling up the time of other texts while his characters remain in the modern world of greater Manchester. His most ambitious novel, *Red Shift*, weaves together a legend, an historical event and a modern love story, all of which 'happened' on Alderney Edge over a span of centuries. As a text, the book needs readers experienced in shifters, not least in shifts of viewpoint, flashback, and the time devices of adult novels. The author makes use of the adolescent's understanding of narrative time that builds up only after a considerable amount of reading experience.

In his later work, *The Stone Book Quartet*, which can be read by much younger children, Garner transmutes autobiographical narrative, at once so clear and so laden with time images, into a fine counterpointing of historical time and the existential now of the chief characters and the reader. It is such a stunning achievement that children respond, as Betty Rosen suggests in chapter 2, with the deep shiftings of their own awareness of themselves as narrators.

An example: Philippa Pearce

From Philippa Pearce's *Tom's Midnight Garden* and *The Way to Sattin Shore* it is possible to study the temporal aspects of narrative discourse in books for the young in such a way as to demonstrate the phenomenology of time that children find in story texts created specifically for them. What follows is only a sketch designed to indicate in summary form something of the reading experience that comes from the reader's interaction with writing of this kind.

Published in 1958, *Tom's Midnight Garden* is still considered to be a paragon of stories for the young. There are many testimonies to its excellence as an example of the writer's craft. The narration has none of the quirky rhythms that made Garner's early work difficult for inexperienced readers. Part of the fluency of Philippa Pearce's prose is its pacing, the result of a versatile use of pauses and the short sentence. The reader reads at a rate clearly marked by the writer, like the tempo of a score. Its most remarkable effect is the way in which the writer's concern with time becomes the reader's.

The story events are these. Tom spends his summer quarantine with a childless aunt and uncle in a town near the Fens. The house has no garden. One night, sleepless after a rich supper, Tom hears the grandfather clock in the hall strike thirteen (its striking is acknowledgedly erratic). He opens the back door and finds, instead of a yard with dustbins, a garden with trees, greenhouses, walls and children, notably Hatty, the visiting cousin who is younger than Tom when he first meets her, a child who lives by 'Biblical heroes and fairies and the people of legend and hearsay and her own imagination'. Gradually life in the garden with Hatty, life in dream time, takes over in reality from Tom's daily round with his uncle and aunt. His boring holiday becomes a time of enchantment. After each episode in the garden he writes to his brother at home an account, a re-telling, of what he and Hatty have done. In response to Tom's letters, his brother begins to dream of them both. At last, of course, Tom must go home, but not before he and Hatty go out of the garden and down the frozen river to Ely. Then the dream-time Hatty disappears and the real one, still alive, is revealed.

The narrative is in two orders of time: daytime and garden time. Within the garden time there is a different order of duration. Hatty grows up to be a fine young lady in the course of Tom's summer holiday. She says, 'sometimes you don't come back for months', but Tom knows he goes to the garden every night.

> He did not always go back at exactly the same Time every night; nor did he take Time in its usual order. The fir tree, for instance, he had seen it standing, fallen and then standing again — it was still standing last night. He had seen Hatty as a girl or his own age who — although Tom would not fully admit it — was outgrowing him altogether.

Tom sorts out his time problem not by reference to his uncle's scientific answers to his question 'What is time?' but by remembering the story of Rip Van Winkle, another game of shifters.

> 'So that I might be able, for some reason, to step back into someone else's Time, in the Past; or, if you like '— he saw it all, suddenly, and for the first time, from Hatty's point of view — 'she might step forward into my Time, which would seem the Future to her, although to me it seems — the Present.'

This resolution comes near the end of the book, after the reader has had time to puzzle out the shifts of people, actions, time and tenses but not before Tom nearly gets out of time altogether. Inside the grandfather clock which gives him garden time that does not show itself on the kitchen clock (shades of Mr Higgins) are the words 'Time no more'. Time he decides, is only temporary. He will live in Hatty's time, in dream time, 'for Time in the garden can go back'. But Tom and Hatty leave the garden to skate on the frozen river, which is frozen time, and,

> Like an ever-rolling stream
> Bears all its sons away.

When it thaws on the return journey, the dreams are over.

Although they are undoubtedly carried along by the narrative and may give scant attention to the surface of the text, readers have to deal with shifters on every page. At the outset, the brothers' anticipated time is spoilt, cancelled: 'They *would have built* a tree house.' 'A child *of your age* needs ten hours' sleep' begins as a threat. Yet in the few moments of clock-recorded time, Tom spends days in the garden which he knew '*was waiting* for him' although it didn't exist. Tom needs skates for a dream exploit. He actually finds Hatty's in the cupboard where she had left them in her time, so, in garden time, there are 'two skaters on one pair of skates'. At this point in the narrative the reader accepts the possibility without question.

Now, it would be foolish to see in *Tom's Midnight Garden* more than some of the elements of *Remembrance of Things Past*, but they are there. Part of my awareness of them is in response to Genette's analysis, to his warning that we must not put too much reading faith in 'psychological laws and realistic motivations', and to his suggestion that,

> We must consider the possible (or rather the variable) narrative competence of the reader, arising from practice, which enables him both to decipher more and more quickly the narrative code in general and the code appropriate to a particular genre or a particular work.[18]

Readers of *Tom's Midnight Garden* come to have an extensive and varied reading experience of time, as order and duration, if not as frequency and repetition. That they also discover how Tom experiences Proust's certainty: 'my dreams were my address', is in itself an anticipation of later literary experiences. My simple point is that literary competences are built up in readers by the discourse diversities of writers. And for all that they are clearly present in Blyton and Dahl, Philippa Pearce offers a wider and more varied play of the text, not least in the matter of shifters.

And yet, the narrative time in *Tom's Midnight Garden* is clearly a device, a way of doing it. Twenty-five years later, years of patient, skilled and meticulous crafting of shorter stories for younger children with whom she has always kept faith and of whose actualities she has always been sensitively aware, Philippa Pearce has written *The Way to Sattin Shore*.

In it there is only linear narrative; no dream time as such weaves a pattern of shifters. This narrative builds the same kind of preoccupation with time as is clear in *Tom's Midnight Garden* into a story that looks as if it were a succession of events in six months in the life of a child of about ten. But it isn't nearly so simple as the surface structure suggests. Here we cannot separate the story from the narration in order to discuss the author's preoccupation with narrative time. Instead, we look at the author's presentation of the complexities of human time to readers who have learned what it is to remember, whose language development can cope with the past and future in the present. They are encountering a story-teller who will teach them how the text is to be read, because it isn't quite like anything they have read before, and who will make their reading into an exploration of narrative discourse about time.

Kate Tranter, the heroine, is the age of most middle-childhood readers of Blyton and Dahl. She is the youngest of three women living in the same house; the other two being her mother and grandmother. She has two brothers. Her father, she thinks, died on the day she was born. The tombstone in the cemetery overlooked by her house seems to indicate this, for all time.

Here on the first page is the author setting Kate in her time at home.

> Here is Kate Tranter coming home from school in the January dusk — the first to come, because she is the youngest of her family. Past the churchyard. Past the shops. Along the fronts of the tall narrow terrace houses she goes.
> Not this one, not this one, not this . . .
> Stop at the house with no lit windows.
> This is home.
> Up three steps to the front door, and feel for the key on the string in her pocket. Unlock, and then in. Stand just inside the door with the door now closed, at her back.

Here 'narrative text borrows time metonymically from its own reading'.[19] Real time and narrative time coincide. A paragraph more of the present tense, and then a pause for the eye to travel.

> Kate Tranter took a slow breath. She made herself ready to start across the floor of the stairs — to cross the dark beam that came from her grandmother's room through the gap where her grandmother's door stood ajar.
> On a weekday, at this time, her grandmother's eyes were always turned to that door, as she sat in her room by the window. Her eyes looked out through the crack of the door, on the watch for whoever came in, whoever went out. Whoever came in must cross her line of vision to go down the passage to the kitchen or to go upstairs. Whoever went out was seen, noted.

Not at all difficult to read. Yet here are moments of actual visual immediacy for the reader (trained by television), the world that children 'half create' by perceiving. Each repetition is calculated to give the impression of being an act in time; the iterative of Genette. So before they have read a page and a half, readers are plunged into a complicated time-scheme of generations and events as they stand with Kate about to cross the hall. They move from events narrated in the order in which they occur to events repeated over time, yet for the reader the events are *now*. On this day, time changes in the

Tranter household and a chapter later Kate needs to know, as part of her own puzzle about being in time, what really happened to her father. Her mother and her mother's mother possess part of the story as memory although each *tells* it differently when the time comes to do so. Kate cannot learn about the past until her mother, her grandmother, her father and older brother fit together for her the time just before she was born. Then she can face the future.

Meanwhile, there are days to be lived through: days at school when thinking helps to put the jigsaw together, especially in mathematics lessons:

> In the time that followed, Kate sometimes said to herself: 'I shouldn't have to think as hard as this — not *think* — at my age.'

There is the memorable day of tobogganing on her grandmother's black tray, the kind of day that is a fixed Archimedean point in a whirling universe, a day to be remembered. Then there is the slow building up of the stories till the past is revealed, some of it to Kate alone. Sometimes time is precise and insistent: 'For three days and nights she thought almost all the time of her father.' Then time has to slow down: 'We must wait for the right time to tell about our dad. The right time, remember, and it's not yet.' Or time to make restitution, for only forgiveness can change the past. What we change is our way of looking at it.[20] Lenny, who has suffered undeserved punishment, says: 'Why didn't you say that before, long ago? Why did you let Mum go on and on at me? You should have said — you should have!' His complaint suggests what might have happened, even before the events being spoken of. Kate and her brother's friend argue about mending a slow puncture in Kate's bicycle tyre:

> 'It's *very* slow', said Kate.
> 'You ought to mend it.'
> 'Yes', said Kate, who hated mending punctures because she was so bad at it. 'I will mend it. I'm only waiting . . .'
> The old strawberry man had been listening.
> He did not raise his eyes from his columns of close black print, but said, as if reading aloud:
> 'If I wait, the grave is mine house.'

Kate, who hates waiting, has to wait to learn what will make the future possible. When it comes, it comes as an intolerable burden, as real as real memory.

> 'You've told me', said Kate, 'and I shall tell. I must tell.'
> 'No', said Arnold West. 'You won't. You can't. They won't believe you. You're a

child that makes things up, they say: mysteries; fairy tales; horrors . . . they'll say
you made this up; and I shall laugh and say so too.'
'Then why have you told me?'
'I've waited ten years to tell someone. Just one person would be enough. You
turned up. You were the right one. I feel better now. *Lighter.*'

That is also, of course, the fate of the story-teller for children: to make plain
the ways by which a child comes to understand, and in so doing, to be
regarded as childish by those who believe that writing for children is a
simple matter.

The Way to Sattin Shore seems to me to present within the conventions of
the realistic novel the 'spots of time' which Traherne saw as characteristic of
childhood and the splendid play of shifters that gives a young reader a grasp
of narrative time as a series of mirror-images. As a book it is less dramatic but
no less powerful than *Tom's Midnight Garden*. Indeed, its very low key is the
more resonant. The plot is a thought; Kate thinking about what it is to
understand what happens, what happened and what will happen. Only once
does the author step out to talk about time. Kate's father is back.

> Within the Tranter family the return made a difference — Kate perceived its
> hugeness like the uprearing of a mountain peak through clearing mist. Years yet
> to come would show the extent of the difference made to them all, Fred Tranter
> included.

By this time Kate has discovered that she has another grandmother alive,
and thus another past, another set of memories. Her mother's mother
doesn't change the past because she can't forgive her son-in-law, so she stays
where she is.

The narrative discourse is very close to the reader. There are some
memorable moments: Kate's mother rubbing flour and Kate's Granny
watching, at the very time when Kate has to ask her mother about her father
and finds she can't. The chance passes. The within-time-ness of the reading
is absolutely governed by the way the sentences stop and start, by the
counterpointing of narrative time that is as subtle as a fugue. In the end, the
story emerges as a perfectly simple read for ten-years-olds and the plot is
thought time.

Many authors work on the time game in stories for children. Most of them
opt for the moralistic futurism of time travel or the serialism of *Dr Who*. But
this is different. The author plays the whole scale of time in language and
includes time in the telling. The reader may read it like a detective story
(which Jakobson acknowledges as a series of shifters) but the author has her
own generation-time problem, Granny, Mum and Kate, as well as her

continuing preoccupation, how to write a book for the young that will engage them as readers over time to come. That is, of course, my problem too, and where I came in with Mr Higgins who began it all.

References

1. Jean Piaget, *Le Développement de la Notion du Temps chez L'Enfant*, Presses Universitaires de France, Paris, 1946.
2. J.L. Austin, *How to do Things with Words*, Oxford University Press, 1962.
3. R. Jakobson and K Pomoroska, *Dialogues*, Cambridge University Press, 1983.
4. Susanne Langer, *Feeling and Form*, Routledge and Kegan Paul, London, 1953.
5. E.G. Pitcher and E. Prelinger, *Children tell Stories: An analysis of fantasy*, International Universities Press, New York, 1963.
6. H. Sachs, 'On the Analysability of Stories by Children', in J. Gumpertz and D. Hymes (eds), *New Directions in Sociolinguistics*, Holt, Rinehart and Winston, New York, 1972.
7. Shirley Brice Heath, *Ways with Words*, Cambridge University Press, 1983.
8. Harold Rosen, 'The Nurture of Narrative', International Reading Convention, Chicago, 1982.
9. Carol Fox, 'Talking like a Book: Young children's oral monologues', in M. Meek (ed.), *Opening Moves*, Bedford Way Papers 17, University of London Institute of Education, 1983.
10. G. Genette, *Narrative Discourse*, Basil Blackwell, Oxford, 1980.
11. Jonathan Culler, *The Pursuit of Signs*, Routledge and Kegan Paul, London, 1981.
12. Maureen and Hugh Crago, *Prelude to Literacy*, Southern Illinois University Press, 1983.
13. Susanne Langer (op. cit., n. 4) says that fiction is 'the illusion of life in the form of a virtual past'.
14. Paul Ricoeur, 'Narrative Time', in W.J.T. Mitchell (ed.), *On Narrative*, Chicago University Press, 1981.
15. Maurice Sendak, *Where the Wild Things Are*, The Bodley Head, London, 1966.
16. Charles Sarland, 'The Secret Seven vs. the Twits: cultural clash or cosy combination?', *Signal*, no. 42, September 1983 (The Thimble Press, Stroud, Glos.).
17. L.S. Vygotsky, *Mind in Society*, Harvard University Press, 1978.
18. Genette, op. cit., n. 10.
19. Ibid.
20. Hannah Arendt, *The Human Condition*, University of Chicago Press, 1958.

20
Community-published Working-class Writing in Context

Gerald Gregory

During the past decade or so there has been in England an impressive development of 'community publishing'. Around the country 'writers' workshops', 'people's history groups' and so on have sprung up to stimulate and publish the work of local and predominantly working-class people. These projects, in their origins, purposes and processes, have been strikingly varied.

As regards origins some arose from WEA classes[1] and some from adult literacy projects[2]; others developed from initiatives to provide bookshops for huge urban and chiefly working-class populations hitherto lacking them[3]; yet others grew out of community action: QueenSpark (Brighton) from a 'campaign to stop Brighton Council turning . . . The Royal Spa into a casino, and to get a nursery school, day nursery and park centre instead[4]; Scotland Road (Liverpool) — the oldest workshop[5] — out of a tenants' campaign and rent strike. One event, Chris Searle's publication in 1971 of East End schoolchildren's poetry and the resultant furore, seems to have been seminal[6]; in fact perhaps only one current project, *Voices*, claims direct continuity with developments prior to 1971.[7] An important factor has been the growing availability of new, simple and cheap means of printing and publishing.[8]

Groups differ widely in orientation and practices, and within groups emphases are constantly shifting. Some welcome writing from 'out there' in the local community with a view to possible publication; others make the workshop central, often promoting participatory processes before products to the point where print publishing is rare. Some groups regard pub readings, agit-prop theatre performances, etc. as their main modes of publication while others combine a wide range of activities. One group will produce chiefly poetry (sometimes a reflection of the interest of an influential member at the group's formation); another, autobiography; a third, people's history; another, black writing; another, feminist writing, and so on.

There are now[9] some twenty-eight independent working-class writers' groups and publishing initiatives loosely linked within the Federation of Worker Writers and Community Publishers (FWWCP); beyond it are many more, small-scale, grass-roots publishing ventures, often remaining unknown to it and to each other. Groups within the FWWCP have some 200 titles currently in print; sales across the board are estimated to have reached one million.[10] The dominant mode of working-class writing, now as in the past, is autobiographical: accounts of life at work and in the dole queue, at home and in institutions of all kinds — schools, children's homes, battered-women's refuges, 'spikes' and prisons. Most of these accounts appear in attractive, illustrated litho booklets; some texts started as tape-recorded interviews; some are by individuals, others by groups. All are the work of beginning writers; all are cheap.[11]

It is the basis of what follows that these developments are potentially of acute interest to educationists. The suggestion is that the initiatives outlined bear close relationship to developments elsewhere over roughly the same period, for example in respect of ideas about the nature and representation of working-class culture, about what it is to become a writer and about the roles of speech and writing. Centrally, a consideration of the products and (especially) the processes referred to suggest fundamental ideas in respect of education itself, both such specifics as the roles of non-standard language and also broad questions of the nature of education and educational processes. Finally, the suggestion will be that the community publishing movement is best seen in the context of certain important social-political trends of the present historical conjuncture.

The nature and representation of working-class culture

> You sit in the same chair
> day in
> day out
> smoking, looking at the wall
> or you put your head in your hands
> and cry quietly . . .
>
> And the Community Health man
> says
> 'There are no rickets in Rotherham,
> no evidence whatsoever of any illness
> caused by unemployment . . .'

He ought to be at our house
at tea-time . . .

Ruth Shaw, 'No Rickets in Rotherham'[12]

Beneath this arc-lit conscious world there is a whole humanity practically unchronicled.

Jack Common (1903–1968)[13]

I had forgotten myself
in the studied books,
lost my own experience
in the history of others,
become the old events,
and I could not write.

Joe Smythe, railway guard[14]

'Culture' is a notoriously slippery word. Two major strands of its reference, usefully disentangled by Raymond Williams, are to 1, 'a whole way of life'[15] (anthropological sense), and to 2, 'the body of intellectual and imaginative work, in which . . . human thought and experience are variously recorded' (documentary sense).[16] In the most public and extensive forms of discourse (in print and via other broadcast communication media) working-class culture in the first sense has, for well-understood historical and political reasons to do with the power relations in our society, only rarely been described, discussed or celebrated. What representation (second sense) there has been of working-class ways of life has been, overwhelmingly, authored by those who either do not or no longer or never did belong within the working class on any definition around which a consensus could be gathered.[17] What has often been thought of as working-class culture has consisted of products extensively consumed by the working class, rather than produced by and for working-class people. (It should, however, be noted in passing that whereas working-class people have been, typically, strangers from print it is by no means clear that estrangement from *writing* has been on the same scale.[18])

It is within the context of such silences — the one about working-class culture, the other and deeper on the part of working-class people — that the recent flowering of working-class writing and community publishing should be considered. Passionate conviction about the intrinsic value of working-class culture[19] (first sense), especially those solidarities that underpin its outstanding and unique institutional achievements (e.g. of trade union, political and mutual help associations); a determined refusal to stay marginalized; indignation and impatience at being represented, misrepresented, patronized and abused by outsiders; these have fuelled the drive to write rather than be written (or not), publish rather than be published (or not) and, increasingly, to theorize rather than be theorized.

The cultural experience that has in community publications begun to be *described*, expressed, explored, celebrated and, for obvious reasons, only more slowly and tentatively *analysed*, is impressively various. The *period* covered is, roughly, from 1910 to the present. The *location* of some of the most prolific groups (Birmingham, Bradford, Brighton, Bristol, Liverpool, London, Manchester, Newcastle-upon-Tyne, Nottingham — plus several smaller towns and rural districts) indicates one sort of variety. A sample of the *occupations* of the writers — docker, miner, farm worker, shipyard worker, domestic servant, 'houseworker', dustman, postman, barber, factory worker, cab driver, bus conductor, office cleaner, carpenter-joiner, Thames lighterman — suggests another. Some dominant themes are: childhood and street life; home life — patterns, conditions and relationships; school, work and unemployment; solidarity and mutual help, resilience and resourcefulness; relationships with the authorities; union and political activity; racism and sexism.

What it means to become a writer and to publish

 . . . producing much in order to find out what our 'bests' are . . .[20]

A list like the above represents an abstraction from hundreds of individual and group writings, a generalization from much particularity. Overwhelmingly, community-published working-class writing is the representation of personal experience and, to some extent, exploration of the self, much of it in the form of narratives or statements, in both the first person singular and plural, where 'we' denotes a known, local group. Readerships, both where explicitly addressed and where implied, vary from the self,[21] to a relatively known, local group[22] ('insiders'), to anyone the distribution system is able to reach[23] (therefore mostly 'outsiders'); and often to all three readerships in the same text. Again, because many books start as taped speech, because most others are the earliest work of first-time writers, and because groups take radically different views of literary quality and operate 'quality-control' criteria distinct from those in play in the mainstream, many texts are sharply different from what is normally encountered in print, including the working-class writing published in the past. Hence those involved have both familiar and unfamiliar senses of what it means to become a writer and to be published.

The sense of group support, of an actual readership and of an access to print unpatrolled by the gatekeepers of mainstream publishing, have for many combined to transform the business of writing from a hated, daunting chore (as so often at school) to a preferred,[24] and occasionally intoxicating,[25] way of life. The advantages to such writers of coming to know writing as another means of thinking about experience and of transforming experience into something permanent, shaped in new ways and open to scrutiny and analysis are formidable.

What has been said so far about working-class culture, its representation and who gets to represent it, and about the move into writing and print, suggests correspondences with developments elsewhere. Parallels are found, for example, in cultural studies, in the purposes of groups like Com-Com (Community Communications Group) which encourage grass-roots initiatives in people's broadcasting rather than the handing down of access facilities from above, especially in education. Here, with roots perhaps in child-centred models of education and the creative writing movement,[26] the same sense of the importance of describing and reflecting on individual and group experiences has flourished, the same recognition, quickened by the findings of research[27] and urgently underlined in reports,[28] of the importance to writers of actual and varied *audiences*. The potential for developing autonomy built into becoming a powerful writer, the chance to gain respect and greater control over one's situation, and to learn how to make and distribute messages and for collaborative work are the same throughout. Such parallels are especially marked in relation to language issues.

Language

The decade or so of the upsurge of working-class writing and community publishing has been in *educational* discourse, as perennially within the society beyond, a marked preoccupation with language issues. In seeking to explain, and to develop strategies to reduce, the under-achievement of working-class pupils (and increasingly of minority groups) theories of language deprivation have been advanced, dismantled, modified, demolished, re-hashed. Again, stemming from the initiatives of the London Association for the Teaching of English,[29] and endorsed by the Bullock Report[30] and the findings of a flurry of surveys, etc.,[31] a sense of the crucial role of language in every part of the curriculum has become received wisdom if not always a springboard to action for curriculum change. Linked with and part of both these strands has grown a body of theory and research into non-standard dialects of English (both British- and Caribbean-based) and into their social-political origins, contexts of use and potential as means of expression, cognition, and learning.[32] This work has taken as axiomatic, and discovered no reason to doubt, that no dialect (or language) is inferior to any other,[33] that no dialect (or language) does not or could not meet all the demands its speakers might make upon it; that the 'differential status' as between standard and non-standard dialects is based on prejudices arising from social judgements about speakers rather than on linguistic judgements about language.[34] The differences are explicable in terms of historical-political determinations. Such is the importance of our mother tongues to all of us, to our sense of ourselves and our relationships, our perspectives and patterns of cognition, that for educators to marginalize, undervalue, outlaw them and to attempt to do business exclusively in standard language is negative, denying, radically disabling. It disqualifies our most potent resource for learning.[35]

While 'non-standard speakers' and 'working-class' are considerably over-lapping categories, the labels are far from coterminous. Arising from a concentration on specifically *working-class* speech — and beyond the context of education — has been a seminal body of work, associated most readily with Harold Rosen,[36] and with the late Charles Parker:

> . . . the language of the working-class is our only hope for the survival of any English identity. I'd put it as strongly as that. It's the last hold we have in our root culture, is this language.[37]

Yet, as both Parker and Raymond Williams have pointed out (with different emphases), non-standard/working-class language has, as a result of a standardization in favour of the dialects of dominant groups, been historically absent not just from print but from *writing itself*.

Community-published working-class writing abounds in non-standard language. However, the purposes and circumstances of its presence are various and some distinctions may clarify this.

Many publications start as taped speech which is then transcribed and edited, collaboratively and with the full involvement of the speaker(s). Where, as very often, non-standard dialect and/or pronunciation is in play, these are often preserved into the written version. Writing-in-non-standard-dialect, roughly:

> I seen Joe at the Kist — then the water came through, that was the lot. There was only one way out. All the air changed. The black damp put 30 of them to sleep, then the water rose, and just covered them over. There are only 8 drownded and that was the 8 I left to my Flat, 6 men and 2 putters — they got the lot.
>
> James Tracey, coal miner.[38]

The next plot to we here was Mrs Doe's and it went right up through. He'd have all different people on his place that never had no ground.

Mrs E. Cooper, 'Romany/Gypsy'[39]

'I think everybody should die on them born spot.'

Isaac Gordon[40]

Given working-class life as subject matter it follows that there is much evocation of working-class speech (often displaying non-standard features) in dialogue or within the narrative mode of entire stories, in prose or verse — and by writers who otherwise operate in standard. Non-standard-dialect-in-writing:

Father Flanagan got to the ozzie a bit puzzled. Only feller 'e could remember called Freddie O' Toole was some geezer 'e married off three years ago 'oo gave 'im the *Racing and Football Outlook* in a sealed envelope 'fer yer trouble, Father'. 'E'd never seen the heathen since.

Jimmy McGovern, Scotland Road, Liverpool[41]

Wha happen black girl
You know here about family planning how you just ah' breed so . . .

Angela Mars, Centerprise Young Writers, Hackney[42]

. . . teacha wunt lerrus
sit next tureachother

went shiwent aht
cockut class cumup
t'me
ansed, 'AH canfaityo
cahnt ah?'
an ah sed eecudnt
an ee sed ee cud
an ah sed ee cuddunt
an eeit me
so ah itim back just
as teacha cumin
shipicked up that
stick as y' point
at bord'we
an crackt m'ovver
edweeit
an sed, 'Widontav
ooligunsere.'

Barry Heath, Your Own Stuff Press, Nottingham[43]

Perhaps a third (rarish) category needs adding: where a speaker's non-standard and highly idiosyncratic use of language (idiolect) is preserved. The outstanding example of this is *Dobroyed*, Leslie Wilson's account of a year in Dobroyed Castle Approved School, near Todmorden:

> . . . the actule city of Todmorden may well of skiped and just jump for joy of freedom exitemants . . .[44]

The work under consideration embodies in products and processes an assertion of the broadest validity of non-standard language, matching the value of the culture it informs and proclaims — an assertion in striking correspondence with the contemporaneous academic/educational theorizing referred to above. While this practice has of course not remained untheorized by the practitioners themselves[45] what especially attracts the attention of those with an interest in the formulative-expressive potential of a language, so often both unwritten and written-off, is the growing body of a rare commodity: *written and printed non-standard*. In time the corpus may provide a means to help students of language move on from expedients like Peter Trudgill's[46] in 'translating' a passage from an anthropology textbook into non-standard West of England dialect so as to explore the latter's functional potential. If it is borne in mind that explorations of *how* working-class speakers use kinds of language and for what purposes are in their infancy, then as more is known (and as may be inferred from remarks such as the following) the very terms of the enquiry may need to be reformulated:

> Jimmy Miller . . . was a branch secretary in Callingly Colliery. He's a Fifeshire man, he used to work in the Michael pits, and he was saying how he refused ever to *not* use the vernacular, and not to use pithy vernacular stories to get over hard political points.
>
> Charles Parker[47]

> . . . working-class speakers had a very strong tendency to use narrative when they wished to make a theoretical point, to clarify an idea or exemplify a generalization.
>
> Harold Rosen[48]

> . . . for social and cultural reasons (working-class speakers) use (dramatic dialogue, i.e. dialogue in which the speaker becomes each of the participants and acts out their voices through direct speech) more readily, more frequently to fulfil functions which other speakers satisfy by discursive methods.
>
> Harold Rosen[49]

Just as fresh territory is being claimed for non-standard language,[50] so also are new arenas for what normally is transacted in speech rather than in writing:

> . . . working-class life should not just be reflected upon in the pub and the front room, but should be published in the long-lasting form of books, as a permanent record and as a means of maintaining an active local class-consciousness.
>
> Ken Worpole[51]

This, written in 1977, seems more urgently true now:

> How can our grandparents' experience of the Depression be effectively presented to the young who seem condemned to re-enact it? How can we get architects to listen to high-rise tenants; bring the thoughts of the unemployed to the attention of the DHSS; persuade the Home Office and the judiciary to take account of what happens inside jails?
>
> Marion Glastonbury[52]

In connection with this new *content* and *form* for writing, that is, what normally is transacted only in speech on the one hand and non-standard language on the other, it should be said that many of the *processes* involved in producing community publications that originate in taped speech develop for participants a sense of the innate differences between speech and writing, a sense that is at least sharpened and often entirely new, and afford new contexts for reflexive thinking. Many of the experiences contingent on involvement in these projects, for example, participation in public readings (which, as the result of understanding their intrinsic value as well as the cost of book production, are on the increase everywhere), and collaborative production of texts and books in 'workshop' contexts, develop a new sense of their provenance and nature and of the relationships between book production and consumption. A fresh, democratic sense of print and books as available, stripped of authority and false dignity, written by flesh-and-blood people with particular points of view and purposes and, therefore, susceptible of reply and rebuttal as well as respect and reverence — all this is self-evidently and powerfully *educational*.

Education and educational processes

In spite of the educational origins of many projects it may be inappropriate to view most of the initiatives under consideration as explicitly, consciously educational. Participants think of themselves as developing writers rather than students in any formal sense. However, for all participants, and especially those involved in the wider processes of the FWWCP, the educational dimension is palpable and undeniable. Viewed as self education and within a long working-class tradition, the model in play resembles closely some influential models contemporaneously developed in more formal educational contexts. Apart from what has already been suggested about language, variety in writing, actual and varied audience, and so on, further marked parallel features include: the democratic, collaborative ethos; the equivalent of a 'student-centred' orientation; the painstaking study of how to make projects inclusive and welcoming rather than exclusive and threatening.[53] Care is taken by leading figures to *enable* rather than to dominate and, in some cases, to regard their intervention as temporary in the interests of group members developing full autonomy.[54] It is these features especially that explain the palpable growth of confidence among participants countrywide. A commitment both to the group and to the difficult business of writing among people who have scant opportunity for practice and, beyond the group, precious little encouragement, accounts for the writers' success.

Community publishing in context

Key terms used in sketching the nature of community publishing in the opening paragraphs above were 'local', 'small-scale', 'grass roots', ' democratic', 'participatory'. Such a list conveys a flavour of what is striven for and realized in the philosophies and practices of worker-writer groups. Individuals and small groups 'dig where they stand'[55] into their experiences and into those of their local forerunners. Locality is of central importance, not out of a deluded harking-back to some golden age of organic community, unqualified solidarity and so on, nor out of an inward-looking cosiness, nor yet in ignorance of the destruction of communities that has taken place since World War II. Rather, in confronting precisely such local transformations,[56] in addressing (in for the most part 'expressive' modes of writing) as primary audience a readership which shares similar experiences and predicaments in the same primary community, groups of beginning (often first-time) writers start both from the known and comfortable in terms of matter, manner and audience, and from the bottom, in terms of their analysis of social, economical and political realities. Objections are sometimes voiced that experience is often *recalled* (with varying degrees of accuracy) but rarely *analysed*; that some writers lack a theoretical framework of political understanding; that they are likely to deal in received (dominant) ideological views. Clearly some work shows such features. But such a critique seems ill-judged and premature: ill-judged in implying purposes which some of the writers would not recognize; premature in that where analysis of lived political realities is on the agenda, writers need first to externalize and give form to experience, to make it into knowledge, before they can analyse, evaluate, and perhaps, finally, act for change. It is noteworthy that examples of just such a trajectory have begun to appear.

'Local', furthermore, is in this context bound up with 'small-scale', and the intimacy this implies is a precondition both of developing the confidence of beginning writers within group projects, and of seeking, through participation, to control and demystify publishing processes. Aside from the determining factors of severely limited resources and problems of distribution, there are clear preferences for the small scale in the thrust to establish 'reciprocal relations between readers and writers'.[57]

When considered in the context of the mainstream, community publishing is marginal. In my experience, a majority of reasonably well-read, well-informed people outside education, and quite a few within, are unaware of it. Thus it attracts such labels as 'alternative' and is awarded a status perhaps comparable with that of other alternative practices, e.g. in medicine, industry and agriculture. Community publishing groups, however, have no intention of occupying a ghetto, nor of settling for a place on the margin. Rather they see their practice as oppositional:

> if the kind of literary production *we* are engaged in were to become the norm — i.e. co-operative, associative, aiming at two-way (many way) communication, cheap, widely available, producing much in order to find out what our 'bests' are — then the conventional norm — competitive, elitist, profit-controlled, labour-dividing, separating producer from consumer — would be impossible.[58]

How far such a development will materialize is clearly bound up with political developments in the wider society. A look at certain of these may, as hinted above, help to place community publishing in a broader socio-political context.

One of the most marked socio-political trends of recent years, currently somewhat obscured by the mushrooming growth of a centralist 'authoritarian populism', has been *away* from the provided and imposed solutions of specialists and of bureaucratic, monolithic political parties and governments, *away* from treating people exclusively as clients and consumers and *towards* decentralism, collective self-help, self-organization and a 'face-to-face politics'.[59] Disillusionment with solutions to problems-as-people-experience-them, for example of housing, education, poverty, injustice and inequality, has led to calls for policy-makers to *listen* much more to those who stand to be affected by their policies once made and enacted (calls heard increasingly in the aftermath of the 1983 General Election)[60] and has fuelled a drive towards a more participatory democracy, vestigially realized in such developments as work-place democracy, workers' co-operatives, tenants' and environmental campaigns, community newspapers, alternative schooling, and teacher, parent, student and community representation on governing bodies within education.[61] Rejection of paternalistic state provision has been in favour of small-scale, 'bottom-up', grass roots (and increasingly networked) initiatives responsive to local and particular needs, and founded on the belief that people must in collaboration describe, analyse, prescribe and act *for themselves*. Related to this Raymond Williams makes a telling point:

> All significant social *movements* of the last thirty years have started outside the organized class interests and institutions. The peace movement, the ecology movement, the women's movement, solidarity with the third world, human rights agencies, campaigns against poverty and homelessness, *campaigns against cultural poverty and distortion*: all have this character, that they sprang from needs and perceptions which the interest-based organizations had no room or time for, or which they had simply failed to notice.[62] (My italic)

Community publishing is recognizably part of the tendency sketched above. While it is easy to exaggerate the importance and potential of such a development, as it is to lose sight of the importance of the *state* to achieving transformations, community publishing has, apart from an intrinsic importance to participants and the provision of alternative and oppositional models of publishing (and to some extent of education), a role to play through giving public and permanent form to working-class experience,[63] thus helping to inform what Raymond Williams has referred to as, 'the wide remaking of a social movement that begins from primary human needs.'[64]

Notes and References

1. Examples include: People's Autobiography of Hackney; Tottenham Writers' Workshop; People's History of Yorkshire; History groups at Heptonstall and Todmorden, Yorkshire, Bristol Broadsides.
2. Examples include: Groups within Centerprise (Hackney), Gatehouse (Manchester), Bradford Literacy Group, Peckham Publishing Project, Write First Time (Bedford).
3. Centerprise (Hackney) and The Bookplace (Peckham) are examples.
4. *Writing*, Federation of Worker Writers and Community Publishers (FWWCP), 1978, pp. 150–157.
5. David Evans, 'Writers' Workshops and Working-class Culture' in Jane L. Thompson, (ed.), *Adult Education for a Change*, Hutchinson, London, 1980, p. 143.
6. Four out of the ten groups whose work is represented in *Writing* (the first

232 Gerald Gregory

anthology produced by the FWWCP) invoke it as inspirational in their initiatives.

7. *Voices* grew out of earlier initiatives in trades union and Labour Party contexts in Manchester. These sought, like Arnold Wesker's Centre 42, to implement TUC Resolution 42 (1960) which recognized 'the importance of the arts in the life of the community' and looked for 'greater participation by the trade union movement in all cultural activities'. See *Voices* 16, pp. 56–60. Also David Evans's brief comment on this in op. cit. n. 5 p. 146. *Voices* became the responsibility of FWWCP in 1980.
8. See K. Worpole, 'Beyond the Classroom Walls' in M. Hoyles (ed.), *The Politics of Literacy*, Writers and Readers Publishing Co-operative, London, 1977. See also *How to Make a Book*, Peckham Publishing Project, 1982: 'We started publishing when we wanted to produce some writing with a group of adult literacy students. We learnt from experience . . . Our experience has shown us that anyone can make a book given a little money and time and the feeling that they want others to read their writing.'(p. 2) See also Minority Press Group *Here is the Other News*, Series No. 1, 1980.
9. Summer 1983.
10. Dave Morley and Ken Worpole, 'Writers at Work', *The New Statesman*, 30 April 1982.
11. For information on what is available see *Writing*, FWWCP, 1978, FWWCP Publications List, 1981; G.T. Gregory, 'Round-ups' of a selection of work produced in 1980 and 1981 in *The English Magazine*, nos. 7, 9, 10.
12. In Rick Gwilt (ed.), *Nineteen Eighty-Three: A First Trade Union Annual*, Lancashire Association of Trades Councils, Preston, 1983, pp. 18–19.
13. 'Christmas Carol', *The Adelphi*, vol. ix, December, 1934; reprinted in Huw Beynon and Colin Hutchinson (eds), *Jack Common's Revolt against an 'Age of Plenty'*, Strong Words, Newcastle-upon-Tyne, 1980, p. 104.
14. Joe Smythe, *The People's Road*, National Union of Railwaymen, London, 1980, p. 39.
15. Raymond Williams, *Culture and Society*, Chatto and Windus, London, 1959, p. xviii.
16. Raymond Williams, *The Long Revolution*, Chatto and Windus, London, 1961, p. 57. See also the discussion of 'culture' in Harold Entwistle, *Class, Culture and Education*, Methuen, London, 1978, ch. 4.
17. See the useful discussion of such classification problems in Raymond Williams, *Towards 2000*, Chatto and Windus, London, 1983, pp. 157–60.
18. See prefaces (and references) in John Burnett, *Useful Toil*, Allen Lane, London, 1974, and *Destiny Obscure*, Allen Lane, London, 1982. See also Ken Worpole, *Local Publishing and Local Culture*, Centerprise, London, 1977.
19. A value consistently asserted by Jack Common: '. . . behind 'mass' there is a humanity as worthy of celebration as any that has been . . . here is a people to believe in, for their qualities are those which the world needs to learn . . . the deep communal loyalties of those people who are incapable of being incor-

porated into the spiky individualist cactus . . .' In Beynon and Hutchinson op. cit. n. 13, pp. 19, 18, 38. Compare the main themes — capitalist attacks on the roots of working-class solidarity and the seductive power of cash values — of Jeremy Seabrook's Channel Four TV programmes, July 1983.

20. D. Morley and K. Worpole (eds), *The Republic of Letters*, Comedia/Minority Press Group, London, 1982, Series No. 6, p. 44.
21. E.g. Harry Harris, *Under Oars*, Centerprise, London, 1978; Stan Rothwell, *Lambeth at War*, SE1 People's History Project, London, 1981.
22. There is a sense of this in the Strong Words booklet, *Hello, Are You Working?*, Newcastle-upon-Tyne, 1977: 'Our hope is that people . . . will gain a greater understanding of their grandparents and of the past' (Introduction, p. 6). See also the statement by People's Press of Milton Keynes (in *Writing*, n. 4): 'In this sort of setting the need to collect and publish the memories of the area's elderly residents seems more urgent and necessary than it does in other more stable areas, for within a few years the majority of Milton Keynes population will be strangers to the area, and probably inquisitive as to what went on before they came' (p. 136).
23. 'As a matter of policy the paper is sold almost entirely door to door. A thousand copies of our first QueenSpark book . . . also sold in less than a month in this way.' *Writing*, op. cit. n. 4, p. 151.
24. '. . . a day without writing something was a day wasted'. Joe Smythe, railway guard, interview with present writer, March 1980.
25. So pervasive is the cultural connection between being published, on the one hand, and becoming famous/doing well out of it, on the other, that the odd case has occurred of a community-published working-class writer becoming confused: some attention, fame even (e.g. via interviews in local papers and on local radio), leading individuals to misconstrue their situation.
26. Itself interestingly traced back through David Holbrook, Marjorie Hourd and Caldwell Cook, in J.T. Hodgson, 'Changes in English Teaching: Institutionalization, transmission and ideology', unpublished PhD thesis, University of London, 1974. See also Chris Searle's reflections in Gregory, op. cit. n. 11, appendix IV, pp. 216–21.
27. E.g. Nancy Martin et al., *Writing and Learning Across the Curriculum*, Ward Lock Educational, London, 1976, pp. 16–22, 132–40.
28. E.g. Department of Education and Science, *A Language for Life*, HMSO, London, 1975, pp. 166, 527.
29. See, for example, D. Barnes, J. Britton and H. Rosen, *Language, the Learner and the School*, Penguin, Harmondsworth, 1969, rev. edn 1971.
30. Op. cit. n. 28, especially ch. 12.
31. See, for example, Department of Education and Science, *Aspects of Secondary Education in England: A survey by HM Inspectors of Schools*, HMSO, London, 1979.
32. For example, P. Trudgill, *Sociolinguistics*, Penguin, Harmondsworth, 1974; P. Trudgill, *Accent, Dialect and the School*, Arnold, London, 1975; D. Sutcliffe,

234 *Gerald Gregory*

British Black English, Blackwell, Oxford, 1982; Talk Workshop Group, *Becoming Our Own Experts*, ILEA English Centre, London, 1982.
33. Trudgill, 1975, op. cit. n. 32, ch. 2; Sutcliffe op. cit. n. 32, p. 224.
34. There are of course dissenting voices: see John Honey, *The Language Trap: Race, class and the 'standard English' issue in British schools*, Kay-Shuttleworth Papers on Education No. 3, National Council for Educational Standards, 1983.
35. The pedagogy implied here is, of course, not without its critics. A view sometimes put is that its outcome is likely to be to confirm working-class children in their subordination; that what is needed, rather, is mastery of patterns of language that 'carry clout'. Presenting these as inevitably mutually-exclusive alternatives seems unhelpful.
36. See, for example, Harold Rosen (ed.), *Language and Class Workshop, 1 and 2*, privately printed, 1974.
37. G.T. Gregory, 1979, 'Workers Writing in the 1970s: An enquiry into the aims and achievements of individuals and organizations.' Unpublished MA dissertation, University of London Institute of Education.; see also C. Parker, *Towards a People's Culture*, Tract No. 3, 1972.
38. James Tracey, *Canary Men and Cobblers*, Strong Words, Newcastle-upon-Tyne, 1977, p. 6. 'Kist': large wooden box in which Deputy kept equipment; also point at which men would stop before being directed by Deputy into work area. 'Flat': station to which putters took full tub. 'Putter': person who brought the full tub from the hewer to the Flat and also took empty tub to him. This version of James Tracey's speech is at times more elliptical than makes for easy *reading*, without, that is, the support of those 'paralinguistic devices' that assist *listening*, especially face-to-face listening.
39. *In West Howe Proper: A part of Dorset remembered by local people*, Word and Action, Wimborne, Dorset, 1982, p. 71.
40. Isaac Gordon, *Going Where the Work Is*, Hackney Reading Centre, Centerprise, London, 1979, p. 33.
41. Jimmy McGovern, 'Compo', in Gwilt op. cit. n. 12, p. 58.
42. Angela Mars, 'Wha Happen Black Girl' in Maggie Hewitt (ed.), *As Good As We Make It: Writing by Centerprise Young Writers*, Centerprise, London 1982, p. 8.
43. Barry Heath, *M'Mam Sez*, Your Own Stuff Press, Nottingham, 1981, pp. 4–5: 'The poems in this book are the voice of 'Barn Lane', proudly written and proudly spoken, without frills. I saw no reason to write like Wordsworth, after all I don't talk like him!', p. 3.
44. Leslie Wilson, *Dobroyed*, Commonword, Manchester 1980, p. 141. '[His] "education" has left Les with an extraordinary range of perceptions and sensitivity but without a standard language in which to communicate them. In place of a standard language, Les has created his own . . . Weeks and months were spent painstakingly writing down, rewriting and copying from exercise book diaries about his year at Dobroyed Castle School. The finished work has been rewritten four times' (Introduction, p. 4). See discussion of this in G.T.

Gregory, 1981, op. cit. n. 11, Part I in *The English Magazine* No. 9, Spring 1982, pp. 49–50.

45. For example, see the discussion between adult literacy students reproduced in *Let Loose*, Write First Time, Bedford, 1978, pp. 69–71.
46. Trudgill (1975) op. cit. n. 32, p. 27.
47. In Gregory (1979) op. cit. n. 37, p. 142.
48. H. Rosen, 'The Dramatic Mode' in P. Salmon (ed.), *Coming to Know*, Routledge and Kegan Paul, London, 1980, pp. 156–157.
49. Loc. cit. p. 157.
50. These shifts — of spoken language (non-standard speech at that) into writing — are not without their difficulties, especially for people who have no experience of their language and thought 'disembedded' (see M. Donaldson, *Children's Minds*, Fontana, Glasgow, 1978, chs. 6, 7. In their Introduction to Les Moss's *Live and Learn: A life and struggle for progress*, QueenSpark, Brighton 1979, the production 'collective' write: 'We have found that people are always shocked when they see word-for-word transcripts of their conversations. They seem jumbled and incoherent: but that is how interesting talk goes.'
51. Worpole, op. cit. n. 18, p. 10.
52. *The Times Educational Supplement*, 13 August 1982.
53. See *Something to Say*, Lee Centre, London 1981, especially Jane Mace's Introduction, pp. 5–9, and Brian Vallins's piece, pp. 36–39. See also T. Blackwell, J. Seabrook, 'Looking for the Working Class' in *New Society*, 9 September 1982, pp. 411–413.
54. See David Evans's discussion of his role in Liverpool workshops in Evans, op. cit. n. 5. Contrast Ken Worpole's approach: in Gregory, 1979 op. cit. n. 37, pp. 165–166.
55. 'Dig Where you Stand' by Sven Linqvist in *Oral History*, vol. 7, no. 2, Autumn 1979.
56. Ken Worpole has commented to the effect that the high-rise flat poem has become almost a sub-genre of working-class writing.
57. D. Morley and K. Worpole (eds), *The Republic of Letters*, Comedia/Minority Press Group Series, no. 6, London, 1982, p. 44. Some of the main argument of this book is endorsed by Terry Eagleton in his *Literary Theory: An Introduction*, Blackwell, Oxford 1983, p. 216.
58. Morley and Worpole, op. cit. n. 57, p. 43.
59. Ibid., p. 3. Parallel trends are observable in the field of educational and related research: realization of the need for teachers collaboratively to define their own problems being currently overwhelmed by insistence on centralist definitions. The case for genuinely 'popular' planning and provision is urged by Socialist Environment and Resources Association (SERA), founded 1973. See, for example, SERA, *Local Socialism*, issues 17 (April/May 1983) and 18 (June/July 1983), 9 Poland Street, London, W1.
60. See, for example, the series of articles 'Debating the Future of Socialism' in

New Statesman, especially 19 August 1983 (Peter Hain), 26 August 1983 (Lynne Segal). See also Peter Hain, *The Democratic Alternative*, Penguin, Harmondsworth, 1983.

61. See Tony Gibson, *People Power: Community and Work Groups in Action*, Penguin, Harmondsworth, 1979.

62. Williams (1983), op. cit. n. 17, p. 172.

63. The need to do this was seen clearly by Jack Common in the 1930s. '. . . we live in a time when the organs of consciousness are almost completely cut off from the mass of the people . . . Therefore we are immensely ignorant of what is happening on any social level beneath that of the petty-bourgeois.' 'Pease Pudding Men', *The Adelphi*, vol. X, July 1935; also in *Jack Common's Revolt Against the 'Age of Plenty'*, Huw Beynon and Colin Hutchinson (eds.), Strong Words, Newscastle upon Tyne, 1980.

64. Williams (1983) op. cit. n. 17, p. 173.

21.
Don't Pull up Your Trouser Legs Before You See the Sea

Young people, culture and the school

Michael Rosen

The word 'culture' is used, misused, abused at least a million times a week. I am not going to try some new and ultimate defining stunt that bottles up the word once and for all. I want to use the word in its loosest, vaguest way, namely to mean 'the way people carry out their affairs together'. What interests me is young people's culture, how this is expressed and how schools react to it.

First, I think it is useful to look at a model of how any individual young person stands in a cultural map or plan. We can think of three spheres:

1. me and my family group;
2. me and my social or peer group;
3. me and my national, or cultural, or ethnic, or class group (depending on how I choose to define myself or how others choose to define me).

Any given cultural form, whether it be a poem, a slang word, a garment, a dance or whatever, can be found to originate from one or more of the spheres. Here is one of those diagrams that are supposed to explain such things.

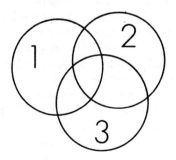

What is the use of all this? Consider the following: four black fourteen-year-old boys get together in a classroom after school with two tape recorders. On one tape recorder a dub version of a Sugar Minott track plays, on the other a blank tape records the dub track and whatever the four boys have to say. They then spend the next half hour 'toasting'. This is an oral technique, part improvisational poetry performed by Jamaican and Black British DJs which has grown up in Jamaica and in Britain. It has now become not merely a means of introducing tracks to dance to, but a form in its own right, with international stars like Yellowman, 'Clint Eastwood' and many others.

Here is an extract of what the boys did:

Danny   Here dem style now
Dem talk 'bout me brown jaja
and no how me black
me get up every morning
me run round the track
me inna track suit
anna shorta bobbysocks
but me atta me atta me no wanna borrow datta
me atta me atta me no wan no more a datta
Winston, I beg yah come inna dis
ribbitta mashitta garatta
lettissa saladda oniona
melanna whatitta gettitta lanitta

Winston   Here no style
Inna O inna O Titan inna O
Inna O inna O Titan inna O
Say go say Titan bum go on de go
Say no DJ coulda touch me any'ow
Me hotta dan de sun in de Colorado
Me cooler dan de breeze dat de West Wind blow
Inna O inna O reek it up and rock it so
Caw when I was a yout me father wan name me Joe
Me father said yes and me mother said No
Bom go say go Tippa Titan on de go
Bom go say go Tippa Titan on de go
Caw inna sweety shop I said dem have Polo
Dem have Marshmallow also Rolo
Dem a chat bout fe gi' your girl your last Polo

Say no DJ coulda touch me any'ow
Me fav'rite programme thatta Hawaii-Five-O
Caw when dey show it me jussa mek de music flow
Bom go say go Tippa Titan on de go.

I have no idea how much of this is totally original or how much is part quoted from other DJs, except that the whole act is totally free-wheeling and improvised. No print, no paper, no writing.

Let's put this on the map. It obviously has origins in sphere 3, as it is a piece of ethnic group culture. By doing it together it becomes 2 — peer group culture to be made and shared. *Some*, though not all, has origins in personal home experience, so is in category 1 (especially as the form enables the DJ to boast, taunt and produce amazing revelations about his personal life or other people's). In other words, as a cultural form for these four boys it is situated right in the heart of our map, where all three spheres overlap.

I think when this occurs the importance of the activity to these boys is very special. They are making and producing something that has reverberations through all three major spheres of their identity. Now let us ask The Beastly Question. What is many schools' response to this activity? A combination of ignorance, indifference, contempt or hostility. In other words, a huge mismatch takes place between boys like these and the school. Let it be said, this was not the case at the school where this went on.

Now, I would suggest, it would be useful to look at any number of cultural forms that children use, and apply the same method. But which ones? And how might we describe the total 'Culture' of a young person or group of young people? How can we do it so as to include the oral diversity, the wealth of personal experience and the network of abstract ideas and opinions? One way of getting to such a description would be to consider the components of any young person's culture:

Fears
Dreams and nightmares
Tricks
Revenges
Trusted people
Thrills
In trouble
Accidents
Sadnesses, regrets
Prides
Shames

Mysteries, things I/we are mystified by

Vows, resolutions

Wishes and hopes

Rumours

Proverbs

Rhymes

Riddles

Games

Laws

Rules

Punishments

Sayings

Stories I've been told, by parents, relations, grandparents, peer group

Happenings and events in the history of my cultural/ethnic group, class/national group

Jokes

Special days

Songs

Attitudes to other members of family, family conversations and arguments

Mucking about, having a laugh, having a good time

Places we go, private/public places to meet and wait for each other, hanging about

Celebrations and feasts

Foods, favourite dishes and recipes

The 'way we do it': garden, hair, dress, style, habits

Hobbies, pastimes, pursuits, activities, crazes

Music, dance, song (participated, performed, spectated)

Sports: participatory/spectator

Kinds of work done by me (as a part-timer), or by parents/grandparents and relations, brothers and sisters, other people, as interviewed, housework, losing work, living without work, activities at work that are not work, like skiving, having a laugh, organizing, strikes, break-times, knocking off

Courtship, marriage, weddings, divorces. Alternatives, like single parenting, gay relationships

Holidaying

Outings

Slangs, dialects, ingroup jargons and new words

Family sagas, stories

Street spectacles and events, as seen or participated in
Superstitions and charms
Oaths and secrets, about secret illicit deeds, for instance
Street cries, market traders, bus conductors
Local legends, myths, urban folk stories
It's not fair: wrong-doers, cheats, conmen, cruel people
Heroes, heroines, anti-heroes, local or historical
Victims and scapegoats — me or others, on the receiving end
Private matters, what I choose to be 'personal'
Irritating things, things that annoy
Attitude to physique — self and others — physical traits, body
Loyalties: taking sides, identifying with groups or individuals
Between two cultures: divided loyalty and identities
Battlegrounds: where and why — home/street/work/
Clubs and organizations
Gender-determined activities — questioning this
Attitudes to change — could things be better for me/my cultural
    group/my family?
The future for me/imagined/for all of us
Death: opinions/observed/bereavement
Supernatural — afterlife, god, ghosts, other-life creatures, magic
Disasters: me/my family, my people
My room
Authority and control; attitudes to it — parental/school/outside
Fantasies — what if I was a ?/my imaginary helper/me as someone else,
    i.e. role play as victim, boss, other people; imaginary worlds: good,
    bad, futuristic
Gangs, mates, friends, rivals
Desertions and separations
Loves and loved ones
Solidarity, not grassing, standing by mates/family/my people
Goings on in and attitudes to, institutions I belong in, like school, work
    place, block of flats, family
Neighbours
Responses to 'natural phenomena', weather, seasons, landscape
Pets
Parties
Encounters with strangers
Arguments, disputes, rows
Disappointments

Promises, made or broken
My moods
My beliefs/strong feelings, me on a soap box

Many of these components are totally different in kind and many overlap with each other or can be mixed, for example, 'Promises' and 'Family'. The list is intended to be useful; the items are not watertight. Also, an approach to any one of them can involve an individual, an individual's description of somebody else or a group. The list has grown out of working with all ages of children and schoolchildren. Mostly, this has been in an informal way in corners of classrooms, libraries and corridors, often nudging alienated people into writing down or taping scraps of their identity.[1]

Given the space it would be possible to illustrate each one of these categories with an example of how they might be expressed. For instance, a piece of writing, a tape-slide show, a tape, a piece of improvised drama, a song or a drawing. In each case the example could be any of the following kind: 'creative', reportage, factual, speculative, or transcripts of other people's words.

So let's take some of the categories.

Proverbs

(From a first-year class in a girls' comprehensive school in East London)

My Mother Always Says . . .
Tracy Parkes is in 1K. Her mother was born in Jamaica. These are some of her favourite sayings. Tracy has also explained what they mean.
1. You can take a person to the country, but you can't take the country out of him.
It means you can't change a person's inborn nature.

2. Show me your company & I'll tell you who you are.
It means people tend to mix with others when they have got the same things in common.

3. If you want to know your friend from your enemy, lie on the sidewalk drunk.
It means how to find a true friend.

4. a. You never miss the water until the well runs dry. b. A cow never knows the value of its tail until called to part with it.
They mean you never know the true value of things until it's too late.

Beyza Beyaztas is in 1K. Her mother was born in Turkey. Her other ancestors come from Romania and from Greece. Beyza has written her family sayings in Turkish and then translated them and told us what they mean.

1. Denizi gormeden pacalarini sivama.
Before you see the sea, don't pull up your trouser legs.
It means don't do something too soon. For example, don't get all your holiday clothes ready before you know where you're going.

2. Samanin altindan su yurutme.
Don't take water from under the hay.
Meaning: Don't do anything without anybody looking, e.g. if you were getting an apple without your mum looking, she would turn and say 'Samanin . . .'

3. Baklavyi azindan cikar.
Take the Bakla out of your mouth.
Meaning: Hurry up and say it, as we would say, 'Spit it out'
(Bakla is a sweet.)

Special days

(By a fourth-year primary boy in East London, tape transcript.)

In St Lucia there's a festival. There's a thing called D Satan, it's all in red and it's got a long white beard and it looks like the devil. They've got a man all in tar with feathers on — he chucks things at you — like a staff, a pole with a handle, and things like that.

It goes all through the streets. There's men that dress up as women and you can go on to Castris marsh, and in the square they have a steel band playing and things like that.

I was there and it's like you're in hell. They chase after you, and if they catch you, they put you in a cart and they take you off. Only they don't really take you away, they just dress you up and you come back with them. It's like a procession. The day is called Festival Day.

Story told by my dad

(Tape transcript from the same boy.)

This story is about a dance hall in Dennery, a part of St Lucia and they used to have a song

De devil day tap, tap
De devil day tap, tap
You defraid Satan
Dat Mysteriuss man
He sure can can.

Everytime they were singing and dancing this song, the door would open and a creature would come in, half man, half cow with wings.

And so now whenever people hear this song, they turn it off. The people ran out of the hall and the thing just danced around the hall and disappeared.

My room

(By a third-year primary boy in East London.)

Mount Wardrobe

On Saturday
I go climbing up on my wardrobe
It takes me half an hour to get up
I climb and climb
The more I climb the tireder I get
Sometimes if we fall off we swim ashore
The shore is the bed
We pretend that the floor is water.
Sometimes I can jump up
from the floor on to the wardrobe.

Local legend

(By a second-year boy in a North London comprehensive.)

One day, ten years ago, where my flats are now there was a factory called Stevens Ink factory and one day one of the foremen was checking up on the machines to see if it was working properly, when suddenly he fell in.

He gave a loud scream, but by the time a worker got there the foreman was dead. He was chopped up into mincemeat.

Now where my flats are, now people say you can sometimes see the foreman scream, then he vanishes.

Games

(A group poem by five first-year primary children)

We play police
out in the playground
we run around
out in the playground
we play 'had'
out in the playground
we play jellybeans
out in the playground
we fall over
out in the playground
we play kisschase
out in the playground
we play mummies and daddies
out in the playground
we get told off
out in the playground
we play kick-ups
out in the playground
we found a coat in the bin
out in the playground
we play bingly-bongly
out in the playground
we play emergencies
out in the playground
we play Grange Hill
out in the playground
we play 'Mother may I?'
out in the playground
we play with our friends
out in the playground.

How we met

(By a fourth-year boy in a North London Comprehensive.)

I was on the train
going to Loftus Road
to see qpr against Arsenal

On the train I saw this boy
on his own.
I went up to him
and said, 'Are you going to this match?'
he said, 'Yes.'
So I asked him his name.
He said, 'Frank.'
He asked me what team do I
support,
so I said, 'Arsenal.'
Then he punched me in the face
and ran off.

Traditional story

(By a third-year secondary boy of Bengali origin.)

The Crocodile and the Monkey

Once there was a monkey he use [*sic*] to live in a tree. At the river side in
the river there was a crocodile. When the monkey eat the sweet fruits and
he use to throw the fruits in the water. The crocodile use to say if I made
friends with the monkey then the monkey will give me more fruits.

One day the monkey went to the river to drink water.
The crocodile said, 'My friend monkey, do you like to be my best friend?'
The monkey said, 'OK I will be your friend.'
The monkey use to give the crocodile sweet fruits to eat.
One day, the crocodile decided to eat the monkey. The crocodile thought
if he eat the monkey's heart he will find a good taste.

So one day the monkey was crossing the river. In his hand he had a
stick. The crocodile came and got monkey's leg.
The monkey said, 'Stop it crocodile. If you want to eat me, you're holding
my stick.'
So the monkey gave his stick to the crocodile and said, 'There's my leg.'

The crocodile got hold of his stick and the monkey swim and he get out
of the river and never again went near the river.

Traditional rhyme

(First-year girl in a South London comprehensive.)

Mary had a little lamb

she thought it very silly
she threw it up into the air
and caught it by his willy
was a watchdog
sitting on the grass
along came a bumble bee
stung him on the ask
no questions
tell no lies
ever seen a chinaman
doing up his flies
are a nuisance
bugs are worse
that is the end of my very silly verse.

A topic on black history

(From a girls' comprehensive in East London.)

Have You always lived in England?

I haven't always lived in England, no, I came here in '69, 1969, no 1959.

Mr . .?

Cleary, my name is, Patrick Cleary.

What country did you live in before?

I lived in the island of Curaçao, that's in . . . I'm a Grenadian. But the island of Curaçao is different to the island of Grenada.

Why did you come to England?

Why did I come? Hmm. I wanted to travel. I wanted to travel. It's, it's the habit of the people in my island, or in the Caribbean as a whole, to travel. When you come of a certain age, you just want to go abroad. And see what's around.

What do you remember about the first day?

Busy. Speed. The trains and the speed that everyone was moving. I think that that was my first impression.

How old were you?

Nineteen. I was nineteen years old.

You didn't have to answer that one anyway!

What sort of reactions did you get from white people?

What reactions? Curiosity, I think, was the main thing. Very curious and ask questions, a lot of questions, I think.

What did you think England was going to be like before you came?

I thought it would be much, mm, much cleaner, and, and umm, look much more prosperous in its appearance, structurally and otherwise.

How do you feel about England now?

Well, I'm earning a living in this island and I feel to survive one has got to work very hard. In every country now you've got to work to survive. So there is not anything particular with England.

Where did you first live when you came to England?

First I lived in Huddersfield; I had some cousins there. And then I went to London in 1962. I live in Ealing now. I have lived in Ladbroke Grove, Tooting.

What work did you do when you first came to England?

My first job was in a stamping forge, stamping metal to make forges for different industries. I've worked in engineering. I've been trained as a tailor and continued at college. I'm a master tailor by profession.

Do you prefer living in England or where you were born?

Well, where I was born has changed quite a lot now to when I left. If I can earn a good living and look after my family the way I am doing here, then I would prefer to live there. It depends.

Would you like to go back?

Yes I would. Yes. But I can't say exactly when.

Where do you come from, anyway?

Barbados. And Pakistan.

Are any of your children Rastas?

Well now, explain the real meaning of the term 'Rasta' to me.

Kinds of work

(Interview with a fireman on a picket line during the firemen's strike of 1976, carried out by third-year girls from a South London comprehensive.)

What do you think a fireman's basic wage should be?

It should be — what we're asking for — the average male working wage

— that's the average of all male people in England who are at work; an average of that plus the government's 10 per cent, which in real terms works out to about £20 a week increase.

How do you think the television are treating your case?

Up till the end of last week we was getting very good TV coverage, as you know. We was on every news bulletin etcetera etcetera and since President Sadat's visit it's not been so good. I think this is primarily because they are taking a direct government line. The government are not directly censoring the newspapers, but they are, how can I put it? directing them not to publish things that it would be politically unsafe for them to publish. i.e. they publish the death figures, the people that get killed but they won't publish how in fact they died and whether they was in direct cause of the strike.

(The girls ask if they are paid while they're on strike and hear that they're not, that they can draw supplementary benefit for wives and children but not for themselves.)

How do you pay for the rent and all that?

The rent? Unfortunately as from December 1st the rent goes out the window, If you're in rented accommodation, the Social Security will make sure you won't lose your tenancy, If you're like me, a mortgage holder, then you've got to make arrangements with your mortgage company to suspend one month's payment of your mortgage.

Do you prefer not doing anything at all instead of going and stopping a fire?

No, of course not. All firemen have got a sense of responsibility. They much prefer to be putting out people's fires and helping the public, which is what they do all the year round, anyway, than standing out there on the picket line getting freezing cold and not getting paid for it. Unfortunately, it comes to this situation where a fireman's pay and conditions were getting so far behind everybody else that the men are leaving the job wholesale for other occupations with more money; and what was left of the union membership decided to take this action to illustrate it to the public and to obtain more money.

Songs

(Composed by second-year girls in a comprehensive school.)

Joanne's eyes are so big

Bird's eyes, bird's eyes
Just as big as fifty pence pieces
Bird's eyes, bird's eyes
And when she comes round the corner
Bird's eyes, bird's eyes
Her eyes always come first
Whose eyes? Her eyes? ah those eyes
Bird's eyes, bird's eyes.

Traditional rhyme

(By a first-year boy at an East London comprehensive.)

Oh where is my smokey
all covered in sand
I killed a Leeds united supporter
with an elastic band
I went to his funeral
I went to his grave
The vicar came up to me
and asked me my name
I answer politely
with a bicycle chain
he took me to court for this
and the judge so did say
you will go to Borstal
for a year and one day
me old woman fainted
me old man dropped dead
and me poor little brother
shot the judge in the head
there's bars on the windows
there's bars on the door
and even the pisspot
is chained to the floor.

Dialect

(By a second-year girl at a South London comprehensive.)

In trouble
Me an me broda was on we wa from school. Me was 6 then an he was 8.

On de way from school me wanted to go tilet. We bote wanted to go in the sweety shop. So we did. While we was sartin out wat we was going fe buy, me wet me self. Dere was a great big puddle on de floor roun abote me. Wen I reach ome me broda tell me muda an she tell me off an tell me sa if me did wan fi go tilet me shoulda go ome straight away an not stop inna sweety shop.

English   I and my brother was on our way from school. I was 6 and he was 8. On the way from school I wanted to go to the toilet. We both wanted to go to the sweet shop. So we did. While we sorting out what we was going to buy, I wet myself. There was a great big puddle on the floor round about me. When I reached home my brother told my mother and she told me that if I wanted to go to the toilet I should of come straight home and not stop in the sweet shop.

I hope that these pieces, by using some of the categories on my list, will suggest the scope of this approach with young people. I don't want to represent all schools as foully oppressive places BUT . . . there is a problem in that many schools ignore these kinds of writing and taping. I often speculate as to why. Is it because many teachers despise young people's culture? Is it because they don't think it's 'important'? Is it because education is supposed to be about giving something to children, not about taking something from them? Is it because many teachers organize classrooms in such a way that interviews and taping and group writing and performing and discussing don't seem possible? Is it because all this stuff seems threatening and could cause children to start throwing things and jumping out of windows?

I won't waste your time by going through each of the pieces placing them in the diagram, as I did with the 'toasting' example, but should you choose to do so, you can easily see how important many of them are to the identities of the people concerned.

From the young person's point of view the situation might seem like this:

I am sitting here in this classroom and you don't seem to be interested in what I do, where I do it, who I meet, my beliefs, my way of talking. You then ask me to write about 'The week-end' or 'A bad day'. I can't do it. You will not be an interested audience.

On the other hand, when the cultural identity of the young person is received with interest, 'many flowers bloom'. In my experience, the 'flowers' have been of many kinds: a study of black history, for instance, a set of poems by a young girl about her relationship with her mother, a book of 'my dad's stories' and so on. In each case, the starting-out point was an interchange about 'culture'.

So what am I saying? There has been a lot of interest taken in the bad 'isms' of education — racism, sexism, classism. But central to the problem, it seems to me, is an adult versus child-ism. We don't actually like children's or young people's culture. To which I would say, how the hell are we supposed to set about any of the other three 'isms' if there isn't the respect for the child in the first place, believed in and shown by the encouragement of writing and taping of the kind I have illustrated?

The result of our ignoring their culture, combined with the constant injection of 'our stuff', is that we choose to influence young people with adult-chosen culture. For many schools this means the culture of the dominant white male media. For some schools, it may mean non-dominant forms are presented. That's fine as far as it goes. But any young person will find it difficult to engage with even these non-dominant forms if their own culture (also non-dominant!) is not given space. Young people have to have the chance to confront new ideas using the tools that *they* produce.

Reference

1. See Chapter 8 in Stephen Eyers and John Richmond (eds.) *Becoming Our Own Experts*, Talk Workshop Group, 1982, ILEA English Centre, Sutherland Street London S.W.1.

22.
Message and Text in Poetic Utterance

James Britton

A lot has been claimed in recent years for writing as a special mode of thinking, a way of capturing meaning in the very effort to communicate it. Sapir long ago anticipated some of the things that are being claimed for writing when he observed that a language, once established,

> can discover meanings for its speakers which are not simply traceable to the given quality of experience itself but must be explained to a large extent as the projection of potential meanings into the raw material of experience.[1]

Today this notion (perhaps applied too narrowly to writing rather than to language) is a prominent theme in the New Hampshire rhetoric of Donald Murray[2] and Donald Graves,[3] and other writers have pointed out that *serendipity*, the art of the adventitious, plays a key role in discovery writing. Fair enough, though it must be added that the idea of a lucky accident, solely and simply, does less than justice to the writer's share in the process; as with the *objet trouvé, recognition* of the random occurrence and its potential significance must be the decisive event.

I want to argue briefly here that there are viable reasons why poetic discourse should demonstrate more frequent and more powerful examples of discovery writing than can be found in non-poetic discourse. By poetic discourse I refer primarily to writings in poetic form (whether metrical or 'free') and secondarily, that is to imply, in diminishing degree, to the language of literature in prose, whether story, drama or essay.* My argument will involve a consideration of writers' procedures; but the picture would be

---

* Works of the *poésie concrète* variety, poetry that does not ask, or even allow itself, to be read aloud is not part of my subject. Such work has its own subtleties as art but seems to me to be related to poetry as we normally know it only as one of the arts to another.

incomplete if I did not then go on to consider the role of a reader of poetic discourse.

The argument centres upon the way words, as we write, find their way on to the page. How accurate is it to suggest that we *choose* our words? More than one writer has objected that it is rather a matter of words choosing them, though that is obviously no more than a fanciful image that satisfies some internal sense of the process. Michael Polanyi makes it quite clear that in his view *denotation*, the fitting of words to phenomena, is a tacit procedure employing unspecified and sometimes unspecifiable criteria:

> In all applications of a formalism to experience there is an indeterminacy involved, which must be resolved by the observer on the ground of unspecifiable criteria. Now we may further say that the process of applying language to things is also necessarily unformalized: that it is inarticulate. Denotation, then, is an art, and whatever we say about things assumes our endorsement of our own skill in practising that art.[4]

We have to conclude that in our co-operative behaviours, what cannot be *proved* succeeds by being *believed*.

Let us say, then — to contribute our own image to the argument — that a writer must be ready to play the conjuror and take words, as the other does pennies, out of the air. But the poet, it seems to me, practises a threefold readiness — trawling, as it were, three nets in the sea of the subconscious. The first, in common with all writers, is a semantic net — the pursuit of meaning in a principally cognitive sense. That implies, for example, that if the mesh of that net drew out the word 'pomp', it would exercise no magnetic attraction over the word 'pump' or over the word 'pimp'. But since a poet's meaning will be in part conveyed by the patterned sounds that words combine to make and by the kinaesthetic echoes or traces that are associated with the articulation of those sounds, he trawls also those two additional nets and shows a triple readiness.

Indeed, for the purposes of serendipity, it must be recognized that there is here more than a threefold gain. A word selected by sound brings with it no clearly established meaning but is potentially suggestive of novel meaning; and a word selected on kinaesthetic grounds similarly represents an alternative, if somewhat less distinct, modality.

Some support for such a notion comes from experiments carried out by two Russian psychologists, Luria and Vinogradova.[5] They found that in different people, and in the same people on different occasions, words formed clusters in the mind on two distinct principles, one a grouping by sound, the other a grouping by meaning.

It would be a mistake to suggest that these additional modalities play no part in the creation of a non-literary text but it can hardly be disputed that the role they play there bears no comparison with the contribution they make to a literary text, and in particular to a text in poetic form. Indeed, the use made of these modalities contributes essentially to the patterning which, in the view of Widdowson distinguishes literary from non-literary discourse:

> What does seem crucial to the character of literature, is that the language of a literary work should be fashioned into patterns over and above those required by the actual language system.[6]

And, of poetic form itself:

> What is distinctive about a poem . . . is that the language is organized into a pattern of recurring sounds, structures and meanings which are not determined by the phonology, syntax or semantics of the language code which provides it with the basic resources.[7]

Jakobson had long since made the interesting suggestion that in poetic form the two fundamental and distinct factors of language, *selection* and *combination*, become interfused. *Selection*, he showed, works by equivalence, similarity and dissimilarity; *combination* is based on contiguity. But in the language of poetry (as also in the private pre-sleep monologues of a young child) lexical, morphemic and phonemic sets are projected from the axis of equivalence on to the axis of combination. That is to say, sets usually subject to the selection process (where one instance in the set survives and the remainder are rejected — to put it in idealized terms) find their way into the combination of items constituting the text. Lexical items, for instance, may systematically occur as doublets in the formal parallelism of biblical verse, and feature in many other forms of planned repetition or successive approximation. And phonological distinctions which in normal language serve only at the selection stage (to provide meaningful units — to distinguish *cat* from *bat* from *mat*, etc.) enter into the combinatory process, manifestly in rhyme, alliteration and the like, but also for the purposes of rhythm and for onomatopoetic and kinaesthetic effect.[8]

What is important is to realize that one effect of these superimposed patterns in poetic discourse is to bind and rebind the utterance into unity. The language code itself, of course, has built into it complex devices for cohesion, as Halliday and Hasan[9] have demonstrated. Rhythms, parallelisms, rhymes, assonances, puns, image clusters — all these patterning devices are further means of creating a verbal object, complete in itself, distinct from the world it exists in, its elements intricately related each to each. Jakobson, whose work is full of fruitful if largely neglected hypotheses, refers to two distinct modes of synthesizing an utterance, one *sequential* and the other *simultaneous*. He goes on:

> In order to comprehend and evaluate a poetic work, we must have, according to Herder, a synchronic insight into its whole, and he gives the Greek name *energeia* to the simultaneous synthesis which enables us to comprehend the entirety of a verbal flow.[10]

We shall pursue this point when we come to look in more detail at the reader's share in constituting a literary text.

*   *   *

All that in support of the idea that a poetic text is fertile ground for serendipitous effects. Let me, with any necessary apologies, illustrate that process at a very simple level from some verses I wrote many years ago as part of a BBC poetry programme for ten-year-olds. I called the piece, 'One is Company' and it began:

> Said an ageing schoolmaster, 'I'm tired of my school
>> And tired of your company.
> I've applied for a permit to live as a hermit
>> And that's how I want it to be.'
>> 'Buzz off,' said he to the bluebottle fly,
>>> And 'Hop it', he said to the frog.
>> At no loss for a word, whatever occurred,
>>> This prince of a pedagogue.

Through a sequence of pun-governed stanzas, I arrived at:

> The day grew dark and the night grew cold
>> And still in the dark sat he,
> Sighing, 'Leave me alone,' to the leaves that were blown
>> From the boughs of a sycamore tree.
>> And they leaved him alone:
>>> And they leaved him right over.
>> And there he lies buried up to his eyes
>>> In all the old leaves of October.

The preoccupation with punning meant that I trawled in particular the net for sounds. The move from 'Leave me alone' to leaves on a tree called into being the final stanza, which was quite unexpected and which gave, I think, the heightened effect needed for an ending. Jakobson, we might note, sees punning as emblematic of the encroachment, in poetic discourse, of the selection principle upon the combination principle:

> Phonemic similarity is sensed as semantic relationship. The pun ...
> (paronomasia) reigns over poetic art, and whether its rule is absolute or limited,
> poetry by definition is untranslatable.[11]

*   *   *

What we do when we listen to someone speaking might be described as looking through the noises he makes in order to discover what he has on his mind, and in much of our reading the process is similar. Michael Polanyi describes how at the breakfast table he may receive letters in several languages, read them through and put them aside having noted their messages. It may then occur to him that his son would be interested to read one of them, but his son knows only English and already Polanyi has forgotten what language the letter was written in.[12]

Bilinguality has been used as a research method to demonstrate this dissociation of text from message. Subjects were given a mixed English and French text and asked to read it aloud as rapidly and accurately as they could; among the errors they made in doing so there was a consistent tendency to *translate* words bordering on the points where the language of the text changed, i.e. to preserve the message at the expense of the text.[13] Similarly, Jacqueline Sachs has shown that readers who, within a few seconds of having listened to a paragraph read to them, are offered either excerpts or altered versions of a sentence from the paragraph rarely fail to identify even minimal changes of form that affect meaning, but show little ability to identify changes of form that do not alter the meaning. She concludes that,

> the findings are consistent with a theory of comprehension which contends that
> the meaning of a sentence is derived from the original string of words by an active
> interpretative process. That original sentence which is perceived is rapidly for-
> gotten, and the memory then is for the information contained in the sentence.[14]

Pursuing for a moment the notion of 'an active interpretative process', we might note that we take to the listening or reading task a complex set of expectations drawing upon a considerable body of knowledge. We have knowledge of word meanings and the rules of syntax. We have knowledge about the kinds of things that might be said concerning homing pigeons or horoscopes, horticulture or horticulture or hamburgers, and a vast range of other topics. From this wide field of knowledge relevant areas will be activated as expectations by whatever clues the situation and the utterance offer us. This, in its most general sense, is the linguist's notion of 'context', described by Lyons as 'the knowledge shared by hearer and speaker of all that has gone before'.[15] Psychologically speaking, it is the frame of reference to which we relate what we see and hear and so construct a meaning.

That we are able to pay attention to so much, and in such variety, is to some extent explained by Polanyi's conception of focal and subsidiary awareness. According to this, we are subsidiarily aware of word meanings and syntax, of the relevant parts of our knowledge of the world and of the speaker and of the situation: we are subsidiarily aware of the words we hear. What we are focally aware of is the emerging message, i.e. whatever we take to be the speaker's or writer's meaning or intention. The text is transparent; we look *through* it to make out the emergent message.

I have suggested that this relation between text and message holds not only for speech but also for a good deal of our reading. However, the persistence of the written text before our eyes does make possible other kinds of response — witness the fact that most of us have felt apprehensive on behalf of the spy in the story who has to swallow his text once he has committed its message to memory!

*   *   *

The fact that my formative years came in the radio age rather than the television age may account for the example with which I open this section. If I have been listening to the radio and someone comes into the room, I may say, 'I've just heard a fascinating talk.' If he shows interest, I give him to the best of my ability the gist of the talk. I cannot recover the script, the text, but I may nevertheless convey adequately the message, so that my listener is in the end little worse off than I am *vis-à-vis* the talk. But if on another occasion I say, 'I've just heard a fascinating poem on the radio', how can I satisfy the interest I may have aroused? Because I cannot recover the text, I cannot convey the message in any form that could create for him the experience I had in listening to it. Here is a clear case of the distinction Rosenblatt made between an *efferent* and an *aesthetic* reading.[16] Any meaning I 'carried away' after listening to the talk can be conveyed to another; my aesthetic 'reading' — my engagement with the text of the poem as I listened to it — can only be recreated by a reiteration of that engagement. In the terms we have taken from Polanyi, the text of the poem is no longer transparent — it has become opaque.

Literary commentators and critics have for long enough been aware of this general difference — making it clear that the meaning of a poem is inseparable from the words, that its meaning, in Auden's expression 'survives in the valley of its saying'. And this must certainly reflect the nature of the verbal object as we looked at it earlier — its intricate and complex cohesion, its isolation and completeness-in-itself. Coleridge used the term 'esemplastic' to describe the form of a poem: 'seamless', but more than that; 'a unity' but also 'unifying'. Bateson has given us in some detail his own explanation of what Jakobson referred to when he spoke of 'simultaneous synthesis':

> The positive function of the various formal devices of poetry — metre, alliteration, metaphor, verbal repetition, etc., — is to ensure that the poem achieves a unity of impression. . . . The continuous verbal links, interconnections and references back (1) prevent the reader from relegating to his memory the beginning of the poem before he has reached its end and (2) are continuous reminders that each sentence in the poem must be read against a background of awareness of the whole poem in all its semantic complexity. Without realizing what is happening we find ourselves forced, in fact, to retain the whole poem in our consciousness all through the process of reading.[17]

The necessity for 'retrospective redefinition' in reading a poem has often been noted. (The word 'sessions' seems to carry no legal flavour when it is met in the first line of Shakespeare's sonnet, 'When to the sessions of sweet silent thought', but it acquires that flavour from the lines that *follow*.) What Bateson claims is a generalization of that process: Polanyi at his breakfast table has derived the message and forgotten the text of his letters, and is satisfied. Substitute a poem for a letter, and that is the *beginning* of the communicative process, not the end. With the message in mind, the reader needs to return to the text and build a network of further meanings, constructing a reinterpretation which takes into account a set of particular relationships between key items in the text and the message. The message becomes, as it were, an important part of the context, part of the knowledge of all that has gone before that is shared by writer and reader. As he reads now he will be subsidiarily aware both of the message and of the words of the text, while he is focally aware of the fuller or modified meaning that is to emerge, as it emerges.

To attempt to exemplify the process at all directly is, I realize, to court disaster. In many of the poems we read it may work at a relatively low level, and much of our subsidiary awareness may barely reach the level of consciousness.[18] It may be that a glance back every now and again may suffice to enable a reader to keep modifying the emergent meaning in the light of both text and message. In describing and explaining I have no doubt already overdramatized the process: to illustrate it by finding a poem that highlights its workings will be to dramatize it even further.

Let me nevertheless suggest that a first ordinarily casual reading of the following poem by Emily Dickinson may (1) indicate as its general message that someone who needs looking after — child or invalid — is in a comforting way being put to bed; and (2) create problems with one or two words that do not conform to this notion:

> Ample make this bed,
> Make this bed with awe;
> In it wait till judgement break
> Excellent and fair.
>
> Be its mattress straight
> Be its pillow round;
> Let no sunrise yellow noise
> Interrupt this ground.[19]

As experienced readers, readers of this paper are probably already disputing my prognostication: yes, 'awe' could be seen as presenting a problem, even perhaps 'judgement', but once that word was processed and by the time the reader came to 'ground', there was no longer intact any 'message' about a comfortable bedtime. Yet I am of the opinion that unless a strong sense of such a bedtime is somehow made to contribute one component of the meaning (that is to say, the sense of it is built up and transferred to apply to a burial), then the major thrust of the poem will have been missed.

It is evident that my original description of the 'double reading process' was a rough approximation that must be amended. We might claim, instead, that it is the nature of a poetic text to impose on a reader a closer-than-casual reading, and that a network of message/text interconnections begins to be formed from our first broaching of the text; and, in particular, that there is something about the close-knit and multi-modal nature of a poetic text that enables a reader to respond in this way. (Indeed, it would otherwise be unlikely that listening to a poem read on the radio would have taken a listener to the point where he found it fascinating.)

It is often remarked that the formal devices of poetry have been exploited as an aid to memory and thus facilitated the preservation of the knowledge-base of an oral culture. Yet these effects have been very little studied. There is experimental evidence to suggest that cues of musical sound may be used to facilitate recall of items from visual memory. Neisser reports the visual presentation of three frames of nonsense syllables under two conditions: one set in silence and a second set with a different musical note accompanying each frame.[20] Recollection of the visually presented material is randomly distributed in the first condition, but biased towards the set that accompanied a note replayed during the recall task. Clearly experiments of this kind might yield important evidence regarding the nature of the poetry-reading process and how it is that a reader is able to apply simultaneous synthesis to a poetic text.

References

1. E. Sapir, *Culture, Language and Personality*, University of California Press, 1961, p. 7.
2. D.M. Murray, *Learning by Teaching*, Boynton Cook, New York, 1982.
3. D. Graves, *Writing: Teachers and children at work*, Heinemann Educational, London, 1983.
4. M. Polanyi, *Personal Knowledge*, Routledge and Kegan Paul, London, 1958, p. 81.
5. A.R. Luria and O.S. Vinogradova, 'The Dynamaics of Semantic Systems', *British Journal of Psychology*, 50, 1959.
6. H.G. Widdowson, *Stylistics and the Teaching of Literature*, Longman, London, 1975, p. 47.
7. Ibid., p. 36.
8. R. Jakobson, *Word and Language* (vol. 2, *Selected Writings*), Mouton, The Hague, 1971, pp. 270, 704.
9. M.A.K. Halliday and R. Hasan, *Cohesion in English*, Longman, London, 1976.
10. Jakobson, op. cit. n. 8, p. 343.
11. Ibid., p. 266.
12. Polanyi, op. cit. n. 4, p. 57.
13. P.A. Kolers, 'Three Stages in Reading' in F. Smith (ed.), *Psycholinguistics and Reading*, Holt, Rinehart and Winston, New York, 1973, p. 48.
14. J. Sachs, 'Recognition Memory for Syntatic and Semantic Aspects of Connected Discourse', *Perception and Psychophysics*, no. 2, 1967.
15. J. Lyons, *Structural Semantics*, Blackwell, Oxford, 1963, p. 84.
16. L. Rosenblatt, *The Reader, the Text, the Poem*, Southern Illinois University Press, 1978.
17. G.W. Bateson, *English Poetry: A critical introduction*, Longman, London, 1950, p. 55.
18. M. Polanyi, *Knowing and Being*, Routledge and Kegan Paul, London, 1969, p. 197.
19. E. Dickinson, *Final Harvest: Emily Dickinson's poems*, Little, Brown and Company, Boston, Mass., 1961.
20. U. Neisser, 'Experiments in Visual Scanning', *American Journal of Psychology*, 76, 1963.

Index